The Death and Life of Sylvia Plath

The
Death and Life
of
Sylvia Plath

By Ronald Hayman

A Birch Lane Press Book

Published by Carol Publishing Group

A Birch Lane Press Book
Published by Carol Publishing Group

Editorial Offices: 600 Madison Avenue, New York, N.Y. 10022
Sales & Distribution Offices: 120 Enterprise Avenue, Secaucus, N.J. 07094
In Canada: Musson Book Company, a division of General Publishing
    Company, Ltd., Don Mills, Ontario M3B 2T6

Queries regarding rights and permissions should be addressed to Carol
Publishing Group, 600 Madison Avenue, New York, N.Y. 10022

Carol Publishing Group books are available at special discounts for bulk
purchases, for sales promotions, fund raising, or educational purposes.
Special editions can be created to specifications. For details contact:
Special Sales Department, Carol Publishing Group, 120 Enterprise Avenue,
Secaucus, N.J. 07094

Manufactured in the United States of America
10 9 8 7 6 5 4 3 2 1

Library of Congress Cataloging-in-Publication Data

Hayman, Ronald,   1932–
    The death and life of Sylvia Plath / by Ronald Hayman.
        p. cm.
    "A Birch Lane Press book."
    Includes bibliographical references and index.
    ISBN 1-55972-068-9
    1. Plath, Sylvia–Biography.   2. Poets, AmericanND20th century–
Biography.   I. Title.
PS3566.L27Z68   1991.
811'.54—dc20
    [B]   91-3835
                                                             CIP

For Anne

Contents

Acknowledgments

I'm grateful to many friends and acquaintances who have talked to me about Sylvia Plath and other people involved in this story. Among those who have been most helpful are Al Alvarez, Gerry Becker, Jillian Becker, Susan Booth, Brenda Hedden, Dr. John Horder, Michael Horovitz, Jutta Laing, Angela Landels, Richard Larschan, Suzette Macedo, Julia Matcham, Jill Neville, Peter Porter, Peter Redgrove, Clarissa Roche, Elizabeth Sigmund, Trevor Thomas, Iain Walker, Fay and Ron Weldon. I also received valuable help from a number of curators, archivists and librarians, including Steve Dalton at the Winthrop public lending library, Sarah Black at the Rare Book Room in the Neilson Library at Smith College, Rebecca Campbell Cape and Marilyn Halkovic at the Lilly Library in Indiana University, Bloomington, and Sally Brown at the British Library.

Catharine Carver and Richard Larschan were generous enough to read through a draft of this book and make comments, while I also received valuable help from Tom Weldon of Heinemann and Hillel Black, Hettie Jones and Donald J. Davidson of Birch Lane Press. I must also express my thanks to Sebastian Faulks, Andy Bull and Robert Winder of *The Independent*: I might never have got started on this book if they hadn't commissioned me to write about Sylvia Plath.

Foreword

There can be no question of telling the whole truth about a suicide. The longest of suicide notes gives only an approximate idea of the pressures and preoccupations that fomented the depression. If Sylvia Plath left a suicide note, it has never been made public, but no suicidal act has been better documented than hers. In verse, in short stories and in her autobiographical novel, *The Bell Jar,* which describes events before and after the suicide attempt she made when she was twenty—ten years before she succeeded in killing herself—she writes with objectivity, precision and an engagingly humorous detachment about how and why her thoughts kept turning to death.

Do we need more biographical information than she gave us in the poetry and the fiction? Some people answer this question with a vehement negative, but many of her letters have been published, and so have some of her journals, though not in the United Kingdom. Three biographies have appeared, and there are biographical facts in the notes supplied by her husband, Ted Hughes, for the collected edition of her poetry. A few book-length memoirs have been published, while several collections of essays contain shorter memoirs. *The Death and Life of Sylvia Plath* is neither a biography nor a memoir—I met her only once—but it is a biographical study, and I must explain why it has come into existence.

Most verse is distilled from experience in such a way that the poem is self-explanatory. To appreciate "Little Gidding" we do not need to know when T. S. Eliot stayed in the village or how long or what happened. Though Wordsworth often wrote auto-biographically, he always told enough of the story to make the poetry intelligible. But Sylvia Plath was strongly influenced by Robert Lowell's confessional poetry, and in the verse she wrote after reading his 1959 *Life Studies,* she frequently assumed there was no more need to incorporate explanations than there would be in a diary.

Her 1961 poem "Parliament Hill Fields," for example, is addressed to someone who is absent but only inconspicuously. The poem gives us clues about the identity of the missing person: "Already your doll grip lets go" suggests she's talking to a small child, and on the nursery wall is a birthday picture of his or her sister, but the poem neither explains the speaker's relationship to the child nor whether the child is still alive. I doubt whether any reader would guess that the child had never been alive, but from the notes to the collected edition of 1981 we learn that Sylvia Plath wrote the poem after a miscarriage. Some readers would have preferred to be left in ignorance of this. Others find the poem more moving when they know the facts.

Her verse is often enigmatic, and there will always be room for argument about whether it's more enjoyable when the mysteries remain unsolved. Her poem "Daddy," which George Steiner calls "the Guernica of modern poetry," contains the statement "The black telephone's off at the root." Is it better or worse for the reader to know that she pulled the telephone wires out of the wall after a conversation between her husband and her rival for his affection?

Many of her poems contain lines which are partially or wholly incomprehensible without biographical explanation. Ted Hughes implicitly acknowledges this by providing notes, but they tell us nothing about the rival woman who features in several splenetic poems written when the marriage was breaking up. It is natural that he should be reticent about all this, but what are we to make of the cryptic complaint in "The Fearful" about a woman on the telephone who says she's a man, not a woman?

Even if her verse had been less personal, Sylvia Plath's posthumous life would depend partly on our knowledge of the biographical facts. Of the three biographies which have appeared, the most informative, *Bitter Fame,* has little to say about her death. The author, Anne Stevenson, told the press: "I don't deal with her death. I was asked specifically not to—it is something that is really Ted's and Assia's life, not Sylvia's." (Assia Wevill was having an affair with Ted Hughes at the time of the suicide.) In my view it's impossible to understand Sylvia Plath's life without understanding the long relationship with death which was eventually consummated in suicide.

Her posthumous life has gone through five phases. *The Bell Jar* was published pseudonymously in January 1963, about a month before she died, but once the secret of her authorship was revealed, it became inevitable that her poetry, her fiction and her life would form a triangle. Though she had started divorce proceedings, she was still married when she died, and Ted Hughes was left in control of the literary estate. It was he who initiated the second, third and fourth phases. In 1965 *Ariel* was published, but it contained only twenty-seven of the forty-one poems she had collected under that title. In 1971 he released most of the poems he had held back, and his annotated collection of her poems followed ten years later.

There was no distinct beginning to the fifth phase, but more biographical facts emerged between 1982, when the *Journals* came out in the United States, and 1989, when the Anne Stevenson biography appeared. Ted Hughes insists that it's not an official biography, although it's described in the "Author's Note" as "almost a work of dual authorship," the co-author being his sister, Olwyn Hughes, whom he had appointed as agent for the Plath estate.

The reader of the poetry is still in an uncomfortable position. The triangular perspective is unavoidable, but important biographical facts are still being withheld. Naturally there can be no question of telling the whole truth about a marriage and its disintegration. Only some of the facts can be rescued from oblivion, and only some can be published without infringing both the laws of good taste and the laws of libel. This book can neither answer all the questions it raises nor solve all the mysteries it explores. My hope is that it will help to correct some of the imbalance created by writers who have been unfair to Sylvia Plath, and to inaugurate a new phase in her posthumous life.

Chronology

1932
October 27   Sylvia Plath is born in Boston, the first child of Dr.
                Emil Otto Plath (age forty-six) and Aurelia Schober
                Plath (age twenty-five).

1935
April 27   Warren Plath is born.

1936   Mainly because Otto Plath is ill with diabetes, the
                family moves to Winthrop, a seaside suburb of
                Boston, Massachusetts, where they will be close to
                Aurelia's parents.

1940
October 12   Otto Plath's leg is amputated.
November 5   He dies.

1942
October   Aurelia and the children move inland to Wellesley.
                Sylvia starts at the Marshall Perrin Grammar
                School.

1944
September   She starts in the seventh grade at Alice L. Phillips
                Junior High School.

1947
Summer   Sylvia makes friends with Phil McCurdy, who
                teaches her to play tennis.

September   She starts at Bradford High School, where she's
                among twenty top students admitted to Wilbury
                Crockett's course on American literature.

Autumn	While the friendship with Phil McCurdy continues, she dates John Pollard and Perry Norton.
1949	She's appointed editor of *The Bradford* and writes a column for *The Townsman*.
Autumn	Sylvia's friendship with Bob Riedemann begins.
1950	She acts in a school production of *The Admirable Crichton* by J. M. Barrie and writes short stories for magazines. "And Summer Will Not Come Again" is published in *Seventeen* and "Bitter Strawberries" in the *Christian Science Monitor.* She wins a scholarship to Smith College, Northampton, Massachusetts.
Summer	Sylvia's still dating Perry Norton, Phil McCurdy and Bob Riedemann.
August	Starts corresponding with Eddie Cohen.
September 28	Her freshman year at Smith College begins.
December	She starts dating John Hodges.
1951	
January	Sylvia makes friends with Dick Norton, later to be her first lover.
March	She meets Eddie Cohen.
October	Dick Norton takes her to watch him dissect corpses and see babies being born in the Boston Lying-In Hospital.
1952	
August	Her prizewinning story "Sunday at the Mintons" is published in *Mademoiselle.*
December	She meets Myron Lotz.
1953	
January	Sylvia fractures a fibula while skiing at Ray Brook, N.Y.
April	She meets Gordon Lameyer.
June	She spends a month in New York as guest managing editor of *Mademoiselle.*
August 24	Sylvia tries to kill herself with sleeping pills, and is found in the cellar of her home and taken to Massachusetts General Hospital, where she's transferred to the psychiatric wing, and moved to McLean Hospital in Belmont, Massachusetts, where she's treated by Dr. Ruth Beuscher.

1954

February	She returns to Smith.
April	Her friendship with Richard Sassoon begins.
Summer	She stays in Cambridge, Massachusetts, attending Harvard summer school.

1955

January	Sylvia submits her English honors thesis, "The Double in Dostoevsky."
June	She graduates from Smith *summa cum laude* and wins a Fulbright scholarship to Cambridge University.
October	She starts her first term there at Newnham College.

1956

February 25	Sylvia meets Ted Hughes at a Cambridge party.
June 16	She marries him in London.
July	They holiday in Spain.
October	They stay with his parents in Yorkshire and settle into a flat in Eltisley Avenue, Cambridge.

1957

June	Sylvia takes her final exams for the B.A. degree.
August	She and Ted Hughes holiday on Cape Cod.
September	She starts teaching at Smith.

1958

May 22	She teaches her last class there and quarrels with Ted Hughes after finding him with a girl.
Summer	They settle into a flat near Beacon Hill in Boston.
October 22	She takes a part-time secretarial job at Massachusetts General Hospital.
October	She attends the seminar given at Boston University by Robert Lowell.
December 10	Sylvia goes to see Dr. Beuscher and decides to resume analysis.

1959

June	Her first pregnancy begins.
Summer	Sylvia and Ted Hughes set out on a camping tour through the States.
September/ November	They spend two months at Yaddo, the writers' colony in Saratoga Springs, N.Y.
December	They return to England.

1960

January	They settle in London.
April 1	Their first child, Frieda Rebecca, is born.
October	Sylvia's first poetry collection, *The Colossus,* is published.

1961

January	Sylvia starts work on a novel, *The Bell Jar.*
February	Her second pregnancy ends in a miscarriage.
March	She undergoes an appendectomy.
July	She and Ted Hughes take a holiday in France.
August 22	She finishes *The Bell Jar.*
August 31	They move to North Tawton, Devon.
November	Sylvia receives a Eugene F. Saxton grant to work on a novel.

1962

January 17	Their second child is born—Nicholas Farrar.
April	Sylvia works intensively on verse.
June	She drives her car off the road and afterward describes the incident as a suicide attempt.
Late June	Her mother, Aurelia Plath, arrives in England and stays till August 4.
July	Sylvia learns of Ted Hughes's affair with Assia Wevill.
September	Sylvia and Ted Hughes go to Ireland, where they stay with the poet Richard Murphy. Sylvia returns to Devon without Hughes. They separate.
October	Sylvia writes at least 26 poems during the month after the separation.
December	She moves with the two children out of the Devon house and into a maisonette at 23 Fitzroy Road, London NW1. She prepares *Ariel,* a collection of 41 poems.

1963

January	*The Bell Jar* is published pseudonymously.
February 11	Sylvia kills herself.

1965	*Ariel* is published in the United Kingdom, a selection by Ted Hughes of 40 poems, including only 27 of the 41 Sylvia had collected.

1966	*Ariel,* with 43 poems, is published in the United States.

1967   *The Bell Jar* is published in the United Kingdom under Sylvia's name; second edition of *The Colossus*.
Assia Wevill gives birth to Shura, a daughter by Ted Hughes.

1969   Assia kills herself and Shura.
Lois Ames is appointed official biographer of Sylvia Plath.

1970   Sylvia's unfinished novel, *Double Exposure*, "disappears."
The Bell Jar is published in the United States.

1971   *Winter Trees* and *Crossing the Water* published, including nine of the poems Sylvia had selected for *Ariel*.

1975   Publication of *Letters Home: Correspondence 1950–63*, selected and edited with a commentary by Aurelia Schober Plath.

1977   Publication in the United Kingdom of *Johnny Panic and the Bible of Dreams*, a selection of stories and prose pieces, edited by Ted Hughes.

1979   Publication in the United States of *Johnny Panic and the Bible of Dreams*, a more generous selection than the United Kingdom edition.
Litigation in the United States over the film of *The Bell Jar*.

1981   Publication of the *Collected Poems*, edited with an introduction by Ted Hughes.

1982   Publication in the United States of *The Journals of Sylvia Plath*, edited by Frances McCullough with Ted Hughes as consulting editor. No United Kingdom edition has appeared.
Collected Poems wins the Pulitzer Prize.

1987   United States and
1988   United Kingdom publication of Lynda Wagner-Martin's biography.

1989   Publication of Anne Stevenson's biography, *Bitter Fame*, written partly by Olwyn Hughes.

The Death and Life of Sylvia Plath

❧ 1 ❧

The End of a Short Life

A t about eight in the evening on Sunday, January 27, 1963, Sylvia Plath went downstairs to ring the doorbell of the ground floor flat. For six weeks she had been living alone with her two young children in a maisonette at 23 Fitzroy Road, in northwest London. Her downstairs neighbor, Trevor Thomas, was a Welsh art historian, working as fine art editor for the Gordon Fraser Gallery. He was fifty-six and deaf. She stood there with bloodshot eyes, tears running down her face: "I'm going to die... and who will take care of my children?" He invited her in and gave her sherry.

At first he had disliked her. Ignoring both his protests and the terms of her lease, she regularly left a big pram in the hallway and went on overloading his trash can instead of buying one for herself. Apparently she had also used unfair means to get possession of the upstairs maisonette, which he had wanted. Deserted by his wife, he was bringing up their two sons, who were at a boarding school, and he needed extra space during the holidays. At first he hadn't invited Sylvia into his flat, but in the last couple of weeks he had begun to like her better.

He tried to reassure her. She wasn't going to die, he told her, and even if she did, her husband would look after the children. She didn't want to die, she said. She had so much to do. But she couldn't go on. Then she became angry, clenching her fists and punching them up and down. It was all that awful woman's fault, she said. They'd been so happy, until she stole him. She was evil,

3

a scarlet woman, a Jezebel. They were in Spain, she said, spending money she'd helped to earn. How she hated them!

But then, in one of her abrupt mood changes, Sylvia asked whether he had the Sunday papers. When he produced the *Observer,* she opened it at the book page and showed him a poem by Ted Hughes. He was her husband, she explained, and then pointed to a long and favorable review by Anthony Burgess of a new novel, *The Bell Jar* by Victoria Lucas. She had written the novel, but her real name was Sylvia Plath. The name meant nothing to Thomas, who knew her as Sylvia Hughes.

Abruptly she was angry again, furiously bouncing up and down in the chair. Ted Hughes would be down there with friends, receiving congratulations on his poem, the center of admiration, free to come and go as he pleased. But here was she, a prisoner in this house, chained to the children. She wanted to be down there too, to know what they were saying about her book and her reviews. It wasn't clear what she meant by "down there," and she seemed to have forgotten she had just said her husband was in Spain. She started to cry again, with her arms locked together, rocking to and fro with grief she couldn't suppress. Thomas gave her a handkerchief.

She kept saying how happy she'd been with Ted until "she" came. The other woman was always "she," as if it would be degrading to mention her name, but Sylvia went on talking about her, furiously. She spoke about him too, more ambivalently, the fury mixed with possessive love, and as she went on talking about him, Thomas wondered whether she was angling for an offer to babysit so that she could go "down there" and join in the celebration, if there really was one in progress. Anyway, she was in no state to go out. She went on talking, saying she had to write poems to pay the electricity bills and to buy food and clothes for the children, but what she really wanted was to be a famous novelist and make a lot of money. The poems were just a means to an end.

The next day, meeting her in the street, Thomas asked how she was. She drew herself up proudly. There was nothing wrong with her, she said, and apologized for being so silly the previous night.

A week later, on February 4, she wrote a fairly cheerful letter to her mother, who lived near Boston. Sylvia had been feeling "a bit grim," she said, having been catapulted into loneliness from the "cowlike happiness" of maternity, but things were beginning to look up, and London was the one city in the world where she wanted to live. Here she had nice neighbors, free medical care from "fine doctors," parks, theaters and the BBC. In May she was going to earn about $150 by taking part in the program "The Critics." This was a fantastic break, and she'd been commissioned to write an article about her school days for *Punch.* Her doctor had referred her to a woman psychiatrist, who was going to start treating her under the National Health Service, which would help her to get through "this difficult time."

At the end of September 1962, when Ted Hughes moved out of their Devon house, she'd been left with Frieda, who was two and a half, and Nick, a baby of less than nine months. In the second week of December she'd brought the two children to London and settled them into the maisonette, where they had to survive a ferociously cold winter, with snow and burst pipes, with flu and head colds. She was close to John Horder, a doctor she liked, who had looked after her in 1960, during her first pregnancy, when she and Hughes were living in Chalcot Square, only a hundred yards away from the new flat. Dr. Horder's office was—and still is—in Regent's Park Road. When she went back to him in January 1963, he could see she was severely depressed, but she struck him as being almost too lethargic to be suicidal, though she had, as he knew, made a serious suicide attempt ten years earlier. To prescribe antidepressants and stimulants was to put her temporarily in greater danger by giving her more energy, and wanting to arrange treatment, he wrote about her to a psychiatrist, but his letter failed to arrive.

An additional risk was that, in combination with certain foods, the drugs could raise the blood pressure, and it was important she should use them as prescribed. To monitor their effects, he told her to keep in close touch, reporting at regular intervals on how she was feeling, either by coming to the office or by calling him. To do this she had either to use a telephone booth or call from a friend's: she was still waiting for a telephone to be installed in her flat. She seemed glad to have regular contact with Dr. Horder, and he formed the impression that she was becoming more active. Directly and indirectly, he made frequent appeals for her to think of her children.

Dr. Horder made sure she wasn't going to be alone with them over the next weekend. The friends who took care of her were Jillian and Gerry Becker, a Jewish South African couple she had met in September. They had young children, a big house in Mountfort Crescent, Islington, and an Irish maid who was good with children. The Beckers both lectured on literature at Hendon Polytechnic (later renamed Middlesex Polytechnic). Jillian, who was to become an authority on terrorism and to write *Hitler's Children,* was passionately interested in comtemporary poetry. Chubby, warmly avuncular and generous, Gerry drove around in an old London taxi. His conversations with Sylvia were less literary. He had read a great deal about the holocaust and visited the camps. Sylvia, who was interested but ill-informed, learned a lot from him, and on his way home from work he'd been calling at her flat two or three times a week for a chat. He also helped by taking the children out to give her time by herself. "You're my real godfather," she told him, and she said this to other people about him.¹ During the afternoon of Thursday, February 7, Sylvia called the Beckers. She was feeling unwell, she said. Could she come by with the children? She was told to come over straight-away, and before leaving she telephoned Catherine Frankfort, a neighbor, asking whether she could babysit on Monday while Sylvia went to her publishers.²

When she got out of her Morris station wagon, she looked thin and frail. Suzette Macedo, the friend who had introduced her to the Beckers, was in the house, but Sylvia, complaining of a migraine, soon went upstairs to lie down. A close friend of Assia Wevill's, Suzette had known from the beginning about her affair with Hughes, and when Sylvia found out, she had been furious with Suzette for not warning her, but before moving to London she had stayed several times with Suzette and her husband, the Portuguese writer Helder Macedo. On Christmas Day Sylvia had dinner with them.

When the Beckers invited her to stay with them for the weekend, Sylvia's response was: "I must. Without the au pair I can't cope." After six strenuous weeks of looking after the children single-handed, Sylvia had found the German girl who had started working for her less than two weeks earlier. Describing the girl as "food-fussy and boy-gaga," she had quickly fallen out with her.

Over the weekend Sylvia saw less of Gerry, who had flu, than of Jillian, who says Sylvia alternated between talking coherently and "raving." She didn't want to be alone, and needed to talk, speaking intensely and almost incessantly, but unrealistically, repeating herself, contradicting herself and jumping abruptly from one topic to another. At first Jillian tried to make occasional interpolations in the monologues, but it became apparent that Sylvia wasn't taking anything in, except when they were making practical arrangements. After Jillian offered to fetch anything she needed from Fitzroy Road, Sylvia made a list of things she wanted.[3]

In the maisonette, on the door of the study Jillian saw a sign: "DO NOT DISTURB, GENIUS AT WORK." The room was extremely neat, but most things were locked away. The books Sylvia had been reading were Jennifer Dawson's novel *The Ha-ha,* which involves mental breakdown, and Erich Fromm's *The Art of Loving.* In her bedroom there was a padlocked box by the bed. She had asked Jillian to bring curlers, makeup and a new cocktail outfit with a glittering blue top. Together with bottles and diapers for Nick, Jillian packed these things into a suitcase. Though Sylvia had said nothing about bringing a change of clothes for the children, Jillian searched in their room, but the drawers were empty. She remembered that the last five or six times she'd seen the children, Frieda had always been wearing the same clothes.

Over the four days in Islington Sylvia seems to have moved through a variety of moods. At times she was animated and lucid, at other times depressed and confused. Jillian Becker uses the word "raving" for some of Sylvia's conversation, and this tallies with the evidence of the critic A. Alvarez, who uses the term "borderline psychotic" to describe the state Sylvia had been in on Christmas Eve. But Gerry, who remembers most of her daytime conversation as being quite lucid, recalls that she took several telephone calls: she had given the Beckers' number to friends and to people involved with her writing and broadcasting. But throughout the four days she struck him as being almost unaware of the children's needs. It was mostly Phyllis, the Beckers' simpleminded, cross-eyed Irish maid, who looked after them. Afterward it seemed to Gerry that Phyllis "had sensed how Sylvia was already part-buried. The attention she gave our small daughter and Sylvia's children was beyond compare. She spent all her time with them as if to ward off the unseen, the unknown."[4]

On Thursday evening Jillian bathed Frieda and Nick, lent Frieda pajamas, fed her and took Nick to Sylvia, who gave him his bottle. At dinner Sylvia ate with a hearty appetite, but afterward said she wanted to lie down and take her pills. She had several

different kinds—sedatives, stimulants and other medication—
and, like a child, she asked Jillian to stay with her till she fell
asleep. Jillian didn't dole out the pills, but gave her water or tea to
swallow them, and tried to persuade her not to take so many.
When the sleeping pills seemed to be having no effect, Sylvia
wanted four more, and they compromised on one more. This sent
her to sleep, and Jillian went to bed, only to be awakened at about
three by desperate calls from Sylvia. Nick was awake too, and
when Jillian took him to her, Sylvia cuddled him. Then Frieda
woke up. When both children were back in bed, Jillian stayed
with Sylvia, who talked as she had to Trevor Thomas about how
happy they had been till Ted betrayed her. The Hughes family
hated her, she said, especially Ted's sister, Olwyn. Sylvia also
talked about her mother as if she were a monster. At 4:30 A.M. she
wanted her antidepressants, because they took two hours to have
any effect. Jillian said it was too early, but Sylvia went on
agitating for them, and at 5:30 took two. After going back to
sleep, she woke at seven. At breakfast she ate heartily, but then
went back to bed.

When Dr. Horder telephoned, he told Jillian to let Sylvia do
things for the children. "It's good for her." Later Sylvia called him
and went on talking for about half an hour, as if he were a
therapist. She spoke to the Beckers about a suicide attempt she
had made in 1953, but it didn't sound as if she were contemplating another, though she did say: "I can't even think about writing
a novel now, because to write a novel you need acres of time." She
talked about hating her mother. Ted had been a father substitute,
she said, but a reconciliation would make no difference now: her
world had been destroyed, desolated, laid to waste. She had seen
herself and him as exceptional, bigger than other people. They
had made love "like giants."

On Friday afternoon, when she went to see Dr. Horder, he
wanted to hospitalize her over the weekend, knowing that a strong
suicidal impulse was at work, and that the antidepressants might
fortify her resolution. But there was no space in either of the first
two hospitals he telephoned, and he decided the third was
unsuitable. He regarded her as one of the sensitive people who do
not always do well in hospital, and though he hadn't read *The Bell
Jar*, it was obvious that after the experiences of electroshock
therapy she had had ten years earlier, she was scared of hospitals.
Her depression was clearly pathological, but in a hospital she

would have been separated from the children, whose presence might work on her 'as an incentive to stay alive. There was no guarantee, in any case, that she would be unable to kill herself in a hospital.

In the limited time at his disposal, and without having read the death-oriented poems she had been writing, Dr. Horder had to make a decision on the basis of talking to her when, as he knew, both her nervous and endocrine systems were affected by the pills. He had arranged for a nurse to arrive at nine on Monday morning, and later in the day she was due to have her first meeting with the psychiatrist he had finally found for her. Dr. Horder was optimistic that if she got through the weekend, she would stand a good chance of recovery. It sounded as though she'd never be on her own, except when sleeping.

On Friday she told the Beckers she had something important to do in the evening. It was obvious she had a date, but was not willing to say who the man was. It's possible that she had arranged to see Corin Hughes-Stanton, the journalist boyfriend of Susan O'Neill-Roe, a girl who had been helping her in Devon to look after Frieda and Nick. He lived in Camden Town. Sylvia didn't mention his name to Jillian, but did talk rather mysteriously about "a journalist friend." In a January letter to her mother, Hughes-Stanton is described as "sweet," and his name appears on the last pages of the 1962 calendar pad she kept on the wall. She had invited him to tea on December 22.

Another possibility is that her date was with Hughes, who was having an affair with Assia Wevill, but had by no means discounted the possibility of reconciliation with Sylvia. At about seven, wearing her new cocktail outfit with the glittering blue top, she set off in her car, taking her jewelry, her curlers and her cosmetics in a small case. Her intention was to put the final touches to her appearance in the flat, but she was already looking elegant when she left Islington. After a long period of wearing old clothes and paying little attention to her appearance, she had been taking trouble over it again, and buying new clothes.

She was in the flat when Hughes arrived—either to see her or expecting to find the children. According to his account of the meeting, she quickly "bundled him out," wanting to lock up and leave, but after she got into her car, she was in no hurry to drive off. Yet another possibility is that she didn't have a date but merely wanted people to think she did. She had told Jillian that she had bought her new clothes with money she had been given by a man; in fact the money had come from Olive Higgins Prouty, a well-established American writer who had made Sylvia into her protégée.

On Friday evening Fitzroy Road was deep in snow, and Trevor Thomas, who'd found the front door wide open when he came home from work, was on the alert. About an hour later, looking out of the window, he saw Sylvia sitting in the old car, staring straight ahead, her hands clasped in her lap. Concerned, he went out. She was pale and seemed ill, with a dreamy look in her eyes. Was she all right? he asked. Why was she just sitting there? She might catch a chill.

She was thinking, she said. He offered to telephone Dr. Horder, but she said she was going away for a long holiday, a long rest, and the children were going to stay with friends. Soon after he went back indoors, she drove away. But when she arrived back at the Beckers' house, it was in a taxi, which may mean she had handed the car over to Hughes. It's possible she felt too confused to go on driving, but she had driven safely from Islington to Fitzroy Road, and after getting out of the taxi, she seemed self-possessed.

She'd been away from Islington for only four hours, and even if the conversations with Hughes and Trevor Thomas were brief, she could have spent little time with any other man, even if they met somewhere near Fitzroy Road. Possibly the man was less sympathetic than the Beckers to the state she was in; possibly he was turned off by it, or said something at which she took offense. It's also possible that he failed to turn up for the meeting, or that he hadn't committed himself to it. Or she may have been desperate for the pills she was due to take at eleven o'clock.

After going to sleep in Islington, she woke, as before, at about three and called for Jillian. On Saturday morning the German au pair rang Trevor Thomas's bell, wanting to know whether a letter had arrived for her. Madam had been awful on her last day there, she said, shouting and screaming at her to go. When the girl asked for her money, Sylvia refused, pushing her, hitting her and telling her to get out.

In the house at Islington, Sylvia spent most of the day with Jillian, talking in the same circular and unanswerable way. In spite of Gerry's flu, the Beckers were both going out in the evening, but not wanting to leave Sylvia alone with Phyllis, they arranged for an ex-student of Gerry's to come in. Sylvia sat on the chaise longue in the study, and he played records for her. It wasn't yet ten o'clock when the Beckers came home. Taking her pills, Sylvia seemed both feverish and hypnotized. She talked incessantly and excitedly, but ignored questions.

On Sunday morning, feeling well enough to go out, Gerry arranged that he and Nest Cleverdon, wife of the BBC producer who'd been working with both Sylvia and Hughes, would take the children to the zoo. Sylvia ate a good breakfast but failed to dress the children warmly enough for the cold day. After setting out, Gerry and Mrs. Cleverdon stopped at her house to wrap Nick up in something belonging to her baby son. It struck Mrs. Cleverdon as strange that it had been necessary to do this; normally Sylvia took such good care of the children.

At lunchtime she again ate heartily, afterward going upstairs to rest. She slept deeply and, waking at about four-thirty, called out to Jillian, who took in tea and cake. Sylvia then said she was feeling much better and wanted to go home with the children. She still seemed disoriented about time, and the Beckers did their best to dissuade her from leaving. After not wanting to be alone even for a few minutes, how would she cope by herself? Why go back to a cold flat? But she was adamant. She thanked them for the four days of freedom they'd given her, but now she was ready to resume her own routine. She had to do the laundry, she said, and get ready for the nurse who was going to arrive at nine in the morning. She also had to get Frieda ready for playschool, and prepare herself for lunch with a publisher. Altogether, she sounded very positive.

Sylvia helped Frieda into her coat and wrapped up Nick. Walking into the outer hall with them, Jillian said, "Look, it's too cold," but without using physical force they couldn't have stopped her from going. Phyllis helped to install Sylvia with the children and the luggage in the back of the old taxi. Finally Phyllis pushed some money into Sylvia's hand, saying "God bless you."

Unable to speak to Sylvia through the glass panel of the taxi, Gerry drove in silence. It was between six-thirty and seven in the evening when they arrived at Fitzroy Road. It was still freezing, and the sky was bright. When Gerry opened the passenger door, Nick was asleep. Sylvia and Frieda were sitting close together. Sylvia was still clutching the money tightly in her fist, and when she picked up Nick, she held him so awkwardly that Gerry told her to put the money away. She had left her coat behind, with her keys in the pocket, and for a hopeful moment Gerry thought he could persuade her to go back with him, but she had another set of keys in her bag.

After helping her to carry the children and the suitcase upstairs, he stayed with her for over two hours. The maisonette was cold when they arrived, but it warmed up after she switched the electric heaters on. After she'd put the children to bed, she made tea and talked about Court Green, the house she and Hughes had bought in Devon. She sounded happy when she talked about going back there in the spring. Marcia, a friend from America, was coming over to stay with her there, and the Beckers should come too. Gerry said he would help with the garden.

In those hours with Gerry she talked to him more than she ever had before about Assia and the infidelity. She was deeply hurt at having lost "the magic and hourly company of a husband so magnificent." Gerry made an effort to convince her that if only for the sake of children, who would be damaged by a broken marriage, reconciliation was in some cases possible. "Not in mine," she answered. When Gerry asked whether she got on well with the Hughes family, she said she didn't at all. She also complained that it was difficult to obtain money from Hughes for the children.

While she was with Gerry, Sylvia seemed clear-minded and reasonably optimistic, except when she talked about Assia and the sense she had of having been deserted. Before Gerry left, he did his best to cheer her up, talking about the nurse who was due in the morning, about Dr. Horder, about her friends. Gerry would pop in to see her during the afternoon, and soon he would take the children to the zoo again. She said she was going to see someone later on in the evening. Gerry didn't want to ask who it was, but assumed she was going to see Hughes.

It's possible she was referring to Dr. Horder, who did call on her during the evening, but thought she would be safe until the nurse arrived in the morning. The last man to see her alive was Trevor Thomas. Shortly before midnight, his doorbell rang. She was looking odd, as if drugged or doped. Her voice struck him as being in slow motion, the vowels drawn out and somehow slurred, making her sound more American than usual. She asked whether he could give her some stamps. She didn't have quite enough and she had letters to mail. He told her there would be no collection till the morning. No, she said, they were airmail for America, and she had to get them into the mail tonight. It seemed useless to argue, but he asked why she had come back instead of spending the whole weekend with her friends. She said the children had been difficult and she wanted to write. He said nothing about the visit from the au pair. When he gave her the stamps, she took out a small purse. He didn't want to accept any money, but she insisted on paying him. Otherwise, she said, she wouldn't be right with her conscience before God, would she? When he said she could leave it till the morning, she asked what time he went to work. He told her he normally left the flat between a quarter and half past eight.

After shutting the front door of his apartment, he could still see light from the hall underneath it. He let about ten minutes go by before opening the door again. She was still standing outside, head raised, and the expression on her face was seraphic. "You aren't really well, are you?" he said. "I'm sure I should get the doctor." But she asked him not to. She was having a marvelous dream, she said, a most wonderful vision. He invited her to come in, but she wouldn't, and when he urged her to go back upstairs, out of the cold, she just smiled. It was now about half past twelve. He had to go to bed, he said, or he wouldn't be able to get up in time. The light stayed on, and after about twenty minutes he opened the door again, but she wasn't there. He went to bed, but couldn't sleep. Although he had taken off his hearing aid, he could still hear her pacing the uncarpeted floor above his head.

Sylvia had in her possession enough sleeping pills to kill her, but she chose to die by gassing herself. Her diary describes how at the beginning of the fifties she chose gas instead of novocaine when she had wisdom teeth extracted. In the dentist's chair she enjoyed feeling the tubes pressing into her cheek, and she tried not to fight the gas, which tasted sickeningly sweet. When the dentist put something into her mouth, the gas seemed to be coming in big gulps. She'd been staring into the light, which seemed to smash into tiny fragments, all swinging rhythmically. Something had taken possession of her lungs, emitting breathy wheezes. As she felt her mouth cracking into a smile, she wanted to describe in writing what it was like to go under. No one had told her how simple it was.

To protect the children from the gas she opened the window of their bedroom. She left bread and cups of milk by both cribs, though Nick was barely thirteen months old, too young to feed himself. She stuffed towels and cloths under the doors of both bedroom and kitchen, as well as sticking adhesive tape around the edges of the doors. All this was done painstakingly. This was clearly a suicide attempt that was designed not to fail. She pinned a note to the pram, which was in the room next door to the kitchen, saying "Please call Dr. Horder" and giving his number. If she wrote a suicide note, its contents haven't been divulged. She knew the nurse was due to arrive in the morning, and it seems unlikely that she had miscalculated the amount of time the gas would take to kill her. She folded a cloth to rest her head on, turned on all the gas jets and put her head deep inside the oven.

When Myra Norris, the nurse, arrived on Monday morning, she heard children crying inside the house, but she couldn't get in though she rang both bells. There was a line outside the nearest public telephone booth, and her agency, when she finally made contact, confirmed that 23 Fitzroy Road was the right address. When she went back to the house, she found a contractor working there. When they forced the front door of the maisonette, the smell of gas was unmistakable. They rushed into the kitchen, opened the windows, turned the gas off and dragged Sylvia into the living room, where Myra Norris tried artificial respiration. The children were still crying and were very cold but unharmed. Charles Langridge, the contractor, went out to a telephone booth, where he called not only the police and Dr. Horder but also an ambulance.

Dr. Horder arrived at about half past eleven.[5] The body was already cold, and his examination of it led him to believe she'd died between four and six in the morning. The ambulance, which arrived five minutes later, took the body to University College Hospital in Gower Street, where Dr. Hill, the doctor there who examined it, said Sylvia had been dead for about four hours. According to the policeman, the ambulance had arrived at the flat at 11:35 A.M., which means Dr. Hill could not have seen the body before midday and that if he was right she hadn't died till about eight o'clock.

Catherine Frankfort, the neighbor who came to babysit, found only the policeman, Dr. Horder and the children. She sat weeping in the doctor's car, while he tried to console her by saying that if it hadn't happened now, it would have happened later.[6] He got in touch with Jillian Becker, who didn't have Ted Hughes's London number, but contacted Suzette Macedo, who did.

Trevor Thomas did not wake up until about five in the afternoon. He had a bad headache, felt sick, and fell over when he tried to stand up. He went to the Gordon Fraser Gallery to apologize for failing to turn up for work, and on his way back to the house met a neighbor who told him the lady upstairs had gassed herself. He realized he had been affected by the gas. The children on the top floor had been in no danger because methane, being heavier than air, sinks. He spoke to Dr. Horder, catching him on his way downstairs from examining them. The doctor, who said Thomas was suffering from carbon monoxide poisoning and prescribed vitamins, seemed upset and almost angry; later he spoke of feeling that Sylvia had let him down.

The autopsy report bizarrely states that Sylvia died on February 11, 1963, and that her body was examined on February 10, 1963. It was the body of an adequately nourished young woman with recent bruises on the right forehead and the right occipital region of the scalp. The hypostatic bloodstains on the flanks were bright pink in color, as was all her blood. There were about six subpleural hemorrhages on the lower lobes of both lungs.[7]

Before the inquest Ted went with the critic A. Alvarez to the undertaker in Mornington Crescent. With a frilly collar around its neck, the stiff body lay in a coffin at the far end of a bare, draped room with a faint smell, like apples beginning to rot. The face was "gray and slightly transparent, like wax." Alvarez scarcely recognized her. "Her features seemed too thin and sharp."[8]

Later in the morning the inquest was held in the coroner's office in a graveyard near St. Pancras Station. Hughes, Alvarez, Dr. Horder, Myra Norris and Thomas were among those present, and so was a man in a dark suit and a white shirt. Contemptuously, Ted pointed him out to Alvarez as a boyfriend of Sylvia's.[9] Describing himself as an author and lecturer in English literature, and giving his address as 23 Fitzroy Road, Hughes testified to Sylvia's long history of mental illness and previous suicide attempts. The coroner put some of the blame on the doctor. The verdict was suicide.

Sylvia had talked about wanting to be buried in Devon, in the graveyard adjoining the grounds of the house, Court Green, where she had lived, but Hughes has written: "My understanding was that she was fond of West Yorkshire."[10] He had her body taken to Heptonstall, the tiny hilltop village where his parents lived, south of the Brontës' Haworth. She was buried in the field that had been annexed as an extension to the graveyard of the old parish church. Other members of the Hughes family had been buried there.

Though the Plaths were not keen on the idea of having Sylvia buried in Yorkshire, her brother, Warren, and his wife, Margaret, came over for the funeral. Her only British friends to make the long journey northward were the Beckers, who took the train to Hebden Bridge. They were met at the station by Hughes and a cousin of his, a young woman. Gerry, who was seeing Hughes for the first time, found him impressive. After worrying about what would happen to the children, Gerry now felt in no doubt that good care would be taken of them.

The four mourners drove to the house, where they sat with Hughes's parents. The impression Gerry formed was that they all resented and disliked Sylvia: their boy had been harmed by an American woman, a foreigner. In Hughes himself the predominant emotion seemed to be anger. When the undertaker asked whether the coffin should be left open, he said no: "She doesn't look as she used to."[11]

It was a very cold day, with thick snow on the ground. Weak sunlight poured in through the stained glass of the church windows. There were about twenty mourners, mostly members of the Hughes family. After a short, simple service, they walked across the snow-covered field toward the one ugly space where the naked earth was exposed. After a brief ceremony, earth was shoveled on top of the coffin. Everyone filed away except Hughes, who for at least five minutes stayed alone, hunched at the edge of the grave. Afterward, catching up with Jillian, he said: "Something of me has died with her."

They reassembled in a room above the Co-operative Store, where places had been laid at two long tables. Tea and pies were served, but conversation was restrained. Hoping to break through the silence, Gerry went downstairs to the shop to buy two bottles of whiskey. There were no glasses, but pouring away the dregs of tea in the cups, he offered whiskey. Several of the women refused, but Ted Hughes was glad to drink some, though nothing could have cheered him up. "Everybody hated her," he said. Later on he said: "It was a fight to the death. One of us had to die."[12] But when he spoke about his last meeting with her, he said he had told her that in six months' time they would be living together again in Devon.[13]

The gravestone he chose was a slab of gray marble inscribed with the words:

SYLVIA PLATH HUGHES

1932–1963

Even among fierce flames
The golden lotus can be planted

This is a translation from the Sanskrit, he explained, and he used to quote it to her when she was depressed.[14]

One of the mysteries that still surround her death is what happened to the Morris station wagon, which she never used again after the Friday night outing. According to a neighbor, it had reappeared in the street during Sunday evening, but had disappeared again by morning. If we knew what happened to the car on Friday night, it might be possible to establish whether the man she was planning to meet then was the man who turned up at the inquest, and whether it was Hughes she was expecting to see on Sunday night.

On the question of whether divorce proceedings were under way, contradictory statements have been made. Sylvia told Trevor Thomas that she had reluctantly signed divorce papers the previous week, and a letter to her mother (October 9, 1962) said she was getting a divorce. Could her brother Warren or her Aunt Dot fly over to be with her for a few days when she had to face the court? She would need help, she said. The hearing would probably be in the spring. But Ted and Olwyn Hughes have protested that no divorce proceedings had been started. He wrote in a letter to the *Guardian* (April 20, 1989): "Whatever she may have said to the advisers who were urging her on, she never touched divorce papers and had no plan to do so. I am able to say that because she and I discussed our future quite freely up to the end." He was unaware, he goes on, of any divorce proceedings.[15]

Meeting Jillian Becker, he asked whether Sylvia had left a coat at their house. When it was found on the coatrack his first question was, "Are her keys in the pocket?" They were—both car and house keys. But Gerry Becker remembered seeing her take a set of keys out of her handbag to let herself into the house. "Were they found later?" Hughes asked. Why did she have two sets, and why were keys uppermost in his mind?

It was ironical that she killed herself without making a will. She cared deeply about the children and her work; the result of dying intestate was to give Hughes total control over Frieda, Nick and everything she had written.

Another question to which contradictory answers are being given is whether she was short of money at the end of her life. Though she had considerable pride, she was putting on a show of being destitute. She even kept a charity collecting box on the mantelpiece, and twice accepted money from Phyllis, although, after the first time, Sylvia said it made her feel she gave off the smell of poverty.[16] This Irish maid, she felt, saw her as an abandoned woman. According to Olwyn, she had fifteen hundred pounds in the bank when she died, and Ted Hughes maintains that between October and her death he gave her about nine hundred pounds, while she was receiving money from her mother, her Aunt Dot and the writer Olive Higgins Prouty, who had for over ten years been a generous patroness. Sylvia was buying new clothes for herself, but when Jillian Becker questioned her about the children's clothes, she said she had nothing. "Can I have anything from your children?"

Another unsolved mystery is about the letters to America. Anne Stevenson's account of Sylvia's visit to Thomas suggests that the stamp-buying was merely a pretext for calling at his flat. "Her real purpose seems to have been to ensure that he would be up before nine the next morning, in time to let in the nurse she expected."[17] In fact, as he told Sylvia, he always left the house between 8:15 and 8:30. She possibly knew the workman would be there, and may have been counting either on him or on Catherine Frankfort to break in and take charge of the children.

It is clear that when she spoke to Thomas, she was deeply concerned about the letters, and apparently one of them was to her mother. Although she obtained stamps, she did not mail the letters. Questioned on October 12, 1990, her mother said that though this last letter never reached her, she was aware of its existence. When she first heard the news of Sylvia's death, nothing was said about suicide, and Aurelia Plath's first impression was that her daughter had died of pneumonia. Later, told about the letter, she was given to understand that it would be better if she didn't see it, and she didn't try to insist.[18]

One of her reasons for not wanting to antagonize Hughes was that she was hoping he might agree to let the children be brought up in America. But even if she hadn't set so much store by everything Sylvia wrote, it still seems odd that Mrs. Plath would surrender her right to read a letter her daughter wrote to her within hours of killing herself.

❧ 2 ❧

My Colossal Father

"She seemed convinced, in these last poems, that the root of her suffering was the death of her father, whom she loved, who abandoned her, and who dragged her after him into death."

A. Alvarez

Sylvia Plath was eight when her father died, but the seeds of her neurosis had already been planted. He was the dominant force in the family, and she loved his praise. Her mother remembers the time when she was starting piano lessons: "She would play for him. He would pat her on the head and praise her."[1] Though he wasn't particularly fond of young children, she did not feel that she was being deprived of his intensely desirable love until illness overtook him, increasing his irritability. Assuming she must somehow be at fault if he was less interested in her, she exerted herself more at the activities which seemed to please him—making up little rhymes, dancing, drawing, playing the piano for him. Without being entirely unresponsive, he soon gave signs that his patience was exhausted, and her longing to stay in his godlike presence was mostly frustrated. Well-meaningly, her mother was trying to protect him by restricting the children to quiet games when he was within earshot, and to protect them by keeping them as far away as she could from explosions of rage and gasps of pain when he had cramping spasms in his leg muscles.

For Sylvia his death wasn't so much a shock as the irreversible

20

conclusion to a series of rejections. She and her brother, Warren, were free to make more noise, but all her chances of winning back Daddy's love had vanished. Either she was at fault for not trying hard enough, or her mother was for allowing her only such brief opportunities.

It wasn't until March 1959, when Sylvia was twenty-six, that she paid her first visit to his grave. The cemetery in Winthrop, Massachusetts, is on the outskirts of the town, on low ground, where you can smell the stagnant salt marshes in the distance. She found three graveyards, separated by roads. With its weather-beaten flat stones and lichen-covered monuments, the old grave-yard is impressive, like country churchyards she'd seen in England, where nothing could disturb the dignity imparted by the ancient stone to the invisible dead. In the newest of the three graveyards everything belonged to the last fifty years. Plastic flowers stood crudely in rusting metal containers.

The flat headstone inscribed "Otto E. Plath 1885–1940" was so close to the pathway that people were regularly treading on his grave. She felt cheated. The tombstone was on a flat grassy area with a view across a barren stretch of land to rows of wooden tenements. Ugly, crude and black, the headstones were crowded together as if the dead were sleeping in a poorhouse. She wished she could dig her father up. "How far gone would he be?" She didn't stay long, but at least she now had a place she could picture: this was where his bones were.[2] If it was fear that had stopped her from coming here sooner, it had been mainly dread of having a place to picture.

Azalea Path, the name of the pathway by the grave, was oddly close to her mother's name, Aurelia Plath. In *The Bell Jar* Sylvia's alter ego, Esther Greenwood, picks a bunch of azaleas from a bush at the entrance to the cemetery, wanting to compensate her father for all the years in which no one has been visiting him. Her mother had said the children were too young to attend the funeral, and Esther, who had been his favorite, now wants to assume the responsibility her mother has always ignored—tending the grave.[3]

Though Otto Plath had been lacking in warmth and had often shown impatience with the two children, this had not stopped Sylvia from feeling close to him and proud of being his favorite. She still thought of him as present inside her, "interwoven in the cellular system of your long body."[4] When she was six or seven, he used to lie on the couch in the living room after supper while she improvised dances for him. Later, as an adolescent, she told herself that the intensity of her longing for male company derived from the absence of an older man in the household, and as a married woman she had an exceptionally strong aversion to being deprived of her husband's company for more than a short stretch of time. Nor could she ever know how different her emotional needs would have been if her father had lived longer. He'd been a lecturer in entomology at Boston University, and at school, following her mother's orientation toward the humanities, she regretted her ignorance of botany and zoology.[5]

Made of mottled pink marble, the headstone is described in *The Bell Jar* as looking like canned salmon. As soon as Esther has arranged the azaleas, she collapses and weeps violently, sitting on the wet grass. Never before has she shed tears for her father's death. Nor has Mrs. Greenwood: trying to look on the bright side, she'd said what a good thing it was he'd died instead of living on as a cripple.[6] In the novel it can be stated categorically that Esther's mother had never wept over the bereavement. In reality all Sylvia knew was that she had never seen Aurelia weeping about it.

Sometimes, when contemplating suicide, as she often did, Sylvia felt as if her father were trying to drag her down into the grave. Though he didn't quite kill himself, he had set a suicidal example. He was fifty in 1936 when he developed a form of diabetes which could have been treated with insulin if he hadn't reacted obstinately and irrationally to the symptoms, refusing to consult a doctor. His health went on deteriorating. He lost weight, suffering from sinusitis and a persistent cough. His irritability increased and his stamina diminished; he needed to spend more and more time lying down. He gave up none of his university work, even during the summer vacation, when he taught a session, but the effort exhausted him, and he worked horizontally, moving from the couch in the living room to the couch in his study as he prepared lectures and corrected written work.

One of his friends, dying of lung cancer, had undergone several unsuccessful operations, and Otto Plath, assuming he too was cancerous, refused to consult a doctor, ignoring Aurelia's persistent attempts to persuade him, though she was supported by her parents and by some of his university colleagues. He was adamant. He had diagnosed his own condition, he said, and would never submit to surgery. He merely grew angry when she begged him to let a doctor examine him. In desperation she asked the family doctor to drop in on the pretext of paying a casual visit, but she was told this would be unethical.[7]

A man with strong willpower and liable to violent outbursts of temper, Otto Plath detested stock responses, received ideas and everything that went by the name of common sense. In the classroom, to demonstrate that human behavior was programmed by prejudices passed on from one generation to the next, he used to skin a rat, cook it and eat it in front of his students. As his health went on deteriorating, he delegated more of his work to his willing wife, who was his junior by twenty-one years, and he withdrew even further from Sylvia and Warren. Otto Plath spent more time in his study, eating many of his meals there, but not welcoming the children when they wanted to see him.[8]

When Sylvia was born, her parents were living in Jamaica Plain, Massachusetts. In 1936, after her father was taken ill, they moved to Winthrop, a suburb of Boston, in order to be near Aurelia's parents, who had a house on Point Shirley, where the spar of land behind the seawall is so narrow that there is space only for two rows of houses and the road intersecting them. The Atlantic beats against the seawall and on the other side are the quieter waters of Boston Harbor. Aurelia's parents, who belonged to the same generation as her husband, lived with her younger sister and her twenty-one-year-old brother. Sylvia's new home on Johnson Avenue was within easy walking distance. Fond though she was of her grandparents, her very young uncle and her young aunt, she resented being sent so often to play in their house. Her parents were getting rid of her, and altogether she saw too little of her father, who seemed to be taking little more than a supervisory interest in his children, concentrating on their education. As she knew, the one sure way of earning his approval was by getting high marks at school. Family life had always seemed to revolve around diligent application to academic work.

The son of a mechanic who worked as a blacksmith, Otto Plath grew up speaking German and Polish, besides learning French in school. One grandmother was Polish but both his parents were German, and his childhood was spent in Grabow (or Grabowo), in the Polish corridor. At school he was first in every subject, and this made such a good impression on his grandparents that after emigrating to the United States, where they bought a small farm in Wisconsin, they offered to pay for him to be educated at Northwestern College—on condition that he go on to prepare himself for the Lutheran ministry. Nothing was more obvious than that hard work paid off: it had won him the right to escape national service by going to live in America and to have a better education than his parents could have afforded to give him.

He was sixteen when he arrived in America with virtually no knowledge of the language. Living in New York with an uncle who owned a food and liquor store, he learned English by sitting in on classes at an elementary school, starting with the youngest children. He sat at the back of the class, taking notes during lessons, afterward chatting with teachers and children. After school he paid for his keep by working in his uncle's shop. As soon as he had improved his vocabulary sufficiently, he promoted himself into the next class, moving through all eight classes in the space of a school year. He had learned to speak English with no accent.

He worked equally hard at Northwestern, studying the classics and getting high marks, but when he went on to the Lutheran seminary, he was forbidden to read Darwin, who had become one of his favorite writers. Most of his fellow students had no feeling of vocation but didn't intend to let this stop them from making a career in the church. Otto Plath had too much integrity to do this, and, hoping to be forgiven by his grandparents, opted for a teaching career. Unforgivingly, they accused him of letting them bring him to America under false pretenses, and this led to a breach with the whole family. Even when his parents, his three brothers and his two sisters came to America, he had no contact with them.

His passion for learning produced a passion for teaching. He worked at the University of California from 1912 to 1914 as a teaching fellow in German. Although his main interest was in biology and entomology, he worked at first as a language teacher and did not receive his Master of Science degree until 1925. After doing graduate work at Washington University, he moved east and taught modern languages at the Massachusetts Institute of Technology from 1915 to 1918. For the academic year 1920–21 he worked as an assistant in zoology at Johns Hopkins University, but he went back to language teaching in 1921. He was a good-looking man, tall, with vivid blue eyes, thick hair, a fair complexion and red cheeks, but he was addicted almost puritanically to the academic virtues, taking less interest in women than they took in him. He married when he was thirty-four, but after about a year with his wife he separated from her and reverted gladly to the habits of an academic bachelor, living in college accommodations or in a furnished room.

From 1922 on he taught German at Boston University; even when he started teaching biology in 1926, he continued the German. His appetite for work was insatiable. Besides his teaching, he was still studying intensely, and in 1928, at the age of forty-three, he got his doctorate in entomology. His book *Bumblebees and Their Ways* was published in 1934. Originally it had been his sweet tooth that got him interested in bees. When boyhood poverty prevented him from buying sweets, he watched out for flights of bees emerging from fields, and, after locating their nesting place, used a long straw to suck out wild honey. But he went on to take as much sensual pleasure in observing the bees as in eating the honey.

He writes about them with unmistakable relish: "If one is fortunate, one may come upon a young queen of the beautiful species *ternarius,* whose orange and yellow pile blends with the colors of the male willow catkins just bursting into blossom. A bit farther on, among the inconspicuous flowers of a female willow, one is almost certain to find a queen of *B. terricola* in her splendid livery of black banded with yellow."[9] By transferring bumblebee colonies to cigar boxes and keeping them in the garden, he won the nickname "Bee King."

He hadn't yet finished his book on bees when, at the age of forty-six, he found a student who drove herself as hard as he did. His favorite pupil in his Middle High German class was Aurelia Schober, a tall, thin, pretty twenty-five-year-old, who was studying for an M.A. degree at the same time she taught German and English at a high school. In the summer, just before the term ended, he was invited to spend a weekend on a farm and to take a friend with him. He had no one to bring, and on the last day of classes, after considerable hesitation, he asked Aurelia whether she would like to join him. While they were on the farm together, she found out he was still married to a woman he hadn't seen for thirteen years.

His friendship with Aurelia developed through correspondence and weekends of hiking. She acquired some of his enthusiasm for entomology and ornithology, while he acquired some of hers for literature and the theater. When they started planning their future together, it was on the assumption that they'd make the most of their opportunities by applying themselves diligently. They'd give time to nature study, travel and writing. After establishing a family of at least two children, they'd collaborate on a book called *The Evolution of Parental Care in the Animal Kingdom.*

When they talked about marrying, Aurelia took it that they would have equal rights in the partnership they formed. But their relationship had started as one between teacher and pupil, and Otto had never discarded the traditional German idea that the man should be master in the household. She had to use her formidable willpower to mold herself into a submissive young wife. After they married in January 1932, he not only made financial decisions without consulting her, he also did the shopping—convinced after years of fending for himself that he was good at getting the best food at the lowest prices. Once a week he shopped for meat, fish and vegetables at Boston's Faneuil Hall Market.[10]

They both wanted to start a family immediately. Believing that girls were usually more affectionate, he was hoping for a daughter, but at lunchtime on the day Sylvia was born, October 27, 1932, he told his colleagues he was hoping for one more thing in life—to have a son within two and a half years. Warren was born punctually. Aurelia applied her energy and willpower to the task of bringing up two young children. When they were babies, she picked them up when they cried, fed them whenever they seemed hungry, rocked them, cuddled them, sang and recited to them. If Otto didn't want her as his partner, she'd have to make herself indispensable as a hardworking and resourceful assistant. When he was invited to write a treatise on insect societies, she worked on it with him, and as his health deteriorated, she took over as much work as he was willing to delegate. After reading and taking extensive notes on sixty-nine texts he listed for use as sources, she wrote the first draft of the treatise, and he revised it.

For over a year he used the table in the dining room as a desk, storing books on the sideboard. More sociable than he was, Aurelia wanted to give small dinner parties when he was teaching at Harvard night school, but didn't dare to ask for permission.

She stood no chance of making him compromise, and the only way to avoid constant friction was to keep him in ignorance of what she was doing. She made sketch plans of the books and papers he'd left on both sideboard and table, entertained her guests and put all her husband's things back in place before he came home.

In mid-August 1940 he was getting ready to leave the house for summer school when he stubbed his little toe against the base of a bureau. In the evening, when he came home, Aurelia asked him to show her his foot. His toes were black, and red streaks were running up his ankle. She called the doctor, who after taking blood and urine samples diagnosed *diabetes mellitus* in a very advanced stage. When Otto developed pneumonia, he went into the hospital for two weeks, and a full-time nurse had to be employed when he was discharged. "How could such a brilliant man be so stupid?" asked the specialist, who confirmed that the gangrenous leg would have to be amputated from the thigh.[11] The operation was performed on October 12, 1940, at the New England Deaconess Hospital. When the children were told, Sylvia asked: "When he buys shoes, will he have to buy a *pair,* Mummy?"

On November 5, Otto Plath died in his sleep. The eight-year-old Sylvia had been praying every night for his recovery, and when the news was broken, her reaction was to bury herself under the bedclothes, saying: "I'll never speak to God again."

Going to see the body at the funeral parlor, Aurelia felt "he bore no resemblance to the husband I knew, but looked like a fashionable store mannequin." She decided against taking the children to the funeral, and managed not to let them see her in tears: she remembered how frightening it had been to see her mother weeping, and it didn't occur to her that they might later accuse her of not having felt the proper grief.[12] In *The Bell Jar* all Esther remembers is that her mother smiled and said how merciful it had been that he hadn't had to live as a cripple, an invalid for life. "I laid my face to the smooth face of the marble and howled my loss into the cold salt rain." Esther forgets that the loss wasn't just hers, and that her mother might have cried when she was asleep.

Otto Plath became more important as a figure in Sylvia's fantasy than he'd ever been as a presence in her life, though her imaginary relationship with him had already started in fantasies and dreams about him. Within eleven days of visiting his grave, she'd started to think about her own death as the unavoidable sequel to his, which she regarded as suicidal. In the poem "Electra on Azalea Path," which she wrote in March 1959, when she was twenty-six,[13] she calls herself "the ghost of an infamous suicide." A less obstinate man would have sidestepped the gangrene that "ate you to the bone." She pictures a blue razor rusting in her throat, and apologizes for knocking at his door to ask forgiveness. It was her love, she says, that did both of them to death. He died after she brought her love for him to bear.

On the day he died, she says, she went into the dirt like a bee going into hibernation. She's been almost asleep ever since, to be awakened only by her visit to his bones in the "cramped necropolis." She's reminded of Sophocles' *Electra* by the dye-stained water dripping from the petals of the artificial red sage among the plastic evergreen on the neighboring headstone. To shut out the idea of his part in her conception, she pictures herself as "Godfathered"—conceived immaculately, with only a stain of divinity left on her mother's sheets. But within a few weeks she'd come to feel embarrassed by the poem, which she dismissed as "forced and rhetorical."[14]

She approaches the subject differently in "The Beekeeper's Daughter," which was written soon afterward. Her father had taken great pride in the magical-seeming power he had over bees. They never stung him when he caught them. If Sylvia made her memories of him into a myth, it was he who almost deliberately started the mythifying process. Once he caught a bee in his fist and held it to her ear; in one of the lines she cut from her 1957 poem "All the Dead Dears," he was "a man who used to clench bees in his fist and out-rant the thundercrack." This links the Bee King with King Lear.

She spent a lot of time with his book, *Bumblebees and Their Ways,* which is the basic source both of the interest in beekeeping she developed in 1962 and of the bee imagery recurrent in many of her poems. But the 1962 series of beekeeping poems is anticipated by "The Beekeeper's Daughter." After drawing on his book for some of the detail in the last stanza, she addresses him as "Father, bridegroom," and symbolically weds him when she ends the poem with a reference to the queen bee who marries "the winter of your year." The idea of wedding the dead father is inseparable from the idea of dying to be united with him. She sometimes thought of the dead as attaching themselves like barnacles to the living, or of "hag hands hauling me down." At the end of "Lorelei" the speaker tells the sirens to "ferry" her down to the depths.

Though Sylvia took pleasure, when she wrote "Electra on Azalea Path," in identifying with a girl whose father had been killed by her mother, she wasn't yet conscious of the extent to which she was blaming Aurelia for Otto Plath's death. By marrying a man so much older than herself, she'd given her children an old father, and then one morning she came in with tears "in her eyes and told me he was gone for good. I hate her for that."[15] It was her fault that Sylvia had to live without "the only man who'd love me steady through life."[16] This made her hate men who couldn't be relied on to go on loving her steadily. She revenged herself by picking holes in them, showing them they wouldn't be any good as fathers, encouraging them to propose marriage, and then puncturing their hopes.[17]

At the same time as blaming Aurelia for the unnecessary death, Sylvia blamed herself—"It was my love that did us both to death"[18]—and assumed her mother was blaming her. Aurelia told Sylvia about a dream in which she was wearing a gaudy dress and was going to become a chorus girl, perhaps a prostitute. Her father, who was alive again, slammed out of the house in a rage. Desperate, Aurelia ran along the beach, her feet sinking into the sand, her purse open, coins falling out. To spite her, he'd driven off the bridge. He was floating face downward in the ocean water by the pillars of the country club, while neighbors watched disapprovingly from the pier.

It's hard to explain why a girl who thought so often about the dead father never visited his grave until she was twenty-six—six years after her first suicide attempt—but it's easy to explain what prompted that visit in the spring of 1959. At the end of December 1958 Sylvia read Freud's *Mourning and Melancholia,* which explains melancholia as developing out of a failure or inability to mourn adequately for a serious loss. At eight she'd been incapable of mourning, and her melancholia was more deep-seated and dangerous than it would have been had the tension been relieved sooner. In Freud's account of it, melancholia consists of profoundly painful dejection, withdrawal of interest in the outside world, loss of capacity to love, inhibition of all activity and a lowering of self-regard, sometimes so extreme that it leads to self-vilification and a delusional expectation of punishment. These symptoms, or variants on them, affected Sylvia over much of her life, and Freud's formulations struck her as an almost exact transcription of her feelings during the depression that had led to the suicide attempt.

Though the 1959 visit to the grave inaugurated a new phase in her feelings about her father, this doesn't mean she'd never previously tried to mourn for him. Among her pre-1956 juvenilia is a villanelle called "Lament," influenced by Dylan Thomas. The dead father is implicitly compared with Christ walking on the waters. The dead father, who was taken away by the sting of bees, trounced the sea like a raging bather, and "rode the flood in a pride of prongs." But the poem is also full of atheistic contempt. God is spelled with a lower case *g* when we're told the father considered the guns of god to be a nuisance. The main emphasis, though, is on the impossibility of replacing such a man. You could ransack the four winds and still fail to find anyone else who could "mangle the grin of kings."

In March 1956, when her grandmother was dying of cancer in Winthrop, Sylvia was in England, and it was painful to think that "Grammy" could "go out of the world and me not there."[19] Divided from the dying woman by an ocean, Sylvia thought tearfully about her and about the father she'd barely known. Photographs of his face at the age of seventeen made her think how much more she could have loved him now than she had as a child of seven. "I lust for the knowing of him." Attending a discussion at the Anchor, a Cambridge pub, where one of the lecturers, Dr. Theodore Redpath, was talking about Shakespeare, Sylvia felt strongly tempted to ask whether he'd be her father. How good it would be to "live with the chastened, wise mind of an older man." She must be careful not to marry an older man with that objective. The best solution would be to marry a young man with a brilliant father. "I could wed both."[20]

What she found by visiting the grave three years later was a new way of expressing her feelings. "Electra on Azalea Path" and "The Beekeeper's Daughter" were both eclipsed by "The Colossus," which became the title poem of her first collection. Here the mythmaking is more deliberate: the dead father is inflated—as he had been in one of her dreams—to the size of a giant. In the dream she was trying to reconstruct a fragmented stone colossus from the scattered pieces.[21] In the poem she addresses them as Father. His body fills the landscape; his bones and hair are littered to the horizon, and the sun rises under the pillar of his tongue. She's again thinking of Electra: the blue sky arching above them is out of the *Oresteia,* while she may also be thinking of *Gulliver's*

Travels. As if trying to resurrect a Brobdingnagian giant, she crawls over the weedy acres of his brow to mend the immense skull-plates and, using disinfectant, cleans the bald white tumuli of his eyes, but the task of gluing him together is too much for her. She's been trying for thirty years to dredge silt from his throat. At night she shelters from the wind inside his left ear.

Of all her attempts to lay the ghost of her father, the most desperate and most notorious is her poem "Daddy." Introducing it when she read it on the BBC's Third Programme, she said the speaker was a girl whose father had died when she thought he was God. This girl had an Electra complex, and her case was complicated by the fact that the man was a Nazi, while his wife might be partly Jewish. The two strains merge in the daughter, who cannot free herself from the "awful little allegory" except by acting it out—once. This camouflages the autobiographical drive behind the poem.

Of course, it's partly a fiction, while the speaker is partly a character, but, as in so many of Sylvia Plath's poems, the tone is so abrasively confessional that we can't be entirely deceived—and perhaps we aren't intended to be—by the pretense of holding it at arm's length as an "awful little allegory." The girl with the Nazi father is a persona, but the mask is designed to become transparent. The statements are too direct, the emotion too raw, the experience too personal. Writing fifteen days before her thirtieth birthday, Sylvia is trying not only to sum up the relationship that hadn't ended with her father's death but to get it under control. There's as much optimism as defiance in the final line "Daddy, daddy, you bastard I'm through." Meaning both that she'd finally worked her way through the problems and that the relationship was over.

The poem opens with a complaint about being imprisoned. For thirty years she has lived inside him like a white foot in a black shoe so tight she scarcely dared to breathe. The rhythm slows down for two contradictory assertions: that she had to kill him and that he died before she had time to kill him. The idea of acting out is a Freudian concept Sylvia may have picked up from her psychiatrist, Ruth Beuscher. Motivated by unconscious drives and fantasies, acting out departs from the normal pattern of behavior—the action is usually more aggressive. Accumulated resentments about a father, for instance, might be acted out in a relationship with a husband. In analysis, the situation encourages the patient to "transfer" the accumulated mixture of positive and negative feeling, and Sylvia, when no longer having sessions with Dr. Beuscher, tended to carry on the therapy, solo, in her writing. At the same time, inevitably, she must have transferred positive and negative feelings to Ted Hughes in such a way that the relationship with him continued the relationship with her dead father.

But there was an element of acting out in all the efforts to excel that she made throughout her life. At school, at summer camp, as a diarist, in college, as a professional writer, she was compulsive and almost heroic in the efforts she made to do well. Her energy was tremendous, and she channeled it relentlessly into her drive for success.

Freud rejected the term "Electra complex." It was introduced by Jung, who believed women could be as violent as Oedipal men in their possessive love for the parent of the opposite sex and in their jealous hatred for the parent of the same sex. In "Daddy" the love and hatred are both focused on the father. The hatred is more apparent—the insistent rhythm makes the poem into a dance of rage—but the rage comes out of frustrated love.

The suggestion of superhuman size—residue from the dream and the earlier poem—emerges in the idea that his toe, as big as a seal, is in San Francisco while his head is in the Atlantic, and, with a fond affectation of contempt, she compares him with the devil by saying he has a cleft in his chin instead of his foot. Though of German origin, Otto Plath had no connection with the Nazis, but he did often stand at a blackboard—this is what he's doing in one of the photographs Sylvia would often have seen— and he did teach German. The daughter in the poem, possibly partly Jewish, is carried off to Dachau by the obscene German language.

But the outsize father blurs into the husband. Brought back to life after the suicide attempt, says the speaker, she was pulled out of the sack, stuck together with glue, and she knew what she had to do. (This "oo" sound thuds repetitively through the poem.) She made a model of him, a man who loved to inflict pain. Like a vampire, he has drunk her blood for seven years. It was almost seven years since she'd met Ted Hughes, and the words "I do, I do" obviously refer to the marriage ceremony, while the conclusive "I'm through" may be aimed partly at him. She's through with both relationships.

❦ 3 ❧

Dearest of Mothers

In February 1953, six months before she tried to kill herself, Sylvia wrote to tell Aurelia what a "superlative" mother she had been. But the suicide attempt was a ferocious act of aggression against her. Both then and in February 1963, when she succeeded in killing herself, Sylvia was following an example both parents had set. Her father was killed by a fanatical faith in his own diagnosis of his disease; her mother was fanatical in denying herself pleasure, sacrificially surrendering her rights, first to her husband and then to her children, refusing to spend money on herself in order to spend it on them. Talking about her to friends, Sylvia called her a martyr. The pattern had started in Aurelia's relationship with her father, who wanted her to have sound secretarial and commercial training. Her own inclinations were literary, but she sacrificed literature to shorthand.

Aurelia grew up during the First World War in Winthrop, Massachusetts, where, thanks to her Germanic surname, Schober, she was victimized by schoolchildren who called her "Spyface." Frustrated when she tried to make friends, she became fiercely competitive in the classroom. Like Otto Plath, she became addicted when young to a self-punishing regimen of intensive academic work; in both of them a basic masochism nourished the soil in which the self-discipline grew. Like his childhood, hers was overshadowed by poverty, but, with encouragement from an inspiring English teacher, she became a passionate reader. Her mother shared both Aurelia's enthusiasms and her books, saying: "More than one person can get a college education on one tuition."[1]

33

Sometimes, however tentatively, the young Aurelia felt she was entitled to greater dividends from her good looks. When she was twenty-one, she was picked to work as a model in an exhibition, appearing in sports clothes with a tennis racquet. Three years later, when a talent scout saw her in an amateur production of *The Showoff* at Brookline High School, he recommended her for a walk-on part—which she was offered—in a Broadway show. But she married within a year, and if she had ever been ambitious, her ambitions from now on were vicarious, for her husband and her children. She didn't set out consciously to make her daughter into a poet, but the early training she gave Sylvia could scarcely have been better if she had.

By the time Sylvia was three, Otto Plath was spending little time with his children, and in their small world Aurelia's influence was dominant. She converted the largest upstairs bedroom into a playroom, and when she made up serial bedtime stories about Mixie Blackshort, Warren's favorite teddy bear, he and Sylvia formed a gratifying audience for a performer who'd been starved of appreciation. Aurelia also read verse. Convinced that babies responded to the cadences of poetry, she recited A. A. Milne, Robert Louis Stevenson, Matthew Arnold, Tennyson, Browning, Yeats, Edna St. Vincent Millay and Rupert Brooke, as well as verse from the anthology *Sung under the Silver Umbrella* and from Dr. Seuss's *Horton Hatches an Egg*.

Sylvia never forgot the first time she heard the stanza about sand-strewn caverns, sea beasts and sea snakes in Arnold's "The Forsaken Merman." Seeing goose pimples on her skin, she asked herself whether she was cold. No, a spark had flown off the poet and shaken her. She'd fallen into a new way of being happy.[2] Soon both children were responding to what they heard by making up their own rhymes and limericks. Left alone while their parents ate dinner, they performed for half an hour afterward, reciting rhymes they'd made up and verses they had memorized. Sylvia played the piano, improvised dances, brought out drawings she'd done.[3] The other kind of performance that infallibly earned parental approval was earning high marks in school.

Aurelia was determined neither to repeat the mistakes her mother had made nor to put the children under the kind of pressure her father had exerted when he forced her to enroll in a two-year course at the Boston University College of Practical Arts and Letters. She'd needed to earn money at the same time by taking part-time jobs. From the age of fourteen Aurelia helped in a public library. During the summer after she left high school, she worked a forty-four-hour week as a secretary. She then persuaded her father to let her sign up for two more years at the college to qualify as a high-school teacher of English and German. After a year of teaching English in a Massachusetts high school, she studied for an M.A. degree in English and German at Boston University, where she met Otto Plath, who was teaching the only course in Middle High German.

Compulsively eager to please by excelling, Aurelia consistently put herself under almost intolerable strain. Always in the subordinate position, first as Otto Plath's favorite student, and then as the submissive wife who doubled as his assistant, she was conscientious, self-disciplined, self-effacing and apparently selfless. After his death she was unexpectedly in the dominant position inside the family, but she was unaccustomed to dominating, and if she'd ever had a talent for taking initiatives, she'd lost it.

On the day her father died, Sylvia came home from school with bloodshot eyes and held out a slip of paper. "I PROMISE NEVER TO MARRY AGAIN. Signed...." Though she was attractive and only thirty-three, Aurelia signed without hesitation. About ten years later Sylvia asked: "That document never kept you from marrying again, did it?" Aurelia assured her it hadn't. But if she hadn't been deterred by the document, she had by devotion to her duties as a mother, and above all as a breadwinner.

From the moment of bereavement she found her freedom financially constrained. The university paid no pension, and Otto Plath had insured his life for five thousand dollars, barely enough to pay for the medical attention and the funeral.[4] Permanently worried about bills, Aurelia went on overworking, just as she had when her husband was alive. In the spring of 1941 she left home at 5:30 in the morning to work as a full-time substitute teacher in German and Spanish at Braintree High School, and later in the year she got a job at Winthrop Junior High School. In the autumn of 1942 she started to teach a medical-secretarial course at Boston University. Spending her earnings almost entirely on household and children, she believed herself to be motivated by unselfish love, with no vicarious ambition in it, and no guilt feelings underneath it. But the strain she imposed on herself had its effect on the children, who felt almost as awkward as they would have if she had sat down to a meal at which they were given caviar while she ate only bread and water. She wanted to give them pleasures she had never had and never would have, but how could they be happy when she wasn't?

Dutifully determined to earn enough for them both to have an expensive education, she paid for their music lessons, their scout uniforms and their summer camps, bought them new clothes and new shoes, while for herself she bought only secondhand clothes. How could they be proud of the figure she cut? She wanted to show there were no limits to her love for them, and that she deserved unbounded love in return, but she never relaxed.

"From the moment Sylvia was conceived," Aurelia wrote in a 1976 letter, "I rejoiced and loved her and served her all her life with all I had in me and with all I could give her emotionally and materially."[5] The word "served" is revealing, for subservience in a parent is at best a mixed blessing.

In Aurelia's iron determination to build the best possible future for her fatherless children, generosity mingled with a masochism that had been exacerbated by guilt when she married a father figure. She punished herself during his lifetime by overworking for him, and after his death by overworking for the children. During the last four years of his illness she developed a duodenal ulcer which hemorrhaged several times. After he died, it remained quiescent for about twelve years but asserted itself again after Sylvia's suicide attempt. The anxiety precipitated more internal hemorrhaging, and in 1954 Aurelia was advised to have a gastrectomy, but even after losing three-quarters of her stomach, she kept her daughter in ignorance of what had been going on.

Consistently well-intentioned, she also kept Sylvia ignorant of a letter which arrived at this time from Otto Plath's youngest sister, saying that their mother, one of their sisters and a niece had all suffered from depression, the mother seriously enough to be hospitalized for it. Not wanting to pass on any information that might conflict with Sylvia's reverence for the memory of her father, or might force her to connect her breakdown with his background, Aurelia kept silent, preferring to take the blame herself. Having taken courses in Freudian psychology, Aurelia did her best not to be a possessive, smothering mother, but she was aware of the fifties tendency to regard all mothers as possessive and smothering, and at least party aware of the problems Sylvia was having.

It had always been apparent to her that Aurelia never seemed happy or relaxed, and there was nothing either of them could do about this. From Aurelia's point of view she worked for the children's sake. From theirs she gave priority to work. At times Sylvia saw so little of her that, feeling in need of another mother, she cast her grandmother in the role, for which she was well suited. The two women even had the same Christian name, and Aurelia Greenwood Schober was four years younger than Otto Plath. In the spring of 1935, when Warren was born, and again during the last stages of Otto Plath's illness, Sylvia was sent to stay in her grandparents' house, where she often had to go later, when Aurelia was too busy to look after her. The adult Sylvia never forgot the telephone number that had become so familiar during childhood. Asking the operator for OCEAN 1212W, and waiting for her grandmother's friendly hello, she was half expecting to be connected instead with the sound of the sea.

During her first stay at the house on Point Shirley, the two-and-a-half-year-old Sylvia felt so resentful about the rival claim on her mother's attention that she asked to stay on with her grandparents for the rest of the summer. She loved being with her grandfather, who adored her, took her for long walks and taught her to swim. The house remained a place where she felt safe and welcome.[6] She called her grandmother "Grammy," a combination of "Granny" and "Mommy."

Both Sylvia's eagerness to please and her tendency to overwork derived mainly from Aurelia, who had little competition as a role model. For at least two years before Otto Plath's death, and at least ten years afterward, the relationship between mother and daughter was uncommonly—and perhaps unhealthily—close. If Warren seemed to resemble their father, Sylvia knew she took after their mother. She felt frightened when she heard the echo of her own voice after she stopped talking: it was exactly as if Aurelia had been speaking. Unable to be wholly herself, the daughter continued the mother. Like her voice, Sylvia's face mirrored Aurelia's expressions.[7]

While it was impossible not to follow the example Aurelia set, Sylvia knew herself to be incapable of selflessness. She had none of this "plodding, practical love."[8] Comparing herself with her virtuous mother, she felt spoiled and self-indulgent, in love only with herself. Guilty at not feeling more grateful and more loving toward the woman who made so many sacrifices, Sylvia tried to compensate with a nonstop show of lovingness. Appreciation gushed out of her. When she was fifteen she reproached herself for not being perfect. "Never, never, never will I reach the perfection I long for." Lovingly, she told Aurelia of her intention to bring up her children "just as you have us," and at eighteen, writing home about another Smith student who was almost suicidal, Sylvia declared: "If you were her mother, she would be all right."[9]

Most of the letters home started "Dearest Mummy," "Dearest of Mothers," "Dearest darling Mother," "Dearest darling adorable Mother" or "Dearest-Mother-whom-I-love-better-than-anybody," and they were signed with the nickname "Sivvy." When *Harper's* accepted three poems on the day before Aurelia's birthday, Sylvia said she was mentally dedicating this triumph "to you, my favorite person in the world,"[10] and a few weeks later, Sylvia told Warren that after twenty years of "extracting her life blood and care" they should start to bring in "big dividends of joy" for their mother. Perhaps they could treat her to a week on Cape Cod at the end of the summer.[11]

Long after she'd helped Sylvia to take her first faltering steps toward writing, Aurelia went on encouraging and instructing. The principal motivation behind the early poems was the desire to please and impress Aurelia, whose praise was the main reward. When she came home from teaching, she'd often find, hidden under her napkin, a poem illustrated by a drawing.[12] At the same time Sylvia was being encouraged to make herself the central heroic figure in a myth she elaborated around her activities and the image she presented in the many snapshots that were taken.

From 1943 to 1945, she received a diary from Aurelia in her Christmas stocking. She then asked for undated notebooks: when the big moments came, one page wasn't enough.[13] The diaries gave her space in which she could talk to herself without being overheard by her mother, but not without paying attention to rules Aurelia had formulated. In the front of the 1945 diary is an instruction in Aurelia's handwriting: no entries are to be made in the diary after 8:00 P.M. The diary Sylvia kept in high school is like a scrapbook, copiously illustrated with snapshots, mainly of herself in different outfits and poses.[14] At the same time, encouraging her to write stories, Aurelia gave her elementary lessons in the art: get your hero up a tree and then get people throwing stones at him.

There are two misleadingly simplistic ways in which the

relationship between mother and daughter can be summed up. A virtuously unselfish mother has an ungrateful and vindictive daughter who not only commits suicide but leaves behind her poems and fiction which portray the mother in an unfavorable light and go on plaguing her for the rest of her life. Or Sylvia can be portrayed as the helpless victim of a woman who makes impossible demands not only on herself but on everyone involved with her. The truth is that both mother and daughter were victims, but neither was a helpless victim, and it's easy to understand why Sylvia had so much difficulty in umpiring the tug-of-war between positive and negative emotions toward Aurelia.

Sylvia once said she'd always felt she could be honest with Aurelia, and wanted nothing more than to "make you proud of me so that some day I can begin to repay you for all the treats you've given me in my two decades of life."[15] Three years after the suicide attempt she was still voicing admiration in the same way. A March 1956 letter eulogizes Aurelia for creating an exquisite home and ensuring that her son and daughter went to the best colleges in the country. It was thanks to Aurelia's teaching, her hard work and her encouragement that the family had "weathered the blackest of situations, fighting for growth and new life." What Sylvia admired most of all was the resilience and flexibility symbolized by the way Aurelia drove her car. This "seems to open new possibilities for a richer, wider life."[16]

But she hadn't forgiven Aurelia for deprivations, discomforts and humiliations, even if they'd been unavoidable. At Bradford High School and then at Smith College, Sylvia had been excluded from privileges and pleasures her classmates enjoyed. Having a smaller wardrobe, she often had to choose between underdressing and overdressing for social occasions. She traveled abroad less than her friends, and didn't have driving lessons until much later than they did. She seldom went outside Massachusetts, and rarely ate in restaurants. Worst of all, Aurelia was a living symbol of the need for parsimony. She worked so hard for the little they had that to ask for money was to demand even more sacrifices, while anxiety about money was inseparable from anxiety about Aurelia's permanent state of stress.

Though Sylvia wasn't consciously putting herself under the same kind of strain, she felt obliged to make the most of educational privileges being bought for her at such a high price. Two years after Otto Plath died, Aurelia sold the house in

Winthrop at a loss and moved the family fifteen miles inland to Wellesley. One of her reasons was that although Sylvia was only ten, it looked as if she'd be capable of winning a town scholarship to Wellesley College. When the time came, she was offered a full scholarship, but by then she wanted to get away from home, and won a scholarship to Smith, a woman's college with an even better reputation. This scholarship, though, wasn't a full one, and to finance her daughter Aurelia had to take on extra tutoring and some ghostwriting as well as economizing with household expenses, while Sylvia felt constrained to work hard, even if other girls at Smith played bridge in the living room all night.

In her first year her scholarship was worth thirteen hundred dollars. Her career at Smith was interrupted in the summer of 1953, when she tried to kill herself, and when she returned to college in February 1954, she wasn't at first on a scholarship. Wanting to free her from any sense of obligation, Aurelia cashed in an insurance policy,[17] but this gave Sylvia an obligation of a different kind until she was voted a new scholarship of twelve hundred fifty dollars at the end of April.[18]

If Aurelia was spending all she had on her children's education, it was their duty to provide plentiful evidence that the investment was going to be profitable, and to maintain a constant supply of good news. When Sylvia won prizes for poems and short stories, or earned fees from newspapers and magazines, the money seemed no less important than the kudos.

The tone of most letters home is strikingly different from the tone of poems, journals and short stories. It would have been impossible to confide in her mother about negative emotions or sexual experiences. Aurelia was generous and self-righteous, loving and smug, perceptive and sanctimonious. She was responsive to the beauties of nature and culture, but if Sylvia tended to gush, it was from this role model that the tendency derived. "We had no money," Aurelia wrote in an unpublished memoir, "save for essentials. Through education we could, however, build a priceless inner life!"[19] Such cracker-barrel philosophizing had both a negative and a positive effect on Sylvia. It made her cringe, but it also influenced her. In 1956, advising Aurelia on how to help a friend's depressive son, Sylvia reminded her of something she had once said: the determination to excel in college should never stand in the way of what mattered most in life—openness to what is lovely among the rest that isn't.[20]

Sylvia sometimes shrugged off the moralistic advice, but at other times she copied passages of Aurelia's letters into her journal. "If you compare yourself with others, you may become vain or bitter—for always there will be greater and lesser persons than yourself.... Beyond a wholesome discipline, be gentle with yourself. You are a child of the universe no less than the trees and the stars; you have a right to be there."[21] Perceptive enough to realize that nothing was more urgent than to edge Sylvia into being more gentle with herself, Aurelia was preaching what she'd never practiced, advocating a relaxation she'd never achieved.

During her first year at Smith, Sylvia, according to her friend Marcia Brown, received a letter from Aurelia every day.[22] In 1962, four months before she killed herself, Sylvia was still ending letters with crosses for kisses and signing herself with her family nickname, "Sivvy." Generally her letters home were designed to express relish for the present and optimism about the future while implying gratitude for the educational opportunities Aurelia had offered. But according to a journal entry Sylvia made during September 1951, her enemies were the people who cared about her the most. "First: my mother. Her pitiful wish is that I should 'be happy.'" But Sylvia's anger is directed partly against herself. She cannot forgive her pathetic efforts to put on a display of happiness and to lash herself forward into achieving more and more. During vacations she exerted herself no less than during the term. Making plans for the summer in 1953, she ordered herself to be cheerful and constructive, scheduling her day as tightly as if she were at Harvard. She would have to "learn about shopping and cooking and try to make Mother's vacation happy and good." Such a giving mother mustn't go unrewarded.

If Sylvia sometimes hit out at Aurelia, it was partly because each of them was too proprietary toward the other. At the same time it was difficult to reciprocate Aurelia's goodness. When the eight-year-old Sylvia demanded what was virtually a pledge of chastity, this was the desperate act of a girl who couldn't afford to lose both parents. But there must have been a grain of disappointment in the child's triumph when the grown-up immediately capitulated. The pattern continued into objections raised by the fifteen-year-old Sylvia when Aurelia was offered a well-paid job as Dean of Women at Northeastern University. Was she so greedy for self-aggrandisement that she wanted to make her children into complete orphans? Once again Aurelia surrendered, only to be told, later on, by Sylvia, that she hadn't had the guts to make the break.

Because of the upbeat tone in the published *Letters Home,* Sylvia is often portrayed as someone who could never release aggression in dealings with her mother. But when Aurelia talked about being used as a model when she was a student, she was told that standards must have been very different in her day. Sylvia often criticized Aurelia's appearance, saying her hair wasn't properly styled or that white blouses did nothing for her or that her suits were too conservative. Aurelia could have pointed out that if her wardrobe consisted almost entirely of secondhand clothes, Sylvia was the main beneficiary of the economies that were being made. But there was no argument that could have compensated for the dowdy image the mother presented to her daughter's friends or made the two of them more sympathetic to each other's viewpoint.

When Sylvia tried to kill herself, aggression against Aurelia was combined with Sylvia's transference to herself of murderous feelings toward her mother. These are revealed most disturbingly in *The Bell Jar* when Esther and her mother go to bed in the same room. In the dim light of the streetlamp filtering through the blinds, the pin curls on the older woman's head glitter "like a row of little bayonets." Sleeping with her mouth slightly open, she begins to snore. "The piggish noise irritated me," and Esther tells herself the only way to stop it would be "to take the column of skin and sinew from which it rose and twist it to silence between my hands."[23]

Aurelia understood that the suicide attempt was aimed partly at her, but whatever grief she felt, she forced herself to concentrate on such practical problems as how to behave when she visited Sylvia in the clinic. Advised not to identify too much with her daughter, she prepared herself carefully for each visit, ordering herself to appear calm. This only made Sylvia angry: didn't she get any more sympathy than this when she was going through hell?

In the novel the stream of visitors makes Esther feel more depressed. Her mother is the worst—consistently careful not to remonstrate, but silently reproachful, sorrowfully and persistently begging for an explanation of what she has done wrong. Obviously she must have done something wrong. Why otherwise would the doctors keep asking questions about Esther's toilet training?

On her birthday Mrs. Greenwood takes her a dozen long-stemmed roses. "Save them for my funeral," says Esther, and dumps them in the wastepaper basket. Afterward she tells the doctor she hates her mother. Surprisingly, Dr. Nolan responds with a pleased smile: Esther will be allowed no more visitors for the time being.

Aurelia's retrospective comment on the incident was: "I bought her her favorite flowers, yellow roses. . . . I knew in my bones she would in her depressed, negative state of mind find fault with that; but I also knew that if I ignored the day, she would write, 'Mother saw fit to ignore my 21st birthday.'"[24]

Another way Sylvia could take revenge was by denying the contribution Aurelia had made to her early development as a writer. Asked how she came to start writing poetry, she was disinclined to mention her mother. Her 1962 answer was that she'd liked nursery rhymes and formed the impression she could do the same thing. She claimed to have been "a bit of a professional" since the age of eight and a half, when she published her first poem in the *Boston Traveler*.

Reluctance to acknowledge Aurelia's usefulness is also apparent in the 1957 poem "The Disquieting Muses," which takes its title from de Chirico's painting of three faceless figures in a clear light that casts a long shadow. The mother who used to make up stories about Mixie Blackshort, "the heroic bear," and who baked gingerbread witches, must have offended some aunt or cousin who sent these mouthless, eyeless creatures to the christening party. The mother who comforted her children with Ovaltine during a hurricane and taught them to sing "Thor is angry: we don't care!" was distracting them from the damage that could be inflicted by hurricanes and witches, and what the daughter later learned, she learned elsewhere, "from muses unhired by you." The poem suggests that she picked up nothing of value from her mother, who praised her piano-playing though her teachers found her tone deaf, with a wooden touch.

Like much of Sylvia's work, the poem mixes autobiography with fiction and myth. In Winthrop Sylvia took half-hour piano lessons from a friend of Aurelia's. These stopped when they moved to Wellesley, but a year or so later Sylvia asked whether she could take one of the afternoon courses at the New England Conservatory of Music, where she did well enough to be offered a half scholarship. She went on with the course for two years.[25]

Another way in which Sylvia takes revenge against her mother is by representing her as more puritanical than she actually was. Though Sylvia couldn't or didn't confide in her about sexual experiences, they did read and discuss Havelock Ellis, Langdon Davies and a book on trial marriage by Professor Rogers of the Massachusetts Institute of Technology. Aurelia wanted her daughter to be better informed than she had been, and Sylvia's sexual education started when kittens were born to their cat. When O'Neill's *Strange Interlude* was banned in Boston, Aurelia went to see it in New York, and she counseled her unhappy girl students about their love affairs. She had conversations with Sylvia about venereal disease, unwanted children and abortion, mentioning that in the Alpine town where her grandfather was born, most brides were three months pregnant.

Sylvia's attitude toward her mother was radically changed by the psychotherapy she had after the suicide attempt. She'd been able, previously, to express hatred for Aurelia in her diary, but, needing an ally against her, she couldn't have found a better one than Dr. Ruth Beuscher, the attractive young psychiatrist at McLean, the private clinic in Belmont, Massachusetts.

In Aurelia's absence during the ban on visitors, the rapport between doctor and patient steadily improved. Back at Smith after being discharged from McLean, Sylvia had regular weekly meetings with Dr. Booth, the college psychiatrist, and occasional meetings with Dr. Beuscher. Therapy helped to loosen her ties with Aurelia. She sent fewer letters home, and traveled more during vacations. The therapy was interrupted for two years, 1955–57, when Sylvia was in England, and at Cambridge she often felt homesick. "I long for Mother," she wrote in her journal,[26] and when Grammy was dying, Sylvia's grief was inseparable from fear that Aurelia might soon kill herself by overworking. She was teaching, cooking, driving, "shoveling snow from blizzards, growing thin in the terror of her slow sorrow." It had once been Sylvia's fantasy that her success would make her mother healthier and more secure, both emotionally and financially. But now, unable to see her dying grandmother, unable to help her mother, she might soon be left with no parents, "no older seasoned beings, to advise and love me in this world."[27]

In the autumn of 1957, returning to the United States and seeing Dr. Beuscher again, she became more emancipated. The story "Johnny Panic and the Bible of Dreams" was a by-product of the therapy. Typing up notes on other people's dreams and problems, the narrator feels as if she's secretary to Johnny Panic himself. In her diaries, Sylvia referred to the Panic Bird on her heart and on her typewriter, but, thanks to Dr. Beuscher, she could get rid of the bird by expressing hostility to Aurelia.

Taking dreams, anxieties and memories to a therapist was like taking essays to an instructor at college. If she had to pay fees to a specialist, Sylvia was going to make sure she got value for her money by working hard at cooperating. No one else had ever talked like Dr. Beuscher, and Sylvia could feel complete confidence in her, as she once had in Grammy. Here was another alternative mother—an older seasoned being who would never stop listening, never start complaining or reprimanding, never be shocked or impatient, but, unlike Grammy, she was young, attractive and impressively clever. Later on, Sylvia came to feel as though permission to hate Aurelia was the same as permission to be happy.

Aurelia had always seen her daughter as an extension of herself, a means of compensating vicariously for the sacrifice she'd made when she gave in to her father and abandoned literature in favor of shorthand. No mother can encroach further on an adult daughter's life than the daughter allows her to. Perhaps Sylvia would eventually achieve enough maturity to overcome her fear of being manipulated. Then she'd be strong enough to let Aurelia enjoy their relationship. But at some deep level, Sylvia wanted to be manipulated.[28]

That Aurelia was having such an unhappy life was pitiable, but unforgivable. What did she know about love? Nothing.[29] The suicide attempt had caused her extra suffering, creating an even greater imbalance between sacrifices she'd made and rewards she'd received. After years of distress over Sylvia's dangerous love affairs and her failure or refusal to marry a nice boy who could give her security, Aurelia went on worrying about her even when she was married to Ted Hughes. Why couldn't they both settle down to teaching jobs which would bring in a steady income? Though Sylvia couldn't shield her from anxiety, she could protect herself from feeling guilty about causing it.

Dr. Beuscher also explained how unconscious fear of Aurelia

and a need for vengeance against her still worked as a deterrent to writing. Anxious that her mother would appropriate stories and poems in the same way as she would take possession of Sylvia's babies if these weren't handed over to her, she tried to spite Aurelia by not writing, while the compulsiveness in the writing was due to a primitive equation between the self and the work. For a long time, writing had been a means of eliciting Aurelia's approval. If you don't love me, love my writing, and then love me for doing it. To be less compulsive about writing felt like a liberation. The need for success had always been inseparable from the need to be rewarded for it with her mother's love.

Before the suicide attempt, Sylvia had been trying to please Aurelia by working for two hours a day during the summer vacation at her shorthand, as well as brushing up her typing. She also intended to write for three or four hours each day, and to spend the same amount of time reading, not at random but from a carefully compiled reading list.[30] It would have been impossible to work as hard as this without resenting the overlap between the mother who wasn't actually telling her to do all these things and the self that was issuing the orders.

❧ 4 ❧

The Hostile Self

*It was as if what I wanted to kill wasn't in that skin or the
thin blue pulse that jumped under my thumb, but somewhere
else, deeper, more secret, and a whole lot harder to get at.*
The Bell Jar

In the space for July 4, 1953, on her wall calendar Sylvia wrote the
word *decision*. On August 24 she tried to kill herself. The other
entries for July 4 show it to have been a day on which she intended to
play tennis, clean the car, and meet her friend Gordon Lameyer. To
delay for seven weeks between the decision and the action was to give
herself plenty of time during which she could have changed her
mind, but the idea had been in her mind long before July 4. There's
no single turning point at which she can be said to have become
suicidal, and to locate a time when it might have been predictable
that sooner or later she'd try to kill herself, it would be necessary to
go back a long way, though not quite so far as she went herself.

Without quite claiming to have attempted suicide when she was
two, she told a story about learning to crawl. After being put
down on the beach, she made for the coming wave, and Aurelia
picked her up by her heels just as she had penetrated the "wall of
green." What would have happened if she hadn't been stopped?
Would she have survived like a mermaid in a looking-glass world,
breathing with gills that had no need to develop on dry land? Her
mythifying reconstruction of the incident hints at a temptation
she didn't always resist, to believe in a utopian alternative to the

real world. Idealizing the self, she saw surrounding circumstances as despicably defective, inadequate to house it. Something would have to be destroyed before it was possible to live in a purer, more fulfilling way.

Her account of the beach incident is characteristic of her prose and verse, which mixes facts from her early life with fiction: whatever it was that happened, the instinct in the infant was different from what the adult makes of it. But a dialectic was at work. Though she was never in real danger, the episode seemed to have brought her close to death. This interpretation proved more dangerous than the event because it revealed and helped to consolidate a habit of thinking that conferred glamor on death, implying an equation between nonexistence and a utopian alternative to the real world. Touching so often on the possibility of suicide, her verse and prose both made it more tempting. She may say that "Daddy" is about a girl with an Electra complex and that "Lady Lazarus" is about a woman with an exceptional talent for dying and being reborn, but the separation between the characters and their author is precariously incomplete, and there was two-way traffic between the writing and the living.

The suicide attempt of August 1953 was by no means the only self-destructive action leading up to the suicide of 1963. She had a skiing accident in January 1953. During 1962 she cut off the tip of her thumb in the kitchen and drove her car off the road in what she described as an attempt to kill herself. Sometimes the compulsion to take high risks is the residue from an early deprivation of love, and it may signal a desire to be looked after, once again, like a child.

Devoted though Aurelia had been as a mother, her goodness had often seemed as hard as iron. One of the phrases Sylvia noted at the end of a diary she kept when she was thirteen was about a voice that hammered at her until it had her nailed down. And though it was Aurelia who inspired her to function as an artist, there was a desperation in all those early attempts to deserve love by achieving distinction. By the age of seventeen she had collected more than fifty rejection slips, and before she had a short story accepted for publication she had made some forty-four submissions. She wrote, drew, painted, danced, played the piano, but the prolific creativity was compulsive.

One of the motivating forces was the drive to compete with Warren for Aurelia's love and attention, but by the age of eleven

Sylvia was also possessed by an exceptionally strong need to talk to herself in a diary. Her first diary was given to her as a Christmas present in 1943. She immediately established a personal relationship with it, addressing it in the second person: "I came home and caught up with you." But though there was enough space for her to write over a hundred words for each day, she didn't leave a single line blank in the whole diary, and often crowded two lines into the space for one. Can a child of eleven ever have been a more devoted diarist? Already her appetite for self-dramatization was insatiable. Diary-writing drops a safety curtain between narrator and performer. Without the long time-lapse involved in autobiography, the diary offers a comfortable space in which you have total control over your account of the experiences you controlled only partially while you were having them. The child was already finding on the empty spaces in her printed diaries the refuge that the adult Sylvia would find in her poetry.

In his book *The Divided Self* R. D. Laing uses the term "false-self system" for the structure which comes into existence when a schizoid individual develops a series of "part-selves none of which is so fully developed as to have a comprehensive 'personality' of its own." It comes to feel as if the real self, only partially implicated in the actions of the false selves, is entitled to be critical of them, and even hostile, treating them as if they were other people. Cultivating her self-consciousness, Sylvia was exacerbating her lack of spontaneity and aggravating her sense of futility. When she was at the head of her class, won prizes, achieved precocious success as a writer, she felt intense pleasure in the short term, but the prestige failed to remedy her insecurity. In Laing's account, the schizoid individual "would appear to be, in an unreal, impossible way, all persons and things to himself. The imagined advantages are safety for the true self, isolation and hence freedom from others, self-sufficiency and control." The disadvantages are that the project is impossible and that the inner world shut up inside the false-self system feels increasingly isolated and impoverished. The feeling of omnipotence is no defense against the overwhelming sense of emptiness.[1]

In her early diaries she was meticulous about chronicling experiences, listing presents, keeping cash accounts. In February 1944 she received two gifts of ten cents and one of fifty cents. She had an allowance of ten cents a week, but she received it only three times during the month, and she noted a loss of $1.50, having started the month with six dollars and ending with $4.50.

At fifteen she grew to her full height, five foot nine. In junior high school she joined the Girl Scouts. Eager for popularity, she was bewildered to find that girls ran away giggling whenever she started to tell a story. It took her some time to find out the reason. Her fear of being abandoned by her friends had got her into a counterproductive habit of rambling long-windedness.[2]

She was sixteen when she wrote "To Ariadne." Still bruised by the bereavement and still angry about it, the abandoned daughter can easily identify with the woman abandoned by Theseus. Her impotent rage is equaled only by the shrieking wind and the waves lashing against the shore. The sweetness of her loving words has turned to brine. She is outsung by the unmusical wind. The thirst for vengeance subsides into futility as the storm retreats, grumbling faintly, while the wind sobs along the beach.[3]

In poems, in her journals and in fiction the violence of the language is proportional to the force of the emotion that has been held back. In a letter to Eddie Cohen, a boy who without meeting her had struck up an intimate epistolary friendship with her, she describes herself as "scared and frozen." While another date was driving back to Boston, his reflection in the rearview mirror, the music from the car radio and the colored lights flowed over her with "a screaming ache of pain." Already she felt a strong urge to dam her life like a river, to alter its direction. She wanted to "stop it all, the whole monumental grotesque joke." Poems and letters were ineffective as a countermeasure. She couldn't explain what she was trying to resist, but she'd seen her mother crying desolately in the kitchen and, looking at Warren, she couldn't believe his potential would ever be fulfilled.[4]

In manic-depressive alternation between exultant happiness and raging despair her mood swings were so abrupt and violent that ecstasy rubbed shoulders with agony, just as hatred for Aurelia jostled against love. After Sylvia started at Smith College in September 1950, she called herself one of the happiest girls in the world. She was seventeen, she was at one of the best women's colleges in America, she was attractive, talented and capable of working hard enough to distinguish herself in the competitive student world, though in most ways she tried to disappear into the mainstream of student conformism.

During the mid-fifties typical Smith undergraduates were eager to be recognizable as college girls. They wore, spring or fall, the uniform of Bermuda shorts, knee socks and shirts with button-down collars; they had their hair carefully styled to look casual. Sylvia cultivated the standard Smith look, even after she was moved from Haven House to Lawrence House, which tended to be less conformist, being one of the houses for scholarship girls. Rebelling against the Smith norms, some of the Lawrence girls modeled themselves on the beat writers and poets and went around in dirty jeans with bare feet. Sylvia disapproved of these rebels.

Education at Smith didn't ignore the body in favor of the mind. Girls couldn't graduate without passing a swimming test and producing a satisfactory "posture picture," which involved a photograph in the nude. Academic work was done mainly during weekdays. The weekends were for socializing: the station at Northampton was packed with girls dressed like fashion models. At some of the bigger men's colleges football weekends and beach parties were organized, with plenty of blind dates on offer, involving brothers and cousins. At Smith the social events included house dance weekends, class dances and a charity dance on George Washington's birthday.

There were about fifty-seven girls in each of the thirty-five houses, where they slept in either double or single rooms. Freshmen had immediate contact with seniors. By the end of April 1952 Sylvia had been elected to Alpha Phi Kappa Psi, which meant she was regarded as one of the two best creative writers among the sophomores. She'd been invited to join the editorial board of the *Smith Review,* which was going to publish one of her sonnets during the fall. She earned ten dollars a month as a correspondent for the *Springfield Daily News.* She'd increased her popularity in the college and had been elected secretary of the Honor Board. The world was splitting open at her feet, she said, like a ripe watermelon,[5] but this was only because of the efforts she was making. Entries in her diary show how relentless she was in verbally lashing herself onward and upward toward prizes, a Fulbright scholarship, publication in national magazines, travel in Europe, relationships with boys. Even if she killed herself in the attempt, she was going to pass her physical science require-ment. Perhaps she could soon go to New York City.

Ambition seemed like the best antidote to the fears of madness and suicide that surged up when she stopped to look inward.

Returning to Smith after four days at home for the Thanksgiving holiday, she told herself that if she had no past or future, she might just as well dispose of the empty present by committing suicide. In Haven House she never needed to be alone for long. Chatty girls surrounded her each time she went downstairs, but in her room she felt loneliness like a disease of the blood, dispersed through her body. She was vaguely homesick, but without her possessions in it, her room at home no longer looked like her own, and the spots on the darkened yellow wallpaper seemed more prominent. Brains and good looks were useless to her. The Smith timetable gave her only a false sense of purpose. She felt as if life consisted of loneliness, as if there were no living being on the earth except herself. Parties were pointless, grins were false.[6]

In June 1952 she took a summer job at the Belmont Hotel in West Harwich on Cape Cod, where she was scrubbing tables when a telegram arrived. Her story "Sunday at the Mintons" had won a five-hundred-dollar prize from the magazine *Mademoiselle*. She screamed with joy and threw her arms around the head-waitress.[7] But when a combination of overwork and overexcitement made her ill, she left for home and lapsed into a depression that inspired the "bell jar" image. A bell jar is a bell-shaped glass jar used in chemical and physical laboratories. She sees it as a container which both isolates you and distorts your view of the world outside. She had been alternating between life and "death-or-sickness-in-life." The days on Cape Cod had been hectic and competitive. Surrounded by attractive young people, dancing, chatting, laughing, kissing, working, she had felt more alive than she did in Wellesley, where she had more freedom but less contact with other people.[8] She used the bell jar image again in a letter to a Smith friend, saying she'd gone around for most of her life as if she were in a rarefied atmosphere, with everything scheduled—four years at college, summer vacations to be filled by taking jobs and never more than two or three weeks of leisure.[9]

Intensely self-critical, she felt at twenty that she was emotionally like a sixteen-year-old. Self-conscious about her height, she avoided high heels, but in flats she looked like a bobby-soxer. Going out with boys, she couldn't stop herself from overreacting and overplaying her bursts of enthusiasm, though she was aware of trying too hard to make them like her.[10]

But she was happy again when, after answering an advertisement in *The Christian Science Monitor,* she got an au pair job for six weeks in Chatham, doing housework, helping to prepare meals and looking after children. When she left, she was thanked on a joke check made out to "the gal with the winning smile, 1,000,000 thanks for the 1,000,000 things so lovingly and cheerfully done."[11] In August the publication of "Sunday at the Mintons" made her euphoric. She drove to the beach with peaches, cherries and the new issue of *Mademoiselle.* Reading her story, she noticed so many flaws that she felt she'd already outgrown it. Chortling to herself, she ran in the sun for a mile through the warm tidal flats, telling herself how marvelous it was to be alive and brown and full of energy and to know so many exciting people. "I never have felt so utterly blissful and free," she wrote.[12]

But within two months she was suicidal. Tearful and unable to sleep properly, she felt envious of her boyfriend, Dick Norton, who was being treated for tuberculosis in the Adirondacks. At least he was being taken care of. The tasks she had to perform were tiresome and pointless: all the effort was leading her nowhere. She felt hollow. Workmen on the roof of the house opposite were intolerably noisy. All her activities had been badly planned, all her potential misused, all her opportunities wasted. The life ahead looked sordid and uninviting, with no idealism, no cause to redeem it. There was no continuity between past and future, no prospect of communicating meaningfully with other people, though she had everything she'd thought she wanted. In three years she had earned a thousand dollars by writing, had bought some beautiful clothes, had found a good-looking, intelligent boyfriend. But she'd never be able to make her life cohere, never succeed in articulating the vague desires seething inside her.

She might have to become a secretary or a housewife, subordinating her ambitions to those of her boss or her husband. She could confide in neither Aurelia nor Dick. During her sophomore year at Smith her confidante was her roommate, Marcia Brown, who lived off campus during her third year, which meant they saw relatively little of each other. No one could help Sylvia, and she couldn't afford psychiatry. The only solution was to wear a mask, hide her terror and self-pity under a pose of cheerfulness and serenity.

She stayed up late at night, working on poems or writing in her diary. It was important to capture mood changes and moments of insight. When she felt something stirring inside herself—a revival of optimistic determination—she could describe it, moment by moment, like a sports commentator.[13]

Four days later she was in despair again. She'd lost all her pleasure in life; she was too indecisive even to go out for a walk. Half helplessly and half deliberately she was cutting herself off from her creativity. She couldn't love, had forgotten how to laugh.[14] Nearly all her letters home give an impression of even-tempered cheerfulness, but the one dated November 19 starts by warning Aurelia to brace herself and take a deep breath. For about a week, Sylvia says, she's been feeling tense and sick, and has almost considered suicide as an alternative to taking the science course. Panicking, she thinks the college authorities will expel her if she tries to evade the science requirement. She's behind in her work and is being driven inward.[15]

She consulted the college psychiatrist about the science course. She also intended to consult the doctor about her insomnia.[16] When she telephoned home, arguments with her mother were audible to other girls in the house, and her letters to Eddie Cohen, her pen pal, had given him an impression of "the agitation, the dissatisfaction, the unrest, the annoyance, the lack of co-ordination, the nervous tensions that mark the time that a person approaches the ultimate breaking point. Syl, honey, I think you've moved much too close over these past few months."[17]

It was apparent during the Christmas holidays, when she went to stay with Dick Norton in Saranac, New York, that he was assuming they'd soon be married, and feeling bad about not wanting to be his wife, she took a suicidal risk. She borrowed skis and, without having had any instruction (except, from Dick who couldn't ski), she took the rope-tow to the top of the advanced slope and tried to ski down.

In *The Bell Jar* Esther does the same thing. The idea of suicide forms in her mind as "coolly as a tree or a flower." She knows she won't be able to stop when she launches herself downward. With the white sun hanging over the hills, she feels happy as an answering point in her body flies toward it. Plummeting past zigzagging skiers, she sees people and trees receding on either side of her, like the dark sides of a tunnel, as she hurtles toward a bright point like "the white sweet baby cradled in its mother's belly." Before she learns her leg is broken in two places, she looks up at the dispassionate white sun at the summit of the sky, wanting "to hone myself on it till I grew saintly and thin and essential as the blade of a knife."[18] Like Kafka, Sylvia enjoyed thinking in terms of violently aggressive images angled at self-destruction. In his life the habit seems to have played a part in the psychosomatic process which engendered the disease that killed him; in hers it possibly helped to tilt her toward suicide.

With her fibula fractured, Sylvia would have to wear a cast on her leg for nearly two months, but she was almost glad to have a handicap which would last only for a measurable time. On January 9, 1953, she told Aurelia she was going to be as cheerful and constructive about her mental difficulties as about the broken fibula. But the next day, pasting a photograph of herself into her diary, she ordered herself to look at "that ugly dead mask ... a chalk mask with dead dry poison behind it." The mouth was pouting and disconsolate, the eyes bored, numb, expressionless. But she vacillated between believing the internal decay irreversible and telling herself that all she needed was a good night's sleep and enough luck to induce a more positive attitude.[19]

She was taking a class in creative writing. The teacher, Robert Gorham Davis, was what Aurelia had once been, the main target for the poetry and fiction she wrote during the year. In January she tried to characterize her depressions in a dialogue. The other speaker, Marcia, modeled openly on her former roommate, is criticized by Alison (an alter ego) for her "rotten layers of middleclass morality." When Marcia ripostes by asking whether making up one's own rules isn't too much of a responsibility, Alison describes what it's like to have no identity. Her eyes are liable to burst like soap bubbles, revealing that there's nothing behind them—only a mess. The rot inside her may erupt in sores and warts, which will scream out: "Traitor, sinner, imposter!"[20]

Sylvia's spirits revived when she was released from the dreaded science course. "Oh, mummy, I am so happy," she wrote on January 19. But on Feburary 21 she said the month would go down in history as Plath's Black Month. When the plaster cast was taken off and she saw "the hairy yellow withered corpse of my leg," she felt as if the doctor were lifting a coffin lid. She could scarcely acknowledge the leg as hers, and was even more depressed when she was told it hadn't completely mended. She cheered herself up—or at least told Aurelia she had—by composing two villanelles which struck her as the best verse she'd written. She sent one to *The Atlantic* and one to the *New Yorker.*[21] By the end of the month her spirits were boosted when she had a talk in the bone clinic with a first-year student who claimed to have read everything she had written for *Seventeen* and *Mademoiselle*. As Sylvia moved away, the girl told a nurse: "She's a wonderful writer."[22]

At the end of April 1953 *Harper's* accepted two of her villanelles and another poem, paying a hundred dollars, and she was elected editor of the *Smith Review* for the next year, the campus job she had most coveted. In May, when Warren got into Harvard, she said she could hardly stop herself from leaping up and down, shouting hooray all over the campus. How well they were both doing, leading a "charmed plathian existence."[23]

Soon afterward, her relish for life was whetted even more keenly when *Mademoiselle* awarded her a guest editorship for four weeks in June. Together with nineteen other girls picked from colleges all over the States, she was to live in New York for a month, working with the staff of the glossy fashion magazine on the August issue. She'd be able to interview, and be photographed with, four writers. The four she most wanted to meet were J. D. Salinger, Shirley Jackson, E. B. White and Irwin Shaw. And perhaps Aurelia could write an article about her teaching job: Sylvia might be able to edit it for her.[24]

The magazine's offices were on Madison Avenue, and rooms were booked for the young guest editors at the Barbizon Hotel for Women on the corner of Lexington Avenue and Sixty-third Street. The indoor swimming pool promised relief from the intense sultry heat of the summer, which, as described in *The Bell Jar,* made the streets waver in the sun, while glittering car tops sizzled, and cindery dust blew down Esther's throat.

Promotional lunches and fashion shows were organized, together with dances, movie previews, visits to theaters and art exhibitions. Assigned to assist the managing editor, Cyrilly Abels, Sylvia was given a desk in her office, from which she could listen "surreptitiously" to all her telephone conversations.[25] Instead of the four writers she'd most wanted to meet, she interviewed Elizabeth Bowen. Commenting on typescripts she was given to read, she found herself criticizing Noël Coward, Dylan Thomas and Rumer Godden. She wrote—and kept having to rewrite—a feature on five rising poets, and (as guest managing editor) contributed the introduction to the August issue. She was also responsible for rejection letters, signing them with her own name. Having been rejected by the *New Yorker,* she enjoyed rejecting a piece by a man on its staff.

She made a good impression on the other guest editors: one rated her as a leader of the group, "one of the smartest and funniest"; another described her as "filled with a healthy love of mankind and great artistic vitality."[26] But Cyrilly Abels said she'd never met anyone less spontaneous, less capable of deviating from a rigid standard of conventionality.[27] By criticizing Sylvia's writing, she appears to have undercut the confidence accumulated through successes earlier in the year. Writing to her old schoolteacher, Wilbury Crockett, Sylvia said he'd never want to see her again, that she'd let him down.[28]

She had applied for a place in Frank O'Connor's course in creative writing at the Harvard summer school, and the darkest fear overshadowing her month in New York was that she would be rejected. She was also disturbed about Julius and Ethel Rosenberg, who were to be electrocuted on June 19 for betraying atomic secrets to the Russians. Hearing radio bulletins and office conversations about them, she felt guilty about buying expensive dresses, hats and shoes for promotional photographs. Indignant that people were eating breakfast as usual on the morning of the execution, she stormed out of the hotel's dining room, pursued by one of the guest editors, Janet Wagner, who didn't want to leave her on her own. As they walked to Madison Avenue, Sylvia kept asking what time it was. At nine o'clock she said, "Now it's happening," and held out her arms, displaying red pinprick bumps, which suddenly lengthened into each other, forming welts. Maybe she had psychic powers, she said, but Janet told her she was suffering from hives.[29]

Later she heard that the execution was arranged for eleven in the evening. She felt sick to her stomach, empathizing with the victim and remembering a journalist's account of another electrocution—the scream, the smoke, the unconcealed fascination on the onlookers' faces.[30]

During her four weeks in New York, Sylvia was, as she told Warren, ecstatic, depressed, shocked, elated, enlightened and enervated. In the final week she visited a large advertising agency, got food poisoning from the crabmeat served by its kitchen, and spent an evening in Greenwich Village, where she nearly fell for a simultaneous interpreter with all the qualities she wanted in a man except that he wasn't tall enough. At a tennis club dance she narrowly escaped being raped by a rich Peruvian delegate to the United Nations. She watched a ball game at Yankee Stadium, and, lost on the subway, felt repelled when deformed men pushed begging cups at her.[31]

Before leaving the hotel she threw her expensive new dresses and most of her other clothes out of the bedroom window. To travel home she had to borrow an outfit from Janet, who was packing and offered her anything on the bed. After choosing a green dirndl skirt and a peasant blouse with ruffles on the sleeves, she insisted on handing over her flowered bathrobe in return.

In the novel Esther, carrying her clothes in a bundle, creeps to the edge of a parapet and feeds her wardrobe piece by piece to the night wind; the gray scraps are ferried off like the ashes of a loved one to settle in the dark heart of New York. On the train home she glances down at the unfamiliar green dirndl which is sticking out like a lampshade. Instead of sleeves the blouse has frills as floppy as a new angel's wings. The face in the mirror of Esther's compact stares back like a sick Indian.[32]

Aurelia, who was waiting at the station with the car, had to break the news that Sylvia hadn't been accepted in Frank O'Connor's class. "I could see Sylvia's face in the rear-view mirror; it went white when I told her, and the look of shock and utter despair that passed over it alarmed me."[33]

Esther in the novel can see bad news in the set of Mrs. Greenwood's neck as soon as she begins to speak. The writing course had seemed like a bright safe bridge through the summer. Watching it totter and dissolve, she sees a body in a white blouse and green skirt plummet into the gap. As they drive through outer Boston, she slumps down on her spine until her nose is level with the rim of the car window, and she slouches down even farther as they approach Wellesley. Passing the identical white clapboard houses with well-groomed lawns, she feels as if she's passing the bars of a gigantic cage from which she'll never escape.[34]

She could have taken another course at the Harvard summer school, but she preferred not to go, and aiming her anger directly at herself, addressed herself in her diary as if she were a delinquent. You've failed to equip yourself adequately to face the world. You're spoiled, babyish, frightened. You must be more honest, more decisive, more constructive. You're not taking advantage of your freedom because you're incapable of deciding where you want to go. You're a hypocrite, plunged so deeply into your private whirlpool of negativism that the simplest actions become forbidding. When you see people who are married or happy or active, you feel frightened and lethargic. You don't even want to cope. You big baby! You just want to creep back into the womb or retreat into a masochistic hell of jealousy and fear. Don't you see how selfish and self-indulgent it is to go on thinking abut razors and suicide and self-inflicted wounds? Start writing. Be glad for other people and make them happy. Go out and do something. It isn't your room that's a prison, it's yourself.[36] Which implies that liberation can be achieved by destroying the prison. The self is dueling with its intimate enemy, the self.

In mid-July, after two nights with almost no sleep, Sylvia was in a panic. Frightening ideas raced through her mind. She couldn't sustain the tempo she had set for herself. Paralyzed by jealousy and fear, she could make no headway in relationships with either men or women; she couldn't stop herself from going against everything she believed in. She saw herself murdering Aurelia, saw herself in a straitjacket. From wanting not to be a drain on the family's resources, she would be more of a drain than ever, running up bills in an asylum, and she would destroy the goodwill and respect she had built up in other people. She had lost her sense of humor and perspective, as well as her ability to think. More than ever, she needed to believe in beneficent forces outside herself, in God and love and mankind.[37]

Her mother and grandmother tried to cheer her up by packing picnics and driving her to beaches in New Hampshire and Massachusetts. There and at home, Sylvia sunbathed joylessly, always with a book in her hand, never opening it. In an effort to pull herself together, she asked Aurelia to spend an hour with her every morning, teaching her shorthand so that she could get a job if she ever needed one. They struggled through four lessons, but even if she had had an aptitude for shorthand, she was in no state to concentrate, and the failure added to her store of grievances against herself. One morning Aurelia noticed some partially healed gashes on her legs. "I just wanted to see if I had the guts," she explained. And then, seizing Aurelia's hand, "Oh, Mother, the world is so rotten! I want to die! Let's die together!"

We can't assume that Sylvia's state of mind when she inflicted these gashes was the same as Esther's when she gives herself some practice in spilling blood. In the novel she's aiming to cash in on the contrast between a laconically comic narrative tone and a seriously self-destructive action. But as many of her friends testify, Sylvia was capable of talking with wry detachment about her suicide attempts, and it is fair to assume that with part of her mind she was watching herself as coolly as if she were a character in a novel she might one day write if she survived. It would be almost as uncharacteristic of Esther as it would of Holden Caulfield in *The Catcher in the Rye* to drop classical names, but she thinks about "some old Roman philosopher" who said he would open his veins in a warm bath.

But the skin of her wrist looks so white and vulnerable that she can't do this. She would have to use one hand to attack the other, and then move the razor to the other hand to inflict a similar wound before she lay down in the warm water. If she watches herself in the mirror of the medicine cabinet, it will be like watching a character in a play. Instead she sits on the edge of the bathtub, crossing her right ankle over her left knee. Lifting the razor, she lets it drop like a guillotine on her calf. She feels no pain. Thrillingly, a red seam appears at the edge of the gash. Blood accumulates and rolls down her ankle into her black patent leather shoe.[38]

Within an hour of seeing the partially healed gashes on Sylvia's legs, Aurelia had taken her to the family doctor. He prescribed sleeping pills and recommended a psychiatrist.[39] The man turned out to be good-looking, and the twenty-year-old Sylvia took an instant dislike to him: he was too complacent and self-involved. He prescribed electroconvulsive therapy. After losing a husband who believed no doctor could cure him, Aurelia was predisposed to trust the first one who offered an opinion. Without consulting anyone else—money was always a consideration—she shepherded Sylvia into outpatient shock therapy, without any follow-up counseling. Soon after the treatment started, the doctor went on vacation, leaving Sylvia in the hands of a colleague.

It's hard to calculate how much harm the treatment did. In *The Bell Jar* Esther isn't given ECT until after her suicide attempt, but Sylvia tried to kill herself after the therapy had started; it helped to demoralize her, and death seemed preferable to a life in which she was regularly submitted to this terrifying, painful and humiliating experience.

The first page of the novel links the therapy to the Rosenbergs' electrocution by speculating about what it must feel like to be "burned alive all along your nerves." In the hospital, after passing a shaggy-haired woman who threatens to jump out of a window, Esther is taken into a bare room with barred windows. A walleyed nurse swabs at her temples with smelly grease as the doctor unlocks a cupboard and drags out a table on wheels with a machine on it. When Esther tries to smile, she finds her skin has gone stiff, like parchment. The doctor fits metal plates on either side of her head, buckles them into place with a strap and gives Esther a wire to bite. She shuts her eyes. Something takes hold of her and shakes her like the end of the world, shrilling through an air crackling with blue light, and with each flash she's jolted fiercely enough to make it feel as if her bones will break and the sap fly out of her.[40] Sylvia never forgot what it felt like. In one of her last poems some god gets hold of her by the roots of her hair and she sizzles in his blue volts.

The new doctor prescribed sleeping pills, which Aurelia kept in a locked steel case. On August 24, 1953, Queen Elizabeth's coronation day, Sylvia was looking well, with sparkling eyes and red cheeks, but she refused to go with her mother to watch the ceremony on a friend's television. Not without misgivings, Aurelia left her on her own, and returned to find a note on the dining-room table. It said Sylvia had gone for a long walk and would be back in the morning. After telephoning the police, who announced her disappearance over the radio, Aurelia found the lock on the steel case broken, and the bottle of pills missing.

The Boston papers carried such headlines as TOP-RANKING STUDENT AT SMITH MISSING FROM WELLESLEY HOME and BEAUTIFUL SMITH GIRL MISSING AT WELLESLEY. Aurelia talked to reporters about the demands Sylvia made on herself to achieve high standards. Neighbors and Boy Scouts joined the police, who were using bloodhounds to scour the woods around Wellesley. They searched Lake Waban and Morse's Pond, but no body was found, and no clues.[41]

On the third day Aurelia, her parents and the eighteen-year-old Warren were eating lunch when he heard a moaning sound from low down in the house. Rushing to the basement, he found that Sylvia had crawled inside a shoulder-high earth-bottomed hole in the wall, under a breezeway which had been added to the house after the cellar was built. The entrance to the hole had been blocked by a pile of firewood, but she'd shifted it when she climbed into the narrow space with the pills and a glass of water. "Call an ambulance," he shouted.[42]

According to the nurse on duty at the Newton-Wellesley hospital when the ambulance arrived, Sylvia was more dead than alive. When she regained consciousness, she felt as if she were trapped inside a nightmare of flashing lights, strange voices, big needles and an overpowering conviction that she was blind in one eye. She hated the people who wouldn't let her die.[43] Her right eye was injured, with festering cuts and bruises under it. Not believing in God or an afterlife, she felt incredulous and disappointed that death hadn't put an end to the consciousness she'd been trying to extinguish.

Although her suicide attempt had failed, Sylvia went on wanting to get rid of something that felt like part of her mind. When she was well enough to get up, she went to see the psychiatrist and demanded a lobotomy. Laughing and shaking his head, he told her she wasn't going to get off that easily.[44]

Her most coherent analysis of her suicidal depression was made in an unmailed letter, written in late December to her pen pal Eddie Cohen. She'd wasted her junior year at Smith by taking the wrong courses. It would have been better to study psychology, sociology and philosophy. It seemed as if she'd been bluffing her way through exams, reading little and writing nothing of value. She no longer even felt confident of her hold on the English language. Her best friends at Smith wouldn't be there next year, and the only boys she would have liked to marry did not want to settle down. After being rejected for the Frank O'Connor course, she told herself that if she were any good as a writer she could manage on her own, but, too depressed to write, she had been depressed still further by her failure to learn shorthand. She felt sterile, empty, unloved, unwise, undereducated, but when she tried to read, she couldn't concentrate. Unable to sleep at night, she found that sleeping pills had no effect even when she increased the dosage, and the electroconvulsive treatment had been terrifying. She had made up her mind to kill herself long before she decided how and when. It was a matter of choosing between a quick clean ending and a joyless life of imprisonment in a mental hospital. Before taking the sleeping pills she had tried to drown herself, but couldn't swallow enough seawater or stop herself from floating back to the surface.[45]

When Aurelia arrived at the hospital, Sylvia's first words were "Oh, no!" Holding her hand, Aurelia told her how happy they were that she was alive and how much they loved her. She answered weakly: "It was my last act of love." All she had to do now, Aurelia said, was rest. Given medical care, she'd recover. "Oh, if only I could be a freshman again," Sylvia said. "I so wanted to be a Smith woman."[46]

In the story "Tongues of Stone," Ellen knows she wants to kill herself after she has struggled with the temptation to murder her sleeping mother. By twisting the life out of that fragile throat, she could end the slow process of disintegration which goes on grinning at her like a death's head. Instead, she creeps back into her own bed, wedging herself into the crevice between mattress and bedsprings, longing to be crushed. Her subsequent suicide attempt is an effort to fight her way back to darkness. Her body is dead, but they jolt her back into it, raising her like Lazarus from oblivion. Her arms and thighs are swollen with purple bruises; the left side of her face is distorted by a raw open scar surrounded by browning scabs and yellow pus. She can't open her left eye and, unable to see out of either eye, expects to go blind. The nurse tries to reassure her by saying there are lots of other blind people. One day she'll meet a nice blind man and marry him.[47]

The uncertain movement between life and death is better described in *The Bell Jar*. After climbing into the hole, Esther wonders when this space last saw the sun. When she has lugged the heavy logs back where they were, the darkness feels as thick as velvet. Holding the glass and the bottle, she crawls to the far wall with her head bent. At first nothing happens when she swallows the pills one by one with gulps of water, but red and blue lights are flashing in front of her eyes as she approaches the bottom of the bottle. The silence draws away, revealing the pebbles and shells and all the tatty wreckage of her life until, at the rim of vision, it gathers itself and rushes her to sleep in one sweeping tide. Feeling nothing but darkness, her head rises like a worm's. Someone is moaning, but the sound stops when a weight smashes like a stone wall against her cheek.

Carried at enormous speed down a tunnel, she feels a cool wind. After it stops, rumbling voices disagree in the distance. They stop. A chisel hits her eye, opening a slit of light, which shuts when the darkness clamps down. She tries to roll away, but hands stop her. Maybe she's in an underground chamber full of people holding her down. Light leaps into her head when the chisel strikes again, and a voice calls: "Mother!" She feels air on her face, the shape of a room around her and a pillow under her head. Her body floats between thin sheets, but when she opens her eyes, she sees nothing. The man with the chisel comes back, but she tells him she's blind.

Esther's first conversation with her mother is different from Sylvia's. Wearing a dress with purple cartwheels on it and looking awful, Mrs. Greenwood comes smiling to the foot of the bed. "They said you wanted to see me." Loving and reproachful, she perches on the edge of the bed and lays her hand on the leg of her daughter, who wants her to go away. Mrs. Greenwood seems to be on the point of weeping. Her face puckers up and quivers "like a pale jelly."

The electroconvulsive therapy had changed Sylvia's relationship with the mother who had betrayed her. Poverty was a factor, and anxiety about fees no doubt deterred Aurelia from calling in another psychiatrist, but it would be hard to forgive the mother who'd put her into the clutches of a man who tortured her with electric shocks. In saying "Let's die together," the suicidal daughter had fulfilled the promise implicit in the contract she'd drawn up when they were both bereaved: you don't need another husband; we'll be as close to each other as lovers. Hatred had been mixed up in Sylvia's love for Aurelia long before the suicide attempt, but from now on the conflict between positive and negative feelings would be fiercer.

Consciously, Aurelia was trying not to put pressure on Sylvia, but parents who make demonstrative sacrifices for their children are making them into debtors. Sylvia exerted herself to repay what she owed Aurelia. Successful though many of her efforts were, she had to live in constant fear of failure. On one level, therefore, she was relieved to feel Aurelia had betrayed her. She now had an excuse for making no more repayments. She'd been riding a roller coaster with no safety belt. The more laurels she won, the more she encouraged other people to expect she would achieve great things, and she hated to feel she was letting them down.

Later, after winning a Fulbright scholarship to Cambridge, she had a heavy workload, but it didn't stop her from trying, in addition, to teach herself German and French. Throughout her life she overtaxed herself as if she could define herself by refusing to recognize limits.

At the end of July 1955, before she left America, the twenty-two-year-old Sylvia sent her twenty-year-old brother a good-bye letter full of advice, wanting him to benefit from the self-knowledge she'd accumulated. Like her, she said, he still had a lot of growing to do, and it was through relationships with other people that they'd both mature. But he must never let his security and love of life depend on anyone else, only on himself, his work and his developing identity. He shouldn't marry until he'd consolidated this identity sufficiently to need no other court of appeal than his own conscience. Even when he felt hungry for sympathy, advice and friendly reprimands, he should resist the temptation to confide in other people about anxieties. He should hold Socratic dialogues with himself.[48] The advice to Warren was also advice to herself. She knew that to survive, to remain intact, she needed to consolidate her identity.

❧ 5 ❧

Boys

In her late teens and early twenties Sylvia Plath was neither short of male admirers nor of dates, but after her marriage, looking back on earlier relationships, she told herself the boys had all been dull, sick, vain or spoiled. Each of them had possessed only some of the qualities she wanted.[1] Although she needed a man, she found the physical need degrading, and though she had brief periods of intense happiness, anxiety predominated. In 1956, when she married Ted Hughes, she was only twenty-three, and the first years of her marriage were the happiest of her life, though by no means free from anxiety and mood swings. She was still in her twenties when the marriage disintegrated, and she could probably have survived if she could have faced the prospect of reverting to her earlier life-style, embarking on one affair after another, or carrying on two simultaneously. But as she knew, she'd have found this intolerable.

Before going back to Smith she had bleached her brown hair blond to make herself more attractive. The only visible evidence of the suicide attempt was a deep brown scar under her left eye. It emphasized the prominence of her cheekbones, but she explained the bleached hair as intended to distract attention from it. She talked about the suicide attempt as a failure: "I couldn't even kill myself." The mistake had been to take too many pills, which made her vomit up most of them.[2] She talked to friends as if she'd been mad and in great physical pain beforehand. "Everything hurt," she said. She'd been "on fire under her skin." If ever she went mad again, she'd kill herself because the pain was intolerable. She couldn't live through it again.[3]

At Smith, where she tried to dress like the other girls, her conformism extended into relationships with boys. If you wanted—as she desperately did want—to be popular among the

66

girls, it was essential to seem popular with boys. Necking was conducted in public places, and you not only had to be dated regularly but to be invited to proms and other dances at Harvard, Yale or Princeton. Nor was this merely a matter of keeping up appearances. In the United States women were marrying younger than ever before; the average age was 20.3, and girls in their late teens worried intensely about finding a husband. Sylvia's values were formed partly by movies with Doris Day and other clean-limbed, ostensibly clean-living stars, partly by such magazines as the *Ladies' Home Journal,* which she read regularly when she came home from school. Implicitly and often explicitly, movies and magazines advanced the view propounded in *Modern Woman: The Lost Sex* by Ferdinand Lundberg and Marie Farnham: women should find their sexual satisfaction through marriage and motherhood. Campus necking was de rigueur, but it must stop at that.

Sylvia did no less—some girls would have said she did more—than her fair share of necking, but it took her quite a long time to fall in love. At first she was so self-conscious about her height that she couldn't take a boy seriously unless he was a good bit taller than she was,[4] and she fantasized about a future husband who'd be very tall. She was only partly joking when she talked about producing superchildren, all male, all imposing in stature, physically and intellectually.[5] She was ambivalent about the prospect of marriage and maternity, half resigned to both, half scared they'd dry up her need to write: writing was one way of sublimating sexual desire.[6]

The story "And Summer Will Not Come Again" is about a girl who falls for her young tennis coach. The boy was modeled on Phil McCurdy, a friend of Warren's who taught her to play tennis when she was fourteen and gradually became a close friend. They went on seeing each other and playing tennis after she started at Gamaliel Bradford High School (now Wellesley High) in September 1947, but more of her dates were with classmates: John Pollard took her to the spring prom and Perry Norton escorted her to other college dances. In her diary the most affectionate mention of Phil McCurdy occurs when he drives her home from Cape Cod. Their hands meet while they're petting his black cocker spaniel in the front seat: she could get "very fond of this guy after all." Pulling up outside her house, he invites her out for the evening, but she says no, and no again when he suggests tennis tomorrow.[7]

Perry, Dick and David Norton were sons of a professor at Boston University whose wife, Mildred, had befriended Aurelia while Otto Plath was alive. The Nortons lived in Wellesley Hills, and the families saw so much of each other that Mrs. Norton was "Aunt Mildred" to Sylvia and Warren, while the Norton boys called Mrs. Plath "Aunt Aurelia." The eldest, Dick, was later to become Sylvia's first lover and the model for Buddy Willard in *The Bell Jar,* but during her last two years in high school she had dates or flirtations with almost forty boys. To reassure herself with statistics she made detailed notes in her diary. In 1948–49 she went on sixteen dates. Nineteen boys invited her out and she went out with twelve of them, taking the initiative herself with the other four boys. Notes she made during the summer before her seventeenth birthday show how conscious she was about the boys' social background. Her main interest that summer was in a boy called John Hall, who made her feel "confident and joyful." They played tennis, went for walks and drives, danced and visited friends on the Cape, driving a Jeep along the beach.

In September 1949 she started her senior year of high school. She visited John Hall at Williams College, but her steadiest date was Bob Riedemann, a sophomore at the University of New Hampshire. He had wavy blond hair, slim artistic hands, "distinguished" purple shadows under his eyes. He had a lazy grin, and when she heard his slow, drawling voice, her hands went clammy and she felt she was melting inside. She spent most of the Christmas vacation with him, seeing movies, skating, dancing, listening to records, going out in his father's car for long sessions of necking. He often hummed in her ear as they danced cheek-to-cheek, "glued" to each other by sweat. In his opinion, women should not have careers, and she once asked what he was "building" for her life. She spent several weekends at the University of New Hampshire, and gave a surprise party for his birthday.

Her sense of identity depended partly on male reactions. On the last day in July 1949, when two truck drivers and a boy whistled at her, the incident was recorded in her diary, as if to keep it alive. After she turned seventeen on October 27, she was aware that each day was precious. At once rapturous and sad, she thought of the time melting away from her. The diary writing was partly an attempt to make more of it. Feeling egoistic, she could both reproach herself and indulge herself. She loved her flesh, her face, her limbs with overwhelming devotion. She had misgivings about her height and her nose, which she considered ugly and fat, but in her bedroom, which she had painted peach gray and brown-gold, with touches of maroon, she primped and posed in front of the mirror, telling herself how lovely she was.

Like the friendships with Perry Norton and Phil McCurdy, the one with Bob Riedemann continued into the summer of 1950,[8] but Sylvia didn't confide in him about her writing, didn't explain how happy it made her to tear "a piece of hurt and beauty" out of her life, transforming experiences into typewritten words.[9] Driving home with him when their time together was running out, she regretted each streetlight they passed. Three days before Christmas 1950, after they'd been to the movies, he kissed her lightly and told her she had been keeping him awake for three weeks. By now she was dating John Hodges, who'd kissed her on the mouth during their second date. He was a tenth-grade boy she'd admired on the basketball team. She put a photograph of him above her bureau, but by the end of November 1950 she said she no longer loved him and watched him sobbing over his steering wheel.

The friend she flirted with least and confided in most was Eddie Cohen, who started writing to her in August 1950, just before she went to Smith, after he read her story "And Summer Will Not Come Again" in *Seventeen*. Her senior by four years, he introduced himself as a "cynical idealist" who'd been at the University of Chicago and wanted to be a psychiatrist but didn't want to attend medical school. Without making any attempt to meet, they regularly exchanged long, frank letters. Knowing he might be drafted to fight in Korea, and half expecting to be killed there, he questioned what life was about and why politicians had so much power. They both felt alienated from society, and if Sylvia's strong streak of conformism made her ambivalent, she at last had an intelligent and articulate partner for a dialogue about ambivalence and about the impossibility of revealing her true self to boyfriends who would be repelled by the chaos underneath the placid exterior. Girls at Smith seldom talked abut politics, but in letters to Eddie Sylvia expressed her contempt for those who succumbed to the anticommunist hysteria orchestrated by Senator Joseph McCarthy. Freedom of thought was being destroyed; the damning label "communist" could be attached to every dissenting opinion.[10]

Correspondence with Eddie alerted her to the disparity between the thoughts she habitually kept to herself and the ones she articulated. People all wore "false grinning faces," and if you ever stopped grinning, you produced shockingly ugly words, rusty from having been cramped inside you for so long. At Smith she felt a sharp discrepancy between the bright chatter that was always available and the gloomy thoughts that took over if she stayed in her room with the loudly ticking clock and the bright electric light.[11] She and Eddie went on confiding in each other uninhibitedly. She could tell him everything, except how much she loved him, never having met him. He was like a dream, and if they met, it would wake her up. He seemed like an invisible extension of herself and her writing, her desire to live her way imaginatively through more than one life.[12]

They were both disappointed when they met at the end of March 1951. He turned up at Smith unannounced and unshaven. After breaking off his second engagement to be married, he had borrowed his parents' car and had driven for thirty hours. Starting her spring break, she was waiting for a lift home when he appeared, and she let him drive her to Wellesley. They were silent most of the time, and when they arrived, she didn't invite him into the house. He was furious with her when he drove away, but their epistolary friendship survived this disastrous meeting.[13]

For some time, Sylvia had been felling desperate about boys. In spite of all the evidence that she was attractive, she felt she wasn't. Perhaps she'd lost the self-assurance that had made her sparkle. Perhaps she'd never sparkle again. She needed a steady boyfriend as soon as possible. "Until then I'm lost," she wrote in her diary. "I think I am mad at times."[14]

She had plenty of dates, some of them blind dates, during her first year at Smith. One blind date was with a disabled veteran who took her on a long walk and made a pass at her. When he moved her hand along his penis, her disgust was mixed with curiosity. She described the soft, writhing flesh in her diary, and used the incident in *The Bell Jar.*

She needed a boyfriend who'd impress other girls at Smith, and in January 1951 she received an invitation to Yale from Dick Norton, who was a senior science student, while his brother Perry was a freshman. Dick would soon be entering Harvard Medical School. Constantly worried about money, Sylvia was glad to be earning twenty dollars a month by writing press releases for Smith, and she could earn money selling stockings in her dormitory. Before the trip to Yale she invested $1.75 at the hairdresser's.

Tall, fair and handsome, Dick had previously seemed inaccessible, but he was so desirable that she decided to study science in order to understand him better. He invited her to the Yale prom. Borrowing most of her clothes for the prom from housemates, she wore a white crinoline dress, silver sandals and a fur, carrying a black bag. On the night of the dance she and Dick stayed out till three-thirty in the morning. After they walked around the campus to a hill behind the chemistry building, he kissed her. She missed the last train back to Northampton, and after arriving at Smith late, she was confined to campus for a week. But when Dick came to Smith the following weekend, it was as the prom date of another girl, Jane Anderson, who had invited him earlier. He merely left a note for Sylvia saying he was on campus.

They saw little of each other during the spring break, but afterward, when he came to Smith for a weekend, they were so absorbed in each other that long walks made them miss most of their meals. In letters to Aurelia she called him the "sweet wonderman." Returning to Smith at the end of April, he helped her get ready for a dance, although she was going to it with another boy. In May she went to Yale for a dance and a beach picnic. Afterward they stayed on the beach, reading Hemingway out loud. He invited her to Yale with his family for his graduation, but after she arrived said he was about to leave for Arizona with friends.

Sylvia had applied for a summer babysitting job at Swampscott on Cape Cod to be near him while he worked as a waiter in Brewster, where his parents had a cottage. She was planning to ask for Monday as her day off, to coincide with his. But when his job ended, he disappeared on a trip out West with some other friends. When he wrote to her from Arizona in June 1952, he mentioned that in Brewster a waitress had been helping him to improve his dancing. He invited Sylvia to Brewster in early July, but she didn't go, and when he visited her a few weeks later, he blamed his affair with the waitress on her absence.

Unable to confide in him as she could in Eddie, she didn't let Dick see how badly he'd hurt her. In Swampscott, when she had time off from her work, she sat on the beach, thinking about death. She tried to widen the focus of her mind, taking in gradual changes in the earth's crust. All anonymous, rocks, waves and grass were momentarily defined in the consciousness of the observer, but it was only impersonal forces that survived; the human organism would decompose in the insentient soil. She felt at peace with the natural forces operating in the environment, but after so many long walks with Dick, sharing reactions to the beauty of the scenery, after feeling she was safe with him, and was saving her virginity for him, she felt shattered by his casualness. Drafting a letter to him, she said her faith and trust had crumbled. She'd thought he was unique. He wasn't.

The letter she mailed was strong enough to leave her with misgivings about the self-hatred it might induce, but with him, as with Aurelia, she camouflaged the desperation she exposed in her diary and her letters to Eddie. Anyway, why should promiscuous men like Dick expect women to be faithful?[15]

It was like another bereavement. The man she'd idolized had shown how little she mattered to him. Sitting in her room, she felt dangerous tensions in her tear ducts. All the festering jealousies, resentments and frustrations might explode in a paroxysm of weeping. But no arms would enfold her comfortingly as they had in childhood. Something inside her needed to be released, but she had to let it go on seething in the space that felt like a prison she herself had constructed.[16]

They agreed to continue the relationship, but she was no longer in love. Whether love meant self-denial or self-fulfillment, she could open herself to it only by subordinating her self-love to it. Love and marriage ought to enhance creativity, but Dick said that as a wife and mother she would be too preoccupied to go on writing and painting.[17] She didn't see why she should have to choose between having a literary career and raising a family, but letters from Eddie warned her she could have only one or the other.[18] Though she disguised Dick's identity by calling him Allen, she confided in Eddie about him, but the response was negative. She was told the relationship was destructive: marriage would lead to unhappiness and possibly violence.

Undeterred, she went to see Dick at Harvard in October 1952 and asked him to show her something of his work. Dressing her up as a student nurse, he took her into Boston's Lying-In Hospital. Together they listened to a lecture on sickle cell anemia and visited seriously ill patients. She watched cadavers being dissected, looked at fetuses of different sizes in jars, and witnessed the birth of a baby. Eight years later she revived the memory in a poem, "Two Views of a Cadaver Room." The corpses are as black as burnt turkey, she says, and a vinegary fume of the death vats is clinging to them. The babies in the jars are snail-nosed, and the man hands the woman a cut-out heart.

In *The Bell Jar,* which was written in 1961, two years later than the poem, and less than two years before her death, Sylvia again recycles the experience. The cadavers look too inhuman to upset Esther as she sits on a tall stool watching Buddy Willard and his friends dissect them. The corpses have stiff, leathery, purple-black skin, and smell like old pickle jars. The only moment of panic comes while she's leaning on a corpse's stomach watching Buddy dissect its lung. A burning sensation in her elbow makes her think the body is still half alive, but when Buddy explains the feeling as due to the pickling fluid, she puts her elbow back where it was.

The smallest fetus has a white head bent over a curled-up body no bigger than a frog; the largest, the size of a normal baby, is looking at her with a little piggy smile. In the delivery room, the pregnant woman is lifted onto what looks like a torture table, with metal stirrups sticking up into the air at one end and at the other instruments, wires and tubes. The woman is swearing, groaning and making inhuman whooing noises, but, as Buddy explains, she's on a drug which will make her forget she suffered any pain. Eventually, something fuzzy appears at the split in the shaven, disinfected place between her legs. It's the baby's head, but it gets stuck, and a third-year student, who has to deliver eight babies before he can graduate, makes an incision. His scissors close on the flesh like cloth, and fierce, bright red blood runs out. The baby that pops into his hands is the color of a blue plum, floured with white stuff. The student is scared he'll drop it, but when the supervising doctor massages it, the blueness disappears, and Esther sees it's a boy. It starts to make croaking noises and urinates in the doctor's face. After the doctor and the student have started sewing up the cut with a needle and a long thread, Buddy Willard asks Esther what she thought. She says it was wonderful. She could watch something like this every day.[19]

Neither Dick's infidelity nor the series of indigestible spectacles stopped Sylvia from going to bed with Dick, but if her experiences are accurately or even approximately paralleled in Esther's, their sexual relationship got off to a bad start. After hearing that Buddy is a fine person—the sort of boy a girl should

stay clean for—Esther assumes there can be no harm in anything
he suggests. Asked whether she has ever seen a man, she says no,
only statues, and agrees to let him undo his chino pants and then
his underpants. Instead of being impressed, she's reminded of a
turkey neck and gizzards. Disappointed at her lack of enthusiasm,
he tells her she should get used to seeing him like this, and when
he asks her to strip, she promises vaguely to do it some other
time.[20]

When Sylvia was with Dick, they alternated between love talk
and arguments about the future, but they tried to probe patiently
into each other's misgivings. If she rejected him, would she ever
find a man who satisfied her in so many ways? Wary of the word
love, they used it, but protected themselves with alternative
metaphors. He was intelligent and articulate enough for amorous
verbal games of elaborating metaphysical conceits. Wary of suc-
culent oysters, they could attach two of them to a string, and
each swallow one. If it disagreed with their digestive system, they
could yank it up before it was too late. There might be a little
nausea and regret, but neither of them would be poisoned.
Marriage, on the other hand, couldn't be attached to a string.
After all, she was only nineteen. It wasn't too late to find a man
no less beautiful, no less companionable, but less threatening to
her creativity.[21]

She knew from Dick's reactions to other girls that he was
unlikely to be faithful. A shorter girl, or one with better breasts or
hair, might catch his fancy. A wife would be a possession he took
pride in, like a new car. He wanted to be a country doctor, with a
wife who made love, cooked meals and brought up children.
Scared of being dominated, Sylvia was accused of wanting to be
dominant. At home he liked to be mothered but, reacting against
his mother, needed to prove his male independence. He tried to
put Sylvia in her place by disparaging poetry as "inconsequential
dust."[22] Doctors on the other hand provided real help.

When writing "Sunday at the Mintons" she began by modeling
Henry on Dick and Elizabeth on herself.[23] She used to get herself
started on a story by listing nouns, adjectives and verbs to
describe the main characters. The words on her worksheets for
Henry are perseverance, firmness, stability, solid, sturdy,
staunch, indefatigable, plodding, obstinate, peremptory, inexor-
able, indomitable, relentless, calculating and designing, while
Elizabeth was to be capricious, irresolute, tremulous, frothy,

volatile, frail, pliant, erratic, fitful, fanciful, whimsical, spontaneous, eccentric, freakish, wanton, giddy.

By the end of the summer Sylvia was trying to avoid Dick.
When he was found to have tuberculosis and sent to a sanatorium
in the Adirondacks, she resented the way his family took it for
granted that she would want to go there for Christmas, but she
didn't refuse, though she no longer relished the idea of settling
down with him. He had used the leisure enforced on him by
illness to start writing, and in his stories the women were
colorless vehicles on which the males proved their sexual prow-
ess. In reality, Dick always arrogated the initiative in sex play, and
when he grew a mustache, he believed it would be a sign of
weakness if he shaved it off merely because she wanted him to.
Now that kissing could be infectious, she thought of his mouth as
a source of germs, and felt no desire to touch him.[24] Her plunge
down the ski slope was partly a way of telling him she wanted to
reject what he was offering.

One of the main reasons was that she'd found a boy who
appealed to her more. At the Nortons' home during the Thanksgiving break in November 1952 she had met two of Perry's
roommates. Hearing that one was top of his class at Yale, Sylvia
had pictured a short, dark boy wearing spectacles, but when she
entered the room, a tall, good-looking boy got up and grinned.
Writing to Warren about Myron Lotz, who was known as Mike,
she said she'd never felt so immediately attracted to anyone. The
son of an Austrian steel worker, and a scholarship student at Yale,
he looked athletic, and he told her that in the summer he had
earned ten thousand dollars playing baseball, pitching for the
Detroit Tigers.[25] She invited him to her house dance at Smith,
where they spent three days together.

Going for an evening walk, they passed the Northampton
mental hospital and heard inmates screaming from behind barred
windows. Sylvia felt curious about the borderline between sanity
and madness. On another walk they saw planes landing in a field.
A pilot offered to take her up in his two-seater. She'd never flown,
and she was ecstatic when, as he did a "wing-over," she saw the
river above her head and the mountains reeling into the sky, while
the clouds floated below. Shouting above the noise of the engine,
she said it was better than God or religion. Invited to take over the
controls, she manipulated the stick to make the plane climb and
tilt.[26]

Unlike Dick, who was no taller than Sylvia, Mike Lotz seemed like a giant physically and mentally. During solitary afternoons after their weekend together she sometimes pulled down the blinds and retreated into bed to lie under the quilt, talking to the absent boy. But she warned herself not to make him into an engine for her ecstasy. This was dangerous. Transmuting him mentally into a lover who constantly desired her, she was giving him a role he'd play inadequately when they were together.[27] But he invited her to the Yale Junior Prom in the spring of 1953, and they spent several weekends together. If she married him, life would have more intellectual dignity than with Dick, but should she crawl into the "paternal embrace of a mental colossus?"[28] With her hankering for the gigantic, yes, perhaps she should.

Another relationship that started during 1953 was with Gordon Lameyer, an Amherst English student who lived in Wellesley. Tall and fair, he'd volunteered for service in the navy and had become an officer in the ROTC. After hearing Sylvia speak at a Smith Club meeting in Wellesley, his mother asked for her telephone number, and when he called Sylvia in April, they arranged to meet for a Coke and sandwich at Toto's, near Lawrence House. Her left ankle was still in a cast. He "didn't know what to make of her effusiveness, her abundant energy. She seemed to effloresce about everything, especially poetry. She loved Dylan Thomas then almost more than life itself."[29] Forced into inactivity by the cast, Sylvia was depressed but reading Yeats, and sometimes, elated, felt as if she were spiraling upward in a Yeatsian gyre, learning from past mistakes. She made up her mind never to get caught in circles of stagnation.

In spite of the suicidal depression which was deepening throughout the first half of July, after her month on *Mademoiselle,* she and Gordon Lameyer saw each other every day, taking trips to the mountains and the ocean, talking about Dylan Thomas and James Joyce, listening to phonograph records of Beethoven and Brahms. But Gordon wrote poetry, not very well, and as a husband he would find it insufferable if his wife were more successful than he was. Mike Lotz was a better candidate, a scientist with a sensitive appreciation of the creative arts and, unlike Bob Riedemann, the New Hampshire sophomore with wavy blond hair, strong enough not to be steamrollered by her dynamism. She'd enjoy making a home for Mike and cooking for him, while stimulating him mentally and physically. When he telephoned her, she felt light-headed and in danger of losing her voice.[30]

During the worst moments she felt weak, phlegmatic and in danger of suffocation, as if there weren't enough air to breathe. But she could fantasize about making love to Mike between bouts of reading and thinking about sex from the perspective of Lucretius as translated by Dryden. "The tragedy of sexual inter-course is the perpetual virginity of the soul." "Sexual intercourse is an attempt to solve the eternal antimony, doomed to failure because it takes place only on one side of the gulf." With her yearning to transcend the human, Sylvia also responded to Swedenborg's description of sexual intercourse between angels as "a conflagration of the whole being."[31]

After inviting Mike to the junior prom at Smith, she celebrated her liberation from Dick by buying silver high-heeled shoes and a strapless silvery gown. She wanted to look "silverly" beautiful, like a sylvan goddess. But she wasn't going to marry Mike, and the intimacy was short-lived. She was still visiting Dick at the clinic, and she spent weekends in New York with a boy called Ray, whom she'd met the previous summer during her job at the Belmont Hotel. He had a good mind, but he was shorter than Mike, with a less impressive body. She alternated between thinking she could live with him and resenting the flat shoes she'd have to wear. When making love to him, she sometimes felt fine but more often like a horizontal Mother Earth being raped by a humming insect who was fertilizing thousands of while little eggs in a gravel pit. Perhaps he'd be unfaithful too. But she liked the way he touched her and the quickness of his mind.

In her absence—she visited Dick at Saranac and spent a weekend in New York with Ray—Mike dated someone else. She was furious at being betrayed, though she had been no less treacherous. Marriage was endlessly on her mind: her ambition was to "live hard and good with a hard, good man." But before the spring term of 1953 was over, she knew she had to go on looking. She still had Dick, Gordon and Ray, as well as Mike. She loved "pieces of" all four, but how could she commit the next fifty years of her life to any one of them? How could she promise one of these boys to love his faults, ignore his infidelities, and go on respecting him even when his behavior was beastly? She'd have to bring up his children, look after his home, cook for him, and be faithful. She hated being alone at breakfast, eating her boiled egg in solitude. But the man she wanted didn't exist.[32]

She needed to love someone because she needed to be loved, and the idea of failure was close to the idea of suicide. She was like a rabbit at night, she said, in danger of hurling itself under the wheels of a car because the lights were so terrifying. Her need for love was desperate, even when she thought of it as an artifice to replace parents who'd turned out to be neither godlike nor omniscient. But she didn't even have as much companionship as she could have had at Smith if only she'd tried to make friends with girls instead of devoting so much time to work and boys. Each day she was stepping closer to death, but death could never happen to her because she consisted of consciousness, which was incompatible with it. Over coffee and orange juice, as she wrote in her journal, "the embryonic suicide brightens visibly."[33]

Her August suicide attempt took Gordon Lameyer by surprise. They went on corresponding, but didn't resume their relationship until the summer, when they saw a lot of each other. He claims they were "unofficially engaged,"[34] and Nancy Hunter, her current roommate at Smith, who assumed they were going to get married, describes him as intelligent, articulate, spectacularly handsome "and obviously devoted to Syl. He seemed the proper middle-class choice. Moreover, he had the one qualification Syl considered crucial: he was well over six feet tall."[35]

But he wasn't strong enough for her. Even when, in moments of loneliness, she longed for him, she felt sickened by his weaknesses. He was going to be secure financially, he swam and he skied, but all the attributes of a god, she said, couldn't compensate for mental and physical weakness.[36] After her suicide attempt they saw less of each other, and in April 1954 she started dating two Yale roommates, Richard Sassoon and Mel Woody, who both called themselves existentialists. In May, when she spent a weekend in New York with the "intuitive and solicitous" Sassoon, they achieved "ecstatic rapport." They saw a play in Greenwich Village, spent two hours over a meal at Steuben's, made love between bouts of sharing wine and poetry, watched the dawn come up. After her suitcase was stolen from a car in the city, Sylvia told Aurelia she had been so short of money at Smith that she'd had to sell all her clothes.[37]

She spent many weekends with Richard in the States and in Europe over the next two years. He shared her passion for food, and together they devoured oysters, snails, avocados, steaks, chops, and strawberries. They drank French wine, went to the theater and the movies, talked passionately about Baudelaire, Rimbaud, Nietzsche, Kierkegaard and Sartre. Sassoon had read more existentialist philosophy than she had.

Writing to Aurelia about Richard, Sylvia said she was forging a new soul, being refined in the fires of pain and love. She loved him "above and beyond all thought"; his soul was the most "furious and saintly" she had encountered. The frailty of his body ceased to matter when his soul spoke to her in words that the gods would envy.[38] In 1959, talking retrospectively to a psychiatrist about her premarital promiscuity, she said that this affair had given her the most pleasure, and that she'd been monogamous throughout most of it.[39]

It satisfied some of the guilt feelings left over from relationships with both parents. Richard wanted to "play daddy" to a girl who was naughty. Sylvia was the only woman he had ever wanted "to please and to punish," while she felt degraded by having a lover shorter than she was. They also took advantage of each other's knowledge. One of her other lovers complained of feeling he was being "cross-examined, drained, eaten."[40]

In the summer of 1954 Sylvia became involved with the man who in *The Bell Jar* is called Irwin. She and Nancy Hunter were both at Harvard summer school. In the novel Esther is still a virgin when on the steps of the Widener Library she meets a tall, ugly, bespectacled young man. At twenty-six he's already a professor of mathematics. When she lets him make love to her, all she feels is a startlingly sharp pain, and she hemorrhages so badly that she has to see a doctor.[41]

Esther is alone when she meets him, but Sylvia was with Nancy when they were accosted on the library steps by a balding, myopic young man with a woebegone expression. Tall, thin and bony, he told them he was a professor of biology. More attracted to Nancy, he tried to seduce her, clumsily but so persistently that she afterward felt she'd narrowly escaped being raped. After telling Sylvia the whole story, Nancy was surprised when she announced that she'd entered into a platonic relationship with him. When she acquired a key to his apartment, she said it was because she needed a quiet place to study, but only a few days passed before she was missing overnight. Afterward she told Nancy she had been raped. She hemorrhaged and had to see a gynecologist, but later, to Nancy's amazement, she went on going out with the man, as well as starting what she claimed was an innocent relationship with a Harvard professor, whose wife—reasonably or unreasonably—became jealous.[42]

But the emotional involvement with Richard Sassoon, which had started in April 1954, survived the Harvard interlude and was still going strong in 1955. That autumn he was in Paris while she was at Cambridge in the first of her two years on a Fulbright scholarship. She'd always tended to mythologize her relationships, but none had penetrated so intimately into her writing. Her letters to Richard were like experiments in a new prose, influenced by Surrealism and Dylan Thomas. Glowing asbestos thorns and whistling flame flowers reflected the cells of the scarlet heart, while the coliseum burned on the brink of blackness.[43] She wrote as if she hoped to bind him to her with incantatory rhythms. Sylvia with a lower case *s* becomes a character in her febrile fiction, burning dahlias on her dark altar as the sun wanes and plants surrender to omnipotent white frosts. He's hector, comforting her by patting her torn and tangled hair. Their lovemaking astonishes the angels and arouses envy in god with a lower case *g*.

The name sassoon is the most beautiful name in the world, containing seas of grass en masse and a persian moon in a rococo lagoon of woodwind tune under a passing ebony monsoon. She equates the name sassoon with the creative word present in the beginning, and she's the weeping, fallen eve, commanding him to be christ and to rise before her eyes, while the blue marys bless them with singing.[44]

Amorous Cambridge undergraduates were fended off. She told them she had a boyfriend in France. Fantasies about him were integral to her oscillation between euphoria and depression. She felt as though she had a great sorrow inside her like a pregnancy. Until she could give birth to it, she'd be clumsy as a dancing elephant, but she lacked the strength to give birth by writing a letter to the world in the form of a poem or story, which would only be rejected by editors who seemed to be pronouncing divine judgment.

Feeling greedy for life, she understood that wanting everything was dangerously close to wanting nothing. There were two ways of wanting nothing. One was to have such a rich inner core of joy that it made external reality redundant. The other was to feel so dead and rotten that nothing could help. She needed him to collaborate on building an exquisite bridge from one grave to another. Or—the metaphors jostle each other impatiently out of the way—she must try to make each day into a brightly colored bead on a string, not kill the present by snipping it up to fit some plan for a future Taj Mahal.[45] It was as hard for her to relax into this feverish writing as into a hammock slung precariously between the poles of life and death.

Spending the Christmas vacation in France with Richard, she mythologized the experience while having it. The blackness of a strange land knifes past the windows of the train as it speeds along the zipperlike railway tracks toward the sunny south, away from the cutting winds of gray Cambridge and the freezing frosts of London. They're raping the land, making France split open like a ripe fig. The stars remind her of Van Gogh, while the cypresses are idiosyncratic pen sketches against the sky. When the train stops at Lyon, they jerk out of their somnolence to buy red wine and ham rolls. They drink from paper cups and eat the sandwiches with the last of their peanuts, dried figs and tangerines. Eventually they're looking at the Mediterranean, the sea Sylvia had associated as a schoolgirl with pyramids and the Sphinx, white Greek ruins, bleeding Spanish bulls and couples in folk costume holding hands.[46]

Back in wintry Cambridge she was still passionately in love with him. When she called up images of what Richard looked like while dressing or shaving or reading, radiance seemed to spill over him. But euphoria dwindled into tearful recognition that the incandescent moments were sprinkled sparsely through a life that consisted mainly of sleeping, cleaning one's teeth and waiting for things to improve or letters to arrive. She couldn't stop herself from wishing for situations, like war, which test us by requiring us to live heroically, using all our resources.[47]

Richard had other lovers, and after their holiday he told her not to write to him until he'd had time to sort out his feelings. In February 1956 she complained to her diary that without him there was no one to love. He was the only man whose child she wanted. His absence was indistinguishable from her depression. She felt terrified, condemned, lost, impotent. While she was crossing a bridge over the Cam, two small boys started throwing dirty snowballs at her. Her tolerant smile felt insincere. After drafting a poem, she noticed that her thesaurus was lying open at 545 Deception, 546 Untruth, 547 Dupe, 548 Deceiver. She believed herself to be a fraud.

Undergraduates seemed to be smiling at her fearfully as if wanting her to confirm their importance by kissing them. She pictured Richard in the arms of either an accomplished prostitute or the Swiss girl who wanted to marry him, while Sylvia felt as if all her earlier affairs had been rehearsals for this relationship. More and more often she dressed in black. To one boy, John, who told her he could love her violently if he allowed himself to, she said she had once been happy and it was Richard who had made her into her present self. She could easily have responded to John's appetite for her, but she playfully told him she wasn't going to let it happen. Or was Richard merely a pretext for keeping her independence? He was small, thin, sickly, moody, nervous. Did his mind and his potency compensate for all that?[48]

She made an appointment with a psychiatrist. She needed someone older and wiser—a father and a mother. She thought about Lazarus, identifying with him. She too had come back from the dead, been rescued from the grave, with the disfiguring scar as evidence. Was it really becoming more prominent, "paling like a death-spot in the red windblown skin"? She also identified with Nina in O'Neill's *Strange Interlude,* wanting husband, lover, father and son at the same time.[49]

The summer before, in 1955, she had begun an affair with Peter Davison,[50] assistant to the director of Harvard University Press. A graduate of Harvard, he had also been at Cambridge, and served in the army. He was twenty-seven when Alfred Kazin introduced him to Sylvia during her final months at Smith, and afterward he looked her up in Wellesley. She went to bed with him on the first evening she was invited to dinner at his apartment.[51] She talked scathingly about both her parents: her father had been "a sort of fuddy-duddy professor who dealt with bugs down in Boston," and her mother was dreadful. Peter was surprised, when she took him to her home, to see how deferential she was toward Aurelia.[52]

He suspected she was affecting more intensity than she felt, and when she talked about previous love affairs and successes at Smith, it sounded as if she were talking about someone else. The only time he sensed he was making contact with the real woman was when she told the story of her suicide attempt.[53] But he liked her energy, her volatility and her alertness. Peter wrote verse; Sylvia loaned him her Dylan Thomas records and discussed Elizabeth Bishop's work with him. He advised her about how to make the most of Cambridge, and gave her letters of introduction to friends and acquaintances in London. In late August, when they went to Martha's Vineyard for a weekend together, she told Gordon Lameyer she was going to meet a prospective agent.[54]

Though there's nothing abnormal in the discontinuity between one youthfully passionate liaison and the next, these relationships of 1952–1955 throw some light on the 1963 suicide. The 1953 suicide attempt had something to do with sexual fantasies and with pressures, physical and mental, set up by sexuality, but nothing to do with disillusionment ensuing from particular sexual experiences. Of all her lovers in 1953–1955, Richard Sassoon seems to have been the only one in whom she confided as freely as she did in Eddie Cohen, who was never a lover. With the other lovers she was nervous about revealing what she called the chaos underneath the placid surface, and when she was hiding this from them, she was also hiding it from herself.

In none of these lovers did she confide less than she did in Dick Norton, but it was he who brought her closest to feeling suicidal, first when he went to bed with the waitress, and later when Sylvia visited him in the sanatorium. He'd seemed like a paragon, like a young god, and the pain she felt in having to withdraw her faith prefigured her pain when she lost faith in Ted Hughes. Having thought Dick was unique, Sylvia had to recognize that he was just like any other man, and the reckless plunge down the ski slope was like a suicide attempt. She'd used the word *madness* for the pain that had precipitated the 1953 suicide attempt, and in the Adirondacks she was mad again, just as she was mad at the beginning of 1963—not clinically mad, but in more pain than she could bear.

✺ 6 ✺

Female Support

Though Sylvia had a great deal of support from other women—both her contemporaries and older women—it wasn't enough to repair the damage inflicted by her family and by men. The neurotic pattern was so deeply ingrained that she tended to wreck her relationships with women, either by asking for too much or by taking generosity for granted. She was good at making friends, and good at losing them.

Arriving at Smith in 1950, Sylvia was given an attic room in Haven House, where Marcia Brown, a sociology student, shared a ground-floor room with another girl. At first Marcia was unimpressed by Sylvia, who struck her as shy, gawky, lacking in general know-how and in the right kind of clothes, but soon they were chatting about intimate subjects.[1] Sylvia seemed to be "in awe" of Dick Norton, but when Marcia met him she found him humorless, bland and sentimental, though likably considerate.[2]

Sylvia spent the spring break with Marcia at her sister's house in the mountains of New Hampshire, and throughout most of July 1951 the girls saw each other every day in Swampscott, where they had babysitting jobs they'd found through the college's vocational guidance office. One day they borrowed bikes and cycled to Marblehead, where they rented a boat and rowed out to Children's Island.[3] It was with Marcia that Sylvia paid her first visit to New York, and in their second year they shared a room. In Sylvia's third year, though Marcia was living with her mother, they occasionally spent an evening together. Before the suicide attempt of August 1953, Sylvia telephoned Marcia and they met for dinner in Boston, where Marcia listened sympathetically to an account of Sylvia's depression and her insomnia.[4] When Marcia married in the summer of 1954, Sylvia was a bridesmaid at the wedding.

At Smith Sylvia had two scholarships. One, worth $450, was funded by the local Smith club; the other, worth $850, was financed by Olive Higgins Prouty, author of the best-selling novel *Stella Dallas,* which had been serialized on the radio. At the suggestion of her scholarship counselor, Sylvia wrote to thank Mrs. Prouty, sending an upbeat letter rather like the ones to Aurelia. In her house at Smith she'd found a startling collection of perceptive and fascinating girls. Never before had she been so alert to the dignity and capacity of women. Mrs. Prouty sent the letter on to the *Smith Alumnae Quarterly,* which published it, and after inviting Sylvia to tea at her home in Brookline, she became sufficiently interested to intervene generously after the suicide attempt. Mrs. Prouty paid for McLean, the private hospital, sent a car to take Sylvia there and visited her regularly.[5]

Mrs. Prouty had once had a nervous breakdown and believed that in the long run she had benefited from it. This was encouraging. But Sylvia alternated between gratitude and resentment based on the feeling of being manipulated. In *The Bell Jar* Mrs. Prouty appears as Philomena Guinea, the silver-haired novelist who comes in her black chauffeur-driven Cadillac with Esther's mother and brother to transport her from the cramped city hospital to a private clinic with golf courses and gardens, like a country club. Esther, who knows she ought to be grateful, feels nothing; she's still under the same bell jar, stewing in her own sour air.[6] Later, when she was back at Smith, Sylvia took her best friend with her to have tea with Mrs. Prouty. Both girls wore white gloves for the visit, but ate so many cucumber sandwiches that the butler had to bring more.

Mrs. Prouty went on taking an almost proprietary interest in Sylvia for the rest of her life. In 1957, when a friend of hers read one of Sylvia's poems in the *Atlantic Monthly* and commented on its intensity, Mrs. Prouty wrote to suggest she should sometimes write with less intensity. Lamps turned too high, she said, were liable to shatter the shade: sometimes Sylvia should be content just to *glow.*[7]

Still wanting to be Sylvia's patron even after she married, Mrs. Prouty went on sending money. When Sylvia and Ted Hughes were furnishing their house in Devon, they bought carpets with money she'd sent, and in August 1962, when she came to

London, she took them to dinner and to see *The Mousetrap*. After the marriage broke up, Mrs. Prouty went on sending money and advice.

The friend who in 1954 accompanied Sylvia on her visit to Mrs. Prouty was Nancy Hunter, an attractive girl who was writing a thesis on "The History of Ethical Culture."[8] Ethical Culture was a kind of secular religion started in late nineteenth-century New York by Felix Adler, a reformed Jew. Otto Plath belonged to the Boston congregation of the Ethical Culture Society. Nancy and Sylvia agreed to be roommates during their senior year. In letters to Aurelia, Sylvia called Nancy her alter ego, and it seemed she was only partly joking when she announced that Nancy's Irish coloring was an appropriate foil for her German blondness, while Nancy was tall enough to be considered an equal.[9]

She noticed that Sylvia's placid demeanor was at odds with the turbulence she expressed in her poetry, but that she was eager to talk about herself and the suicide attempt.[10] At the end of the term Nancy was invited to spend a weekend at the Plaths' home, and in the summer of 1954, when they both had scholarships to Harvard summer school, Sylvia and Nancy shared a bedroom in an apartment on Massachusetts Avenue in Cambridge, renting it from two graduate students, and taking two other Lawrence House girls as lodgers. Compulsively proprietary about the things she owned, Sylvia marked many of them with her name, and kept them meticulously neat. "If anyone ever disarranged my things, I'd feel as though I'd been raped intellectually."[11] But Nancy felt as if they were "Siamese twins, joined at the ego."[12]

Their relationship deteriorated as a result of the demands Sylvia made on Nancy after the balding biology lecturer had raped her and made her hemorrhage. When she reappeared in the late afternoon, after spending part of the night at his apartment and part at a hospital, she looked pale and ill. It was after collapsing in a pool of blood on the bathroom floor that she told Nancy she'd been raped. Worried that she might be bleeding to death, Nancy called a doctor, who gave advice over the telephone about how to stop the bleeding. When it resumed, Sylvia was terrified of going back to the hospital. After promising to stay with her all the time she was there, Nancy called the biologist, who drove them to the hospital emergency room.

Keeping her promise, Nancy stayed with her, but they quarreled when Sylvia tried to maker her go back with her at noon the next day when the vaginal packing was to be removed. Nancy has been invited to have lunch with Professor Hans Kohn, who was teaching her course at Harvard and had promised to tell her about his friend Morris Cohen, the philosopher-educator who was to be the subject of her honors thesis. But how could she possibly expect Sylvia to go to the hospital alone after everything that had happened to her in hospitals? They agreed to go there together at ten, so that Nancy could still keep her lunch date with the professor.

The friendship cooled further when, within a week, Sylvia had resumed her relationship with the biologist and started one with a Harvard professor. According to her, this was platonic; according to the professor's wife, Sylvia was a blond bitch. To Nancy it seemed that Sylvia was counting on crises to give her creative inspiration; for the sake of her poetry and her stories she was taking risks and depending on other people to rescue her from dangerous situations. [13]

The suspicion grew stronger on the morning of Nancy's final exams. She was awakened by screams. Sylvia was lying on a bed, shrieking with pain and recrimination. "My head is flying off. I can't stand the pain. Do something; I'm dying." After telephoning a doctor, who promised to come, Nancy had to decide whether to leave for her exam, which started at eight, or submit to Sylvia's pleading and stay with her till the doctor arrived. One of the other Lawrence girls was willing to sit with Sylvia, and Nancy left. Afterward there was no recrimination, but she felt Sylvia was being "driven, periodically, to stage a symbolic salvation with herself as the suffering victim and me as the deliverer, almost as though only by being snatched from the brink of death she could confirm her worth." If the message behind all the drama was that a key was missing from the elaborate clockwork that kept Sylvia going, Nancy had to recognize with a mixture of sadness and relief that she couldn't go on acting as that key. They went on sharing a room in Lawrence House during their last year there, but the intimacy was over. [14]

It was thanks to Mrs. Prouty that Sylvia had met the woman who became her most powerful ally against Aurelia. Dr. Ruth Beuscher, a psychiatrist at McLean, was unlike any of the other psychiatrists Sylvia had seen either before the suicide attempt or in the Framingham Hospital, where she was taken by ambulance after being found by Warren, or in the closed psychiatric wing of

Massachusetts General Hospital in Boston, where she had insulin shock treatments. Dr. Beuscher continued the insulin therapy, which made Sylvia put on weight. Her unhappiness about this is reflected in her story "Tongues of Stone," in which the girl is caught "in the nightmare of the body, without a mind, without anything, only the soulless flesh which got fatter with the insulin and yellower with the fading tan." In Sylvia's opinion, Dr. Beuscher looked like Myrna Loy, which probably helped her to overcome her young patient's distrust of psychiatrists and her terror of electroconvulsive therapy. In *The Bell Jar,* when Esther threatens to kill herself if she has to undergo the blue flashes, the jolting and the noise, Dr. Nolan says it doesn't need to be like that. If it's done properly, it's like going to sleep. But she promises to give Esther advance warning if she's to have this therapy.

When the warning is delivered, only a few hours before the first treatment, Esther feels betrayed. The doctor puts her arm around the girl and hugs her like a mother. The only reason she didn't tell her yesterday evening, she explains, is that anxiety might have kept her awake overnight. She has come especially early to tell Esther, and she's going to stay with her until she regains consciousness after the treatment.

Esther is led to a room with white tile walls and bare bulbs. Keeping her eyes half closed, she sees a high bed with a tight sheet and a machine behind it and people in masks around the bed. A nurse talks to her soothingly, rubbing salve onto her temples and fitting small electric buttons on either side of her head. When something is put on her tongue, she bites down in panic and the darkness wipes her out like chalk on a blackboard. When she wakes out of the deep, drenched sleep, Dr. Nolan's face is swimming in front of her and calling her name. The heat and fear have purged themselves. She feels at peace as she's let out into the fresh air. She's to have the treatment three times a week. [15]

Electroconvulsive therapy was combined with insulin therapy. By the end of 1953 Sylvia was discharged from McLean, and by February she was back at Smith, but she went on seeing Dr. Beuscher until she left for England in 1955. After going back to America in 1957, when she taught at Smith, Sylvia resumed psychotherapy with Dr. Beuscher, at first keeping her husband, Ted Hughes, in ignorance. Alongside him, Ruth Beuscher became an almost mythical repository of value. By living and writing, Sylvia could be "worthy" of them both.[16] Sylvia also interiorized a great deal of what Dr. Beuscher said and felt.

In May 1958, suspicious about Hughes's feelings toward other women, Sylvia felt she already knew what Dr. Beuscher would say. Making promises to herself was like making promises to Dr. Beuscher. No, she wouldn't jump out of a window, or smash the car into a tree or fill the garage with carbon monoxide or slash her wrists. No, she could go on teaching and writing.[17]

She'd started viewing Aurelia in a perspective which included all the other mother figures, such as Mrs. Prouty and Mary Ellen Chase, a teacher at Smith who had given generous help but seemed resentful when Sylvia steered her own course. They both disapproved of the marriage, and Mary Ellen Chase was disappointed when Sylvia abandoned academic work. Thanks to Ruth Beuscher, Sylvia came to realize how much hatred and rage she had been accumulating against all these mother figures. Dr. Beuscher didn't advise her on how to handle this hostility, but it became easier to acknowledge and confront it.[18]

The therapy stopped again when Sylvia left Boston in June 1959, but her patterns of thinking had been permanently altered, and she continued in many of the habits Ruth Beuscher had inculcated. One of these was to list the jobs she intended to do each day, and check them off when they were done. Presumably the objective was to increase her realism and minimize her anxiety about how much could be done and should be done. But it is questionable whether therapy could have helped to liberate her from her compulsive habit of overfilling her day. Her energy was phenomenal. The letters she wrote in addition to poems and stories, the amount of hard work she did in typing out her own writing and Hughes's, the housework, and by the spring of 1960, the extra work of looking after the children—what she accomplished during the course of one day was prodigious. But at the cost of overloading her nervous system. There was a suicidal element in the way she overworked, and the accumulated exhaustion helps to explain the state of mind she was in when she killed herself.

In the last six months of her life Sylvia again asked for help from Dr. Beuscher, who wrote back to her on September 27, 1962, saying she couldn't treat Sylvia by correspondence, but offering all the love and support a friend could give. Dr. Beuscher said she was "furious" with Hughes for his immature behavior and that Sylvia should try to keep control of her life in her own hands.[19]

At Cambridge the most important mother figure was her supervisor, Dr. Dorothea Krook, who lectured on Henry James and on the moral philosophers. Writing home in April 1956, Sylvia described Dr. Krook as "more than a miracle." Talking about Plato, she'd been whetting Sylvia's mind "like a blue-bladed knife."[20] Meeting Sylvia once a week to discuss the essays she wrote, Dr. Krook gave the impression that they could soon become friendly. After a conversation about the Trinity, Sylvia was aghast to think how much she'd missed by refusing to take account of religious ideology. Now standing "at the juncture of Greek and Christian thought," she felt as if her mind had never been so keen to make "leaps and sallies into new understanding."[21]

From the moment they saw each other, Dr. Krook recognized Sylvia as someone who took an intent interest in everything that went on. Coming into the small living room in Dr. Krook's home in Grantchester Meadows, Sylvia always looked neat and fresh, her hair held in place by a broad bandeau. Dr. Krook describes her typical expression as eager, mobile, tranquil and serene. She was a movingly responsive student: writers mattered to her in a personal way.[22] Plato provided the main perspective for all their discussions about love and beauty, justice, the pleasant and the good, knowledge and opinion, the contemplative intelligence and the practical intelligence, rationalism and mysticism; when Mary Ellen Chase arrived in Cambridge, Sylvia talked about Plato and Mrs. Krook in a way that suggested she admired them equally.

Mrs. Krook found Sylvia more impressive in conversation than in her essays, which, though they were all on a high level, neither seemed to contain enough of herself nor to penetrate deeply into the subject matter. Trying to explain this retrospectively, Mrs. Krook wondered whether the striving for excellence in the essays had been part of a campaign "against the forces of disintegration within her." Planning to teach English literature at Smith, she was perhaps struggling to consolidate a firmer hold on "normalcy."[23]

In the autumn of 1956, when Sylvia, who had broken the rules by marrying and was fearful of dismissal, admitted what she'd done, Mrs. Krook advised her to tell her tutor. There was no disciplinary retribution, and the married couple settled down to live in Eltisley Avenue, around the corner from Grantchester Meadows. Sylvia seemed so extremely happy that Mrs. Krook felt worried about what might happen if anything should ever go wrong with this marriage.[24] It was a cold winter, and when Sylvia complained of feeling degraded and diminished by the cold, Mrs. Krook lent her an oil heater, for which she seemed almost excessively grateful, frequently saying how much difference it was making to their lives.

February 11, the day she died, was Dorothea Krook's birthday, and Sylvia's former supervisor has followed the Jewish custom of commemorating her death by lighting a candle. "Though I hate and fear death, I am glad I am prevented from forgetting hers."[25]

❧ 7 ❧

Marriage

Ted Hughes and Sylvia Plath had a partnership that tangled
literature with sexuality. Though they produced no writing
under a joint signature, they shared experiences which would serve
as raw material for literary work and maintained a dialogue about
both experiences and work. "You begin to write out of one brain,"
Hughes has said. "We were like two feet, each one using everything
the other did."

Many people have praised his generosity in encouraging other
writers and giving them confidence in unfinished work. When he
was living with Sylvia, there were no bounds to their opportunities for literary intimacy, and it took a long time for the
relationship to deteriorate to the point at which she decided that if
she achieved fame by the age of fifty, she would never write any
tributes to the loving husband whose help had been indispensable
to her success.

Sylvia Plath met Ted Hughes on February 25, 1956, when she
was twenty-three and he was twenty-five. Her last meeting with
him was shortly before she committed suicide in February 1963.
In finding him she found what seemed like a powerful and
inexhaustible source of love. He looked like the best possible man
to replace the father whose death had robbed her, she believed, of
the man who could have been trusted never to withdraw his love.
Hughes was big, strong, good-looking, creative, brilliant, successful, helpful. He could teach her, look after her, bring out the
best in her, make love to her, side with her against the rest of the
world.

On another level, her relationship with him was, from the outset, a relationship with the death that awaited her. In so far as her suicide was an act of aggression, it was aimed against him and his new lover, Assia Wevill. In *After the Fall,* the autobiographical play he finished in 1962, shortly after the death of Marilyn Monroe, Arthur Miller wrote: "A suicide kills two people, Maggie, that's what it's *for!*"[1] Sylvia's suicide was meant to kill three. If Hughes and Assia regarded it as the worst blow she could have dealt them, they were right.

It was the final aggression in a series of violent exchanges that started on the day Sylvia met Hughes. The question of whether her death was inevitable is bound up with the question of their conscious and unconscious motives for starting the relationship. They were both highly intuitive people; both must have had strong inklings of what they were taking on.

She seems at first to have been attracted almost as much by his reputation as by the physical impression he made. In Cambridge his reputation as a poet was based on solid achievement; his reputation as a seducer was based, even then, on stories that mixed fact with fiction. Clive James, who was at Pembroke, the same college, and had rooms on the same staircase, says Hughes invited women not only to spend the night but to advertise their presence by hanging stockings to dry outside his window, which overlooked the Old Court.[2] Many other stories were told about him, some true, some exaggerated, some invented.

Ted Hughes was born in a small Yorkshire Pennine town, Mytholmroyd. His father, who had been a carpenter, was one of seventeen survivors of a regiment massacred at Gallipoli in the First World War. Ted had an older sister, Olwyn, and an older brother, Gerald. When Ted was seven, the family moved to Mexborough, where his father took over a newsagent's and tobacconist's shop. After winning a scholarship to Pembroke College, Hughes did his compulsory military service before matriculating in 1951. For two years he studied English, but he was soon disillusioned with the way it was taught. Instead of going to lectures he spent much of his time reading folklore and Yeats's poetry. There was a time, he claims, when he knew the whole *Collected Poems* by heart.[3]

Hughes says the account in Sylvia's journal of their first meeting is "ridiculously exaggerated,"[4] but he offers no alternative. A party was being held in Falcon Yard, Cambridge, for the poetry magazine *St. Botolph's Review.* Sylvia describes him as big, dark, and hunky, the only boy in the room huge enough for her. As soon as she arrived, she wanted to know who he was, and watched him "hunching around over women." He is tall, but to her he was "colossal." She describes their conversation as if they were shouting to each other.

Eventually he ripped off her hairband and kissed her, first on the mouth, and then on the neck. She responded by biting him "long and hard" on the cheek, making blood pour down his face. There's no doubt about the bite: his Cambridge friend Lucas Myers didn't witness it but saw that Ted had been bitten,[5] and in Ted's poem "Lovesong," which he published in the 1970 volume *Crow,* the woman who bites, gnaws and sucks the man wants him "complete inside her." Sylvia, when she intended to write a Cambridge novel, thought of making Falcon Yard a central image. Love would be equated with a falcon, which struck once and for all. The central chapter would feature the "irrefutable" experience which had involved a blood sacrifice.[6]

There is nothing surprising about the desires she felt, but the language in her journal is surprisingly violent: she was "screaming" in herself, she wanted to "give myself crashing, fighting, to you." He was the one man who could "blast" Richard Sassoon.[7] Still feeling "desperately vengeful" when she recollected the emotion in comparative tranquility, she assumed they would never be lovers, though she would have liked to "try just this once, my force against his."[8] The fantasy is of lovemaking as a fight, and her excitement spread immediately into plans for future writing. She wanted to write a detailed account of the electroconvulsive therapy, "tight, blasting short descriptions with not one touch of coy sentimentality." She did this five years later in *The Bell Jar.*

Two days after meeting Hughes she wrote a poem called "Pursuit," which she described as a poem about the dark forces of lust. She dedicated it to him.[9] A male panther is stalking her down. In the end he will kill her. His greed has set the woods on fire, and in his wake lie the charred corpses of women who have been lit like torches to give him pleasure. To slow him down, she throws him her heart, and she tries to quench his thirst with her blood, but nothing can appease him or liberate her from the spell he casts with his voice and his secret desire.

In the biography by Anne Stevenson this poem is interpreted

as an invocation of Sylvia Plath's libidinous double, the "deep self full of violence and fury she was suppressing under her poised and capable appearance."[10] But the panther is emphatically male, and women are his victims. The emphasis on the spellbinding voice is probably an allusion to Hughes's, which had made a strong impact on her. In other respects the panther in the poem has less to do with the real man, whom she'd met only once, than with what she knew of his reputation, while the poem reveals less about him than about what she expected—half fearing it, half wanting it—from him. There is gleeful celebration as well as frightened revulsion in her loving account of predatory animality.

But was the fantasy grounded in reality? According to Lucas Myers, Hughes was never violent, even in his gestures; the violence in his poetry reflected the violence of the universe.[11] But in his Yorkshire boyhood he enjoyed fishing, shooting and trapping animals on the moorland. Between the ages of twelve and thirteen, he listed his killings in a diary which was subsequently stolen by one of his girlfriends. In Sylvia's May 1962 poem "The Rabbit Catcher," which centers on the pleasure he still took in killing—this was a poem she intended for *Ariel*, but he held it back until 1971—she identifies with his victims. Those little deaths, she says, waited for him like sweethearts. They excited him. She too is caught. Their relationship is like the tight wires of a trap, fixed to pegs which are too deep to uproot, and his mind is like a ring "sliding shut on some quick thing."

The story of that first meeting on February 25 has sometimes been told as if she immediately felt committed to him, but on March 6, she wrote to Richard Sassoon, asking for a spring meeting in Paris. When, describing her room at the end of March, she says she's as happy as she could be without her man, she's referring to Sassoon. We don't know what it was that provoked the fight with Hughes or whatever it was that left her hurt, but when she arrived in Paris on March 26 her mirror reflected a battered face smeared with a purple bruise. Her neck was raw and wounded too.

To mention bruises and wounds he inflicted is not to imply he was any more to blame for them than she was. Knowingly and happily, she chose a man capable of physical violence. Afterward she drew it out of him, partly through provocation, direct and indirect, partly through mythicizing him in both verse and prose. "Pursuit" is only one example of a poem partly about him, partly addressed to him like a coded message about her desire to be pursued. To write like this is to acknowledge an appetite for violence, if not to invite it.

Apprehensions of impending conflict disappeared in euphoria when they were together, but he was no longer living in Cambridge. After a brief stint as a zoo attendant, he was working in London, reading film scripts for J. Arthur Rank, and the next time he came back to Cambridge it was to find a girl called Shirley.[12] Sylvia found out about this only later. It took some time for her fury to subside, and toward the end of March she sent a frenzied, tear-stained letter, begging him to come back to Cambridge. In April she saw him in London. Sometimes he talked to her about the way women offered themselves to him, and she wondered how many he had slept with since she last saw him.

At last, after all the affairs and agonized hesitation about boyfriends who wanted to marry her, here was a man she could wholeheartedly want. As a poet she excitedly ranked him above Yeats and Hopkins. They went for long walks, and he seemed to know the name of every bird, tree and plant they saw. He told her spellbinding stories mined from Irish folklore or from his fertile imagination. In his indifference to clothes there was an inverted panache: he always wore the same thick black sweater and the same khaki trousers.

He appeared to have as much power over owls and hares, who came when he whistled, as her father used to have over bees. If he gave the impression of caring primarily about himself and secondly about a few male friends such as Lucas Myers, giving them more consideration than the women who threw themselves at him, this was a challenge that appealed to Sylvia. She could penetrate beyond the rough exterior; she could tame him. Describing him to her friend June Anderson,[13] Sylvia made him sound formidable, but said she thought she could cope with him. She took pride in his reputation for being successful with girls, and she told Mrs. Prouty he was destructive. His behavior was sometimes unruly, she said, and there was much ruthless force in him, but writing to her mother, she claimed to have penetrated beyond the mask of cruelty, the ruthlessness and callousness, to reach the essence of his true self. In a letter, Mrs. Prouty tried to warn her of the dangers. "You don't really believe, do you, that the characteristics which you describe as 'bashing people around,' unkindness and I think you said cruelty can be *permanently* changed in a man of 26."[14]

In the months before and after she married him, Sylvia was incredulous that so much happiness was available. She was so full of love and joy, she told Aurelia in April, that she could "scarcely stop a minute from dancing, writing poems, cooking and living."[15] She thought her seven latest poems made the rest seem like baby talk. When Ted read poetry to her in his irresistible voice, radiance and love seemed to come surging out of her as if she were a sun, and as she sat with him listening to Beethoven, she felt certain that in using every fiber of her being to love him, she was also being totally true to herself. Without expecting the future to consist entirely of bliss, she felt strong enough to take pleasure in the "deadly blasts of whatever comes." Memories of unhappiness before and after her suicide attempt—she still felt as if she'd had, like Lazarus, the experience of being dead—made her all the more confident that the rest of her life could be an uninterrupted "song of affirmation and love."

They happily prepared food together, and she delighted in his reactions to her cooking. After one meal he lay groaning by the hearth with giantlike ecstasy. Sylvia loved both his sense of humor and his inventiveness. He made up stories for her about kings and knights and about Snatchcraftington, a wizard who looked like a stalk of rhubarb. At the same time he supported her faith in her writing. No other woman had ever written poetry like hers, he told her, and with his help she felt certain that within a year she could produce a book of thirty-three poems that would "hit the critics violently."

From this new perspective, all previous relationships looked tawdry and insecure. Even when she was with Richard Sassoon, an opportunistic mental court had been in session—hadn't it?—drawing her attention to his weaknesses and proposing stronger, healthier alternative men. Now, for the first time, she felt fully satisfied with the man she had. She loved the "virile, deep, banging poems" he'd written, loved relaxing with him at Cambridge. Punting on the Cam, they saw cows, baby owls and even a water rat; at Grantchester they picnicked in an orchard.[16]

When Aurelia came to London in June 1956, Sylvia and Hughes decided to marry immediately. Less than four months had gone by since they had met, and he didn't tell his parents about the wedding. Although it was difficult to get a license in time, they were married on June 16 at St. George's Church in Bloomsbury. They chose the day partly because of James Joyce— June 16 is Bloomsday. Their witness was the sexton, who had been on the point of escorting a group of mothers and children on a church outing to the zoo; they were all kept waiting outside in a bus. Ted had come in the old black corduroy jacket he wore every day, Sylvia was in a pink knitted dress her mother had bought for herself but never worn. The church was empty, and bathed in the watery yellow light of a rainy day. [17]

They spent the summer in Spain, going first to Benidorm, which was still an unspoiled fishing village; she did several sketches of it. Later they moved inland. When they watched a bullfight, her sympathy was with the bulls. She was pleased when one of them managed to gore a plump picador, who was carried out with blood spurting from his thigh. [18]

They had to live cheaply. In the early morning they went to the market for fish and vegetables, buying potatoes from the stand that sold them at the lowest price. They wrote from eight-thirty in the morning until twelve, and again from four to six, studying French and Spanish from eight to ten. [19] Sylvia was still ecstatic at possessing and being possessed by a man who tallied so closely with her fantasies. *Magnificent, handsome,* and *brilliant* were the words she used to describe him. Living with him was like listening to a story that never stopped, or like living in a country that kept on extending its frontiers. She could feel his energy pouring directly into her work, and it was an adventure just to buy a loaf of bread or step over goat droppings. [20]

But within six weeks of the wedding, quarrels were threatening to capsize their happiness. Incredulous at her vulnerability, she felt the hurt "going in, clean as a razor, and the dark blood welling." In the unfamiliar landscape, under the full moon, with crickets chirping and donkey bells jangling in the distance, she felt "wrongness" growing between them and making his skin hard to touch. Alienation seemed to fill the house, like a carnivorous plant. When he said he was going out for a walk, she went with him, knowing it would be intolerable to stay indoors alone, but she felt foolish as they strode toward the hills, past the railway station. When they sat down, it was with a distance between them. They walked back in silence and slept separately. In the morning she felt as if the house were choking with wrongness, but their sense of togetherness revived when Ted found an anthill and they played with their superiority by lifting the stone above it, throwing the colony into confusion. To a spider who had captured two ants they tossed a third, and they gave the ants a big dead fly.[21]

Generally the habits Hughes had acquired were quite different from hers. He went on wearing the same clothes day after day, apparently untroubled when they were too thick or too thin for the current weather. Sometimes he was suspicious of food she gave him, complaining she was trying to kill him with a protein diet. When he couldn't find what he was looking for, he accused her of hiding his things or secretly destroying them. Periodically he sank into black moods, and when he took his clothes off, he tended to throw them on the floor, while she was always careful to keep her things neat. But though she wrote in detail about their life together in the diaries she kept, she speculated remarkably little about what was going on in his mind. Sometimes they talked to each other about dreams, but, endlessly interested in her own inner life, she seems to have been uncurious about his.

Toward the end of August they left for Paris, and when they returned to England in early September, they went to stay in Heptonstall with his parents, who readily forgave him for not telling them about the wedding until he wrote to them from Benidorm. They were friendly and welcoming. Sylvia describes them as "dear, simple Yorkshire folk."

Having spent all their money in Spain and France, she and Hughes stayed in Heptonstall until school began.[22] His Uncle Walt took them by car to see the Brontës' Haworth, and they picnicked in the heather. She reread *Wuthering Heights,* which helped her to enjoy the wild landscape of bare hills, the deep-creviced valleys and the heather purpling the moorland. Half-Irish, wiry, white-haired, and still a tobacconist, Ted Hughes's father drove every day to his shop in Hebden Bridge, while his plump, arthritic wife told stories about the neighbors and made starchy pastries and meat pies for her son and her new daughter-in-law. Sylvia was allowed to do most of the cooking for Hughes and herself in the tiny kitchen.[23] One night he took her out to stalk rabbits in the woods, but when he shot a beautiful doe with its fawn, Sylvia didn't have the heart to take it home to make a stew.[24]

Back at Cambridge, she confessed and was forgiven. She and

Hughes were at first extremely happy together, in spite of living in a shabby flat which wasn't self-contained: they had to share the bathroom with their upstairs neighbor. She was depressed by the dirt and grime. Soot seemed to be ingrained in everything. Domestic surroundings obviously mattered less to Hughes, who had lived at Cambridge with Lucas Myers in a hut which had once served as a chicken coop, and later in a tent in Myers's garden.

Wendy Campbell, a friend of Dorothea Krook's, was allowed to sit in on Sylvia's sessions and immediately liked her: "She was so alive and warm and interested. She seemed to be entirely collected and concentrated and in focus."[25] When she came with Ted Hughes to a party, they were both "smiling and smiling, almost incandescent with happiness.... They seemed to have found solid ground in each other." She'd at last found "a man on the same scale as herself. Her vividness demanded largeness, intensity, an extreme," while he seemed unfettered and unafraid. "He didn't care, in a tidy bourgeois sense, he didn't give a damn for anyone or anything."

In their flat in Eltisley Avenue they used to get up at five in the morning to write before the day began. Sylvia struck Wendy Campbell as having a natural excellence at everything she attempted. The flat was well kept, she cooked superbly, and "her very remarkable efficiency" seemed to be "very natural to her and was never accompanied by any sense of strain."[26] In fact there was a great deal of strain, physical and financial. But like a ballerina who keeps a radiant smile on her face while executing dance steps that involve both anxiety and pain, Sylvia knew how to appear happy and exhilarated.

Dorothea Krook was amazed at how much marriage had changed her. Antonia Byatt, who met her at the beginning of her Cambridge career, found her "very hard to talk to: she was very gracious, very deliberately outgoing, almost aggressively an image of the healthy American girl, blonde hair, red mouth, full of bouncy wonder."[27] After she married, her extreme happiness was unmistakable but almost worrying. What would happen, Dorothea Krook wondered, if anything should go wrong with this marriage? Her fears were allayed by Sylvia's "serenity, her tranquility, her confidence and (most of all) her marvelous vitality which seemed a guarantee of limitless powers of resistance."[28] But Sylvia, who knew these powers weren't limitless, was aware of being dangerously dependent on Hughes.

Ever since the suicide attempt she'd been struggling to rebuild her identity, making it flexible and strong. What she needed was a solid core of self, but everything that constituted her existence had become interwoven with Hughes's. Within twelve months of meeting him, she found life without him inconceivable. She told herself that if she lost him, she'd either go mad or kill herself. After spending twenty-five years searching for someone just like him—so she told herself—she knew he was the only man in the world who was right for her.[29]

Her father's death had pushed her into a symbiotic relationship with her mother; the suicide attempt had put an end to the symbiosis, and Dr. Beuscher had become a surrogate for both parents. By leaving America Sylvia had lost Dr. Beuscher; Hughes now had to serve as a replacement for father, mother and psychiatrist. At first he seemed to be offering all the love and protection Sylvia needed. If her life was like a sea, he appeared to be holding it steady and spreading his deep, rich colors through it. She focused on him all her capacity for hero worship, all the adulation she'd lavished on poets such as Auden and on the teachers who'd helped her most. Hughes seemed like a classical god she'd conjured up from the depths. He had surfaced with his spear shining and rare fish trailing in his wake.[30] She had always been a perfectionist. Now she was committed to perfectionism *à deux*. The balance was going to be precarious.

For nine pounds ten shillings they bought a huge, soiled, second hand sofa for the living room, but they were finding it so hard to pay for food, electricity, gas and coal that by the middle of November it looked as if Hughes, who had been hoping to work as a teacher, would have to settle for a laboring job.

Before the end of the month Sylvia had her first meeting with his sister, Olwyn, who came to stay for a weekend on her way from Heptonstall to Paris. After taking an arts degree at London University, she had settled in Paris, doing secretarial work. Her relationship with Sylvia was uneasy from the start. Olwyn, who had never married, had dominated her younger brother during childhood, and Sylvia formed the impression that as children they had slept in the same bed. Olwyn's attitude toward Hughes struck her as proprietary, and writing to Aurelia, she described her sister-in-law as selfish and extravagant over clothes and cigarettes. Not long afterward, she started sketching out a story about a "diabolic" sister who is jealous of her younger brother's marriage and finds things intolerably different from what they used to be.[31]

Though it had been too late for Hughes to get a Cambridge teaching qualification, he managed to land a job at a day school for boys, teaching English and helping with sports. At last he would be earning a regular salary, but Sylvia went on typing and retyping his poems to have fresh-looking copies she could send out to magazines in England and the United States. The poems that were returned she immediately sent out again. After promising to place at least fifteen poems a year for him, she exceeded this quota. She collected forty and submitted them to *Harper's,* which was running a competition for a first book of poems. The judges were W. H. Auden, Marianne Moore and Stephen Spender. Sylvia didn't see how they could do anything but give the prize to Hughes, who in her opinion was writing the richest, most powerful verse since Yeats and Dylan Thomas.[32]

Her confidence was vindicated. He won the prize, which meant his first book, *The Hawk and the Rain,* would be published. As Lucas Myers testifies, Hughes would not have established himself so quickly if it hadn't been for her help. "Without Sylvia, Ted Hughes might have had to go on working in rosegardens and warehouses for quite a few more years."[33]

Sylvia was elated when he won. "We will publish a bookshelf of books between us before we perish!" she predicted. "And a batch of brilliant healthy children."[34] Euphoria boosted her energy: in addition to studying, cooking, cleaning and typing both Hughes's work and her own, she sent out a number of poems by Lucas Myers and offered to type out a long piece of his fiction.[35]

At the same time she was studying for a Cambridge B.A. in English and sketching out a Cambridge novel about an American girl who would go through several men, one modeled partly on Richard Sassoon and one on Gordon Lameyer, while one of the female characters would derive partly from Nancy Hunter. Sylvia's aim was to write at least two or three pages every day, not worrying about plot, but describing a remembered incident with dialogue, characterization and description. By the beginning of the summer vacation she expected to have about three hundred pages which she could revise later.[36]

Fearful of becoming enmeshed in domesticity, she studied the diaries of Virginia Woolf, who cheered herself up by cleaning the kitchen or cooking sausages when her work was being rejected.

Sylvia, who had felt in 1953 that she was "reduplicating" Virginia Woolf's suicide, still believed their lives were linked.[37] She also thought Virginia Woolf was helping her: "Her novels make mine possible."[38] They showed how much you could leave out when telling a story and how you could modulate effortlessly into the subjective.[39]

Though Sylvia was irritated by the unevenness of the writing, which alternated between finely fluent sentences and ungainly, ugly ones, she saw her own problem reflected in the last fifty pages of *The Waves,* which focus on the deadness of someone who can no longer overcome the forces of depression by working creatively. Sylvia reread the pages again and again, underlining heavily and resolving to do better.

She promised herself to have no babies until she had succeeded. The life of the creative mind must come before the life of the creative body. Health consisted of writing poems, stories, novels. She mustn't live her life without simultaneously reliving it by giving permanent form to moments of experience. Loss, transience, evanescence would be insufferable unless they were counterbalanced by artistic activity. Observations and passing thoughts could be preserved. She made up her mind to be stronger than Virginia Woolf, to go on writing "until I begin to speak my deep self."[40] She would never be prepared to let her duties as a wife pull her away from literature.

8

Panicky Wife

In June 1957, when Sylvia completed her exams at Cambridge, four months before her twenty-fifth birthday, she was finally bringing her education to a close. Child of two teachers, she'd always lived in a partly educational structure, responding to didactic pressures. Although she got only a Two-One—a second class degree, but of the upper grade—in the Cambridge Bachelor of Arts exam, she could have stayed on to do a Ph.D., but she had a stronger urge to write than to go on studying, and she would now have to meet the challenge of finding a structure for her daily activity in tandem with a husband, but with no supportive timetable, and no "supervisor."

Before completing her two years at Cambridge, she had been offered a year of teaching at her old college, Smith, for a salary of four thousand dollars. She and Hughes agreed she should accept the appointment. He could probably get a job nearby at Amherst College or the University of Massachusetts. Remembering the sexually predatory habits of Smith girls, she didn't want him to teach there, even if an invitation should be forthcoming.

Once the exams were over, they spent the first part of their vacation in Heptonstall, before leaving for Cape Cod, where Aurelia had taken a seven-week lease on a cottage for them as a wedding present. In Yorkshire they wrote in the mornings, walked in the afternoons, and spent the evenings with his parents and Olwyn, who was staying there. Though Sylvia made efforts to adjust, there were times when she couldn't conceal the strain. Finding herself excluded from the conversation when Hughes's old English master, John Fisher, came to tea, she rushed out of the house, banging the front door. After about ten minutes Hughes went out to look for her, and when they came back, she went straight upstairs.

He was being tugged between two sets of loyalties. Unwilling or unable to side with her against the family, he wrote ambivalently about her in a letter to Olwyn when they were crossing the Atlantic on the *Queen Elizabeth.* It had been obvious, he said, that she'd felt anxious after the exams. When she was in a panic, she clutched at stereotypical American niceness, putting on a show of openness and charm when she met new people, allowing her poise and intellect to disappear in a rush of "vacuous receptivity" and saying "stupid things," which mortified her afterward when she could bring her intellect to bear on them skeptically, penetratingly and subtly. But she couldn't use this part of her mind when talking to people she didn't know well.[1] This criticism may be valid, and it helps to explain what many people described as her tendency to gush. But Hughes was obviously finding it hard to compromise between defensiveness on her behalf and solidarity with those who condemned her moody behavior.

He'd never lived abroad before, and after they arrived in the States, he felt uneasy at parties, especially when extrovert American well-wishers offered him their friendship. He also found it harder to write than it had ever been in England. In Wellesley, where they arrived in late June, Sylvia seemed radiant when she introduced him to about seventy American friends who came to a catered reception held in a large tent behind the house. The Cape Cod cottage was at Eastham, where they immediately gave themselves a timetable. Their aim was to do four hours of writing before noon, when they'd cycle to Nauset Beach for an afternoon of swimming and running. In the evening they read.

It was hard for her to settle back into a writing routine. Though she took delight in the way her mind worked, it had been pushed like a corpse under the floorboards, so she felt, by the pressures of living in the "slovenly" Cambridge flat, scraping for money, cramming for the exam, preparing for the move, and packing.[2] Abruptly liberated from all this, and gradually recovering from the exhaustion, she could lie supine, letting sensations and memories well up as if she were painfully giving birth to some "endless and primeval baby." It was a joy to wake up, because consciousness released her from bad dreams. But why, after a year of marriage, was she having them? Were they still exorcising terrors and insecurities that had started when she lost her father? Emancipated from the academic rhythm, she felt sure the best way to achieve equilibrium was by writing. A life of eating and cooking would be bestial unless she could also think and create.[3]

She ordered herself to start from specific experiences, such as encountering mat green fungus in pinewoods or the smell of vanilla flavoring in a brown bottle.[4] Besides writing poems, she wanted to warm herself up for the Cambridge novel by writing stories for such magazines as *Good Housekeeping,* the *Ladies' Home Journal* and the *Saturday Evening Post,* but she hadn't published any fiction for five years. The new stories were all rejected, while her efforts to concentrate were stultified by the growing fear that she was pregnant. Panic-stricken, she reproached herself for being so casual about contraception. The chance to teach at Smith had been doubly alluring: she could go back as an equal of teachers who had seemed like superiors, and she could prove her competence at what both her parents had done.

But if she was pregnant, she'd lose all these opportunities and jeopardize her togetherness with Hughes, who didn't yet have a job in America. Within four years they could have established themselves sufficiently to start a family, but she was scared of hating the baby if it arrived too soon and killed their "spiritual and psychic selves" by forcing them to give up writing in favor of earning. She felt almost as depressed as during the suicidal summer of 1953. She wept in the doctor's office when she had a blood test, and, after she and Hughes were soaked to the skin— caught in a thunderstorm while on their bicycles—she succumbed to fantasies about divine judgment.

The anxiety was dispelled when her period came, two weeks late, but the elation was punctured by the rejection of her collection of poems, *Two Lovers and a Beachcomber,* which she'd submitted for the Yale Younger Poets series. Getting the poems back was like retrieving the cancerous body of a lover who should have been at the morgue. Willing herself not to feel jealous of the success Hughes was enjoying, she told herself she had married him knowing he was the better poet. She must go on working and waiting.[5]

In fact it wasn't at all easy for her to overcome her jealousy of Hughes's success. In theory she had always wanted, if she married a poet, to be less successful than he was, but in the family she had found it easy to outshine her younger brother. Hughes was now like an older brother outshining her. His first collection came out in 1957, but, hard though she tried, she didn't succeed in publishing her first collection until 1960, the same year she wrote her story "Day of Success," about a young wife and mother who has to cope with bitter envy of her husband's breakthrough into fame and success. When the story opens she's carrying a load of freshly folded diapers into the bedroom and looking at drapes she hemmed by hand while waiting for the baby to come.

For Sylvia 1956 had been a tremendously eventful year. She had met and married Ted Hughes, graduated from Cambridge, honeymooned in Spain, and she was about to make her triumphant return to Smith, a married woman and a teacher. But as the summer began to fade, she was so depressed that she convinced herself she hadn't deserved any of her previous success—she should have worked ten times harder. She commanded herself to "feel the pain of work a little more," to stockpile five stories and five or ten poems before she started hoping to publish. Anyway, she should write in order to become a better writer, not in order to publish. In her agonies of self-reproach she felt guilty at succumbing to the temptations of beach and sun instead of staying in and working.[6] But the anxiety was, as usual, concealed from Aurelia. "We're happy as chipmunks," Sylvia wrote.[7]

The depression wasn't lifted by the move to Northampton in late August, or by the start of her teaching at Smith, though she'd looked forward to the work. She liked her students, and they generally liked her, but when she was with them she felt insufficiently in control, while her colleagues gave her neither the welcome nor the warmth she'd been expecting. She didn't have to lecture, only to lead discussions, and all her classes were on Thursdays, Fridays and Saturdays, leaving her free to write on the other days, except when she had to correct written work. Once every three weeks a stack of at least sixty-five papers arrived.

As it had through so much of her life, anxiety about money was eroding not only her security but her sense of identity. Though it was comforting to think she was now Ted Hughes's wife, marriage had compounded the problem of identity. Who were they? They could assert the reality of their existence by writing, and, as he reminded her, their faith in their work was more important than how soon they published it. They must go on exercising their imagination by turning out poems and stories. But when they walked into a shop, wanting to open an account, they had no credentials to offer. He had no job, they didn't own a television set or a car (the one they were driving belonged to Warren) and they were buying no furniture on time.[8]

At the beginning of October she confronted what she saw as the duality between her two selves—the good one and the murderous one—by addressing a letter to her demon. She'd had a sleepless night. With her nerves "shaved to pain," she'd listened to an inner voice which accused her of incompetence. She couldn't write, couldn't teach, couldn't think, couldn't do anything. As in a bad dream, she was the sole author of what was being said; she had to defend herself in her diary against the self that was attacking her—defy the voice, disprove its prophecies, reverse the tide of negativity. If she couldn't ignore the murderous self, at least she could refuse to identify with it. What made her vulnerable was her perfectionism. In writing, teaching and living she set herself such high standards that any frustration, any whiff of failure, was enough to make her feel worthless.

She went on arguing with herself as Ruth Beuscher might have argued four years previously. With no experience of teaching, how could she have expected to be a first-rate teacher? She had no advanced degrees, had published no books. Why not just think of herself as moderately good? Already she was doing better than she had on the first day of the term; surely she could go on gaining confidence and improving. Her good self responded to bright colors, tasty food, ideas, hills, skies. This self deserved better than to be murdered by the demon. She mustn't retreat in panic whenever she was too shy or tired to exert herself. She confided in other people too much, talked too often about anxiety. She should fight the demon silently, achieve something positive every day, observe, think, teach. If she relaxed more in class, the girls would share her enjoyment.[9] All this was good advice, but she was assuming she could tear up her habits like a rough draft.

Sometimes she confided in Hughes, who cooked breakfast and lunch for her,[10] and did his best to reassure her, but confided his misgivings to Olwyn: Sylvia was working twelve hours a day, he wrote, and often cracking under the strain.[11] Sometimes she preferred not to confide in him, finding her fears were magnified when he echoed them. She tested her self-control by refusing to

1. The house in Johnson Avenue, Winthrop,
near Boston. This was Sylvia's home
between the ages of three and ten.

2. Her grandparents' home in Shirley Street.
She used to sit on the bottom step,
staring out at the ocean.

3. Sylvia with Ted Hughes
at Eastham, Cape Cod,
in the summer of 1956.

4 and 5. Sylvia with the children
at Court Green, Devon,
their home between August and December 1962.

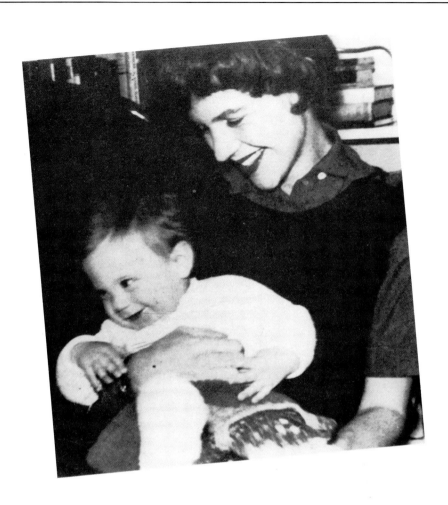

6. and 7. Sylvia with Frieda and with Nick.
Snapshots by Susan O'Neill-Roe,
who was helping her with the children.

8. Assia Wevill, who was having an affair with Ted Hughes when Sylvia killed herself.

9. and 10. Jillian and Gerry Becker. Sylvia spent the last weekend of her life in their Islington house.

11. Trevor Thomas,
the last person
to see her alive.
Or was he the
last but one?

12. The house
in Fitzroy Road
where W. B. Yeats
once lived, and
where Sylvia died
in February 1963,
after living there
with the children
for two months.

13. Assia with Ted Hughes.

14. Assia with Shura, her daughter by Ted Hughes, born in 1967. Assia killed herself and Shura in 1969.

ask for sympathy. Picturing herself as staggering lugubriously about, bleak and sick, she stiffened her backbone.[12] Her determination to appear calm made it impossible for her Smith colleagues to know how painfully she was floundering. Her poem "The Disquieting Muses" ends with the resolution that no frown must ever betray the company she keeps; smiling to conceal anxiety, she deprived herself of sympathy and put herself under enormous strain.

Favorable feedback made her more confident about teaching. Hearing that students thought she was "brilliant," she began to agonize less. But feeling stifled by the "neat, gray secondary" air of the college, she resented the waste of time and energy that could have been used creatively. On November 5, after correcting sixty-six essays on Hawthorne and before settling down to prepare for the next week's classes, she wrote to Warren about her worries. If colleagues sat in on her classes, she'd be found inadequate, and fired. She needed contact with other people—it gave her copy for her writing—but it was frustrating to meet only teachers and students. She was forced to approach literature academically instead of reading to let herself be stimulated and influenced. After studying the way Henry James used metaphor to convey emotion, she would have liked to go straight into making up her own metaphors.[13]

She found that far from being in danger of dismissal, she would probably be promoted if she came back for a second year of teaching, but his experience at Cambridge had convinced Hughes that creativity was incompatible with the academic life. He was to start teaching at the University of Massachusetts in the spring, but they decided to do no more teaching after the summer. They would rent a cheap apartment in Boston while he worked full-time and she part-time, but neither job must involve homework: early mornings, evenings and weekends should be entirely their own.[14]

By December Sylvia was worrying less about her teaching. She was no good, she decided, at speaking without detailed notes, and would still be preparing them at the last minute. She felt more confident, though, until mid-December, when she succumbed to the virus that had been spreading an epidemic of flu through the campus. Having broken a bone in his foot by getting up out of a chair too abruptly when his foot was asleep, Hughes was in no state to look after her, and he didn't realize how ill she was. They had arranged to spend Christmas in Wellesley, where they arrived five days early. At first Aurelia attributed the pinkness of Sylvia's face to the cold wind, but, touching her daughter's forehead, found it was feverishly hot. Sylvia had a temperature of a hundred and two. Aurelia put her to bed and called the doctor, who diagnosed viral pneumonia. Robbing her of the Christmas holiday, the illness left her debilitated and behind in preparation for her classes.

Her image in the mirror no longer gave her the pleasure it had eight years before, when she was seventeen and pursued by boys asking for dates. When she was depressed, her face struck her as ugly and froglike, with thick-pored skin exuding dirt and pus, with yellow in the white of the eyes and crust in the corners. But she made ambitious plans for the summer vacation, intending to study Berkeley and Freud, as well as reading French literature and studying German. [15] But she was still sleeping badly, being kept awake at night by coughing, and on January 7, the day before school began, she felt "mad, petulant, like a sick wasp." For a long time—to her it seemed like two days—she lay under the maple coffee table, intermittently weeping. The telephone rang, and she ignored it. Perhaps she'd go on lying there, rotting, till her body was thrown out with the rubbish. [16]

At the college, steeling herself to go on teaching until May, she encountered cold disapproval of her decision to quit. "Do you really hate it here so much?" The question dangled in the air. How dare she feel so superior? What entitled her to liberate herself from the routine that gave her colleagues their identity? But for much of the time she felt inferior, incapable of organizing her life, inadequate as wife and housekeeper. When she felt under attack, mortified by hostile glances and unspoken criticism, she forced herself to go on behaving politely. But she would have liked either to punch or to spit at the colleagues who showed their disapproval by dropping her from the exam committee or by superciliously admonishing her not to give students advance information about questions. [17]

When the poems she had entered for a competition failed to win it, she consoled herself by typing out Hughes's, and telling herself she could live through him till the end of May. When she thought about her novel, her mind focused on the story of their meeting in Falcon Yard, as if she'd been a combination of the sleeping beauty, Cinderella and Brünnhilde, and as if he were a princely hero. Married to the statue of a dream, and ringed by flames, she meets a man who liberates her with a kiss that changes her rhythm permanently. But in making vague plans for future writing, she reached out for disparate models. Reading stories in the *Saturday Evening Post,* she warned herself against set pieces that climaxed in a declaration of love. The stories were full of babies, dowagers and the technical language of jobs. She could aim to copy them, but when she read the anthology *New Poets of England and America,* edited by Donald Hall, Robert Pack and Louis Simpson, she advised herself to work on rhythms and to find a bigger, more relaxed, tougher voice. For prose, as for poetry, much depended on having a distinctive voice. The influence of Virginia Woolf was still irresistible, but she wanted to sound tougher, and to make her minor characters more vivid.[18]

Laying plans for writing she couldn't start for five months, she was trying to distract herself from the rage that threatened to unbalance her. She was seething with malice and anger. She felt furious, envious, humiliated and isolated. She was aware of Hughes's physical presence. This was the man she had chosen. She would be his wife forever, but he was a stranger in a black sweater and black trousers that has superseded the khaki pair. She heard him sighing, heard floorboards creaking under his weight, but at the college, patronized and cold-shouldered by colleagues, she still felt like a student, naughty and presumptuous. She was also a stranger when she caught sight of her reflection in shop or car windows, her face sharp enough to seem unfamiliar, a black coat flowing behind her. Perhaps it had always been like this, with a world full of well-meaning enemies. Trying to preserve her equilibrium by keeping herself busy, she earned a hundred dollars by marking papers for a senior colleague, the critic Newton Arvin.[19]

Financial insecurity was receding. When Hughes was teaching, their annual income would be eight thousand dollars, but beyond this comforting figure she had a vision of his death and hers "smiling at us with a candied smile." She went on planning, though, compulsively. A year of writing to start in June; then a year of traveling in Europe; then the first baby. Self-confidence flooded fitfully back. Reading stories in the *New Yorker,* she believed she would one day see her own stories and poems there. She used the diary as if it were a Polaroid camera she could focus on herself. She could also map her position in time, calculating on February 23 that this was her twenty-sixth February 23. Alive for more than a quarter of a century, she'd accumulated enough memories to spend several years fishing for the monsters sunk in the Sargasso of her imagination. The relics of her past selves could be woven into new fabrics. [20]

It was two years since she had met Ted Hughes. Looking back on aborted impulses to leave some indelible imprint on him and to murder Shirley, his Cambridge girlfriend, she congratulated herself on wrenching chaos and despair into a rich and meaningful pattern. Without copying Virginia Woolf or D. H. Lawrence, she must distance herself from her own experience as she converted it into her novel. [21]

Even in March and April 1958, when there was more money in their bank account, she vacillated between confidence and desperation. Sometimes she luxuriated in peace and joy. [22] When she looked back on October and November, it seemed as if she'd been struggling to stop herself from "flying into black bits." Now, so long as she remained healthy, she'd be able to survive bad days and exhaustion without running away or weeping. Getting his poems accepted by all the magazines he approached—or she approached for him—Hughes kept a foot in the door to the golden world. No wonder he was more even-tempered than she was. When she talked to him about her depressions, he sometimes managed to cheer her up, but she couldn't always accept his astrological diagnoses: he talked about the moon and Saturn "to explain the curse which held me tight as a wire." He never seemed rooted in their day-to-day existence, often saying he wanted to get clear of this life. And they quarreled about buttons she'd failed to sew on his jacket.

Exhausted, she found it hard to cope with domestic chores. Unwashed dishes piled up in the kitchen, the garbage can overflowed with coffee grounds, rancid fat and vegetable peelings. The world was full of foul smells, and she felt like a dead woman offered the joys of the world on the condition that she stood up and moved. [23]

Sometimes, feverishly reacting to the noise of cars and the sense of being trapped, she doubted whether she was really alive. Perhaps she was an automaton, her mouth only a tube that trumpeted dead words about life and suffering. She had nightmares about maps and deserts and people in cars. America consisted of a line of cars with people jammed inside, moving from gas station to diner. Her nails were splitting and chipping. She almost fell asleep during a lecture by Newton Arvin.

Her spirits revived when the vacation started at the end of March, and she wrote eight poems in eight days. They were all based on paintings. She told Aurelia she'd just discovered that art was her deepest source of inspiration, and she was overflowing with ideas, as if she'd been bottling up a geyser for a year.[24] She was hoping to complete another thirty poems by the end of December.

But the outpouring didn't stop her from feeling vengeful. When she saw the orange glow of a fire below the high school, she felt hungry to see parents jumping out of windows with babies, and afterward she wandered around the streets, hoping to see a child crushed by a car, or another fire, or someone thrown by a horse into a tree. Even when she felt rapturously at one with Hughes, relishing the comforts he offered, enjoying the food he cooked and the drinks he brought to her in bed—iced pineapple juice and coffee—she felt possessed by hatred for men like the ones she had rejected. She would go on using her mind, her "ice-eye," to kill men who were weak or false or sickly souled.[25]

During her period of promiscuity she had wanted to be reviled: her lover was to confirm her guilt feelings by abusing her. Now that she was monogamous, she liked the feeling of being mastered, used so fully that she felt on fire with love, but she slept fitfully, waking after weird sexual nightmares. In one she was in a dark high place, watching a new comet pass overhead until she was lifted up and hung in midair with a pole through her and someone twirling her on it. As she spun, distant voices discussed what should be done about her.[26] Sometimes, when she got up in the morning, she thought about rising out of a grave, collecting moldy, worm-eaten limbs into a final effort. At other times, tingling with vitality, she felt solidly confident about having the power to eclipse Adrienne Rich or any other rival woman poet. But the confidence melted into tears when the *New Yorker* rejected another batch of poems. Depressed, she thought about death, about dying prematurely, having seen so little of the world, about the pains and humiliations of childbirth (she was never to forget her visit to the maternity ward with Dick Norton) and about falling short of the standards set by Dorothea Krook.[27]

She hated to be separated from Hughes, even for a few hours, and when she thought of calling her first collection "Full Fathom Five," it was partly because the association with *The Tempest* and the sea made her think of her father as a buried male muse and divine creator who'd risen to be her mate.[28] But in May, catching Hughes with a girl, she panicked. How could she have invested so much trust in him? The incident occurred after a reading of *Oedipus* in a new translation by Paul Roche. Hughes, who was cast as Creon, asked her not to come, but she went. Aware of her presence as soon as she entered the hall, he seemed to be ashamed of something. He read badly, almost inaudibly. Hypersensitive to any hint of betrayal, she sensed a faint flare of disgust or misgiving, and to find him afterward she had to ask the janitor where the readers were. In the small room he was sitting hunched over a piano "with a mean wrong face," banging out a tune with one finger.

The next day, May 22, when she came out of her last class, she ran jubilantly to the parking lot, expecting to find him waiting in their car, but it was empty. She searched in the reading room, and after a flash of intuition told her what was about to happen, she saw him coming up the road from the pond where boys took girls for necking sessions. He was smiling into the eyes of a lipsticked girl with brownish hair and khaki Bermudas on thick legs. When she saw Sylvia approaching, she gave a start and began to run, without saying good-bye. Sylvia started thinking about times when he had come home late, and about a vision she'd had while brushing her hair of a black-horned, grinning wolf.[29]

Perhaps it was no more than an innocent flirtation, but she reacted as if all her faith in him had been misplaced. Thinking of what Dr. Beuscher might have said, Sylvia held an imaginary conversation, answering no, she wouldn't jump out of the window or kill herself in a deliberate car crash or gas herself with exhaust fumes or slit her wrists in the bathtub. If she had to go on living without her faith, she could survive by teaching and writing. There were still a few people for whom she felt a little love, and she wanted to keep her dignity intact.

Hughes said little by way of explanation, but what he did say struck her as untrue. She had a sleepless night, sometimes trembling with rage and disgust. In the morning she went on reproaching herself for being naive: she had trusted him completely, loved him sincerely, spent Aurelia's hard-earned money on buying clothes for him, spent hours, days, typing his poems. She scratched him so fiercely that his skin was marked for a week; he hit her so hard that she saw stars.[30]

But the marriage remained intact, and within three weeks she was able to make light of the incident, telling Warren they had such rousing battles "every so often" that she emerged with a sprained thumb and Ted Hughes with a missing earlobe. But as a wife, she said, the best she could do was demand nothing more than to find workable schemes by which they could both write and spend lives dictated by inner needs for creative expansion and experience.[31]

Some of her aggression got transferred to a group of schoolgirls they found in a public park, stealing rhododendrons they needed for a dance. Sylvia and Hughes had gone there to steal a rose, but the girls were stealing wholesale, and Sylvia was so angry that she had to recognize in herself a violence "hot as death blood." She could kill herself, she admitted in her diary, or kill someone else—kill a woman or wound a man. The girls were shameless, and one of them said: "This isn't your park." As she stared into the eyes of the defiant girl, Sylvia felt stars flashing in her head. She would have liked to rush at the girl and tear her to pieces.[32]

🔖 9 🔖

Boston

In the early morning of Tuesday, August 20, 1957, while they were on Cape Cod, Sylvia and Ted Hughes went to collect mussels in Rock Harbor Creek. The tide was low, the water colorists hadn't yet arrived with their easels, the mud flat was pervaded by a salty stench of seaside decay, while the brittle grass stretched away toward the salt marsh. The damp mud was alive with evil-looking fiddler crabs, who scuttled away as the human beings approached. Holding one big pale green claw erect, the crabs near the bank retreated sideways into holes in the mucky earth, while others, closer to the center of the drying pool, dug themselves into the mud, until only claws protruded. But eyes seemed to be looking out from the roots of the dry grass and the clustered mussel shells. A fishy world had swung its hinges shut.[1]

To survive a suicide attempt is to be alive in a different way from everyone else. Having escaped death, you take a special interest in durability, in decomposition, and in what remains of a body after it has died. The poem "Mussel Hunter at Rock Harbor" shows Sylvia's fascination with the silent otherworld in which shellfish followed instincts different from ours, governed by different relationships with the vegetable and mineral worlds. Grass could seem to grow claws; mud could be fitted over the head like a helmet, but she couldn't judge whether contact with wet earth gave crabs any sensation. Nor could she know what they made of the two-legged mussel pickers. Trying to look from this alien perspective at the human world is to make it both alien and familiar.

116

Incomprehensible though the shellfish were, it was clear there were deviants among them. Why had a fiddler crab ventured so high in the grass? Resisting the otherworld's inclination to shut her out, she struggled, with a mixture of dry humor and pathos, to empathize with the dead crab that had strayed from the herd. Had it been adventurous, reclusive or suicidal? Her consciousness of fragility helps her to identify with the vulnerable crab. Now only its husk remains; its innards have been dried by the sun and scattered by the wind. But it is in a more dignified position than the shells, the dead crabs and the fragments of crab being bounced around by the waves. Instead of giving any direct expression to the suicidal urge she was secretly nourishing, she concentrated on the dead crab, while the poem derives some of its strength from the underlying conviction that she and Hughes were also deviants, separating themselves defiantly from the herd.

They had come to America because of her job at Smith; having now opted to free-lance, they could live anywhere they chose. To stay in Massachusetts was to continue the life they had led during the last year. In the summer of 1958 they settled into an apartment on Willow Street, near Beacon Hill. For Sylvia, the decision to live in Boston had many advantages. She would be within reach of her mother, and have easy access to Cape Cod and the seaside scenery that played a star role in her childhood memories. She would at last cut herself free from the academic routine. Though she had taught at Smith instead of having to write essays, she had remained in an academic environment, still working on literature and adapting her week to a timetable imposed by higher authorities. Structured tightly around scheduled reading, the work had still climaxed in deadlines. Now, suddenly, she had discarded the academic framework. Without it she was to survive less than five years.

At least partially aware of how hard it was for her to live without clear-cut tasks and incentives, Hughes did his best to fill the empty space in her routine. He did not find it difficult to be didactic and encouraging. He suggested subjects for poems and exerted a strong influence on her reading, edging her into anthropology. Without him she might never have become interested in Aztec civilization, or astrology. He had various semi-meditational disciplines, and before starting to write he concentrated for ten minutes on the base of the spine and several points along it.[2] He initiated her into some of these practices, and he prodded her with questions: "What are you thinking? What are you going to do now?" He even tried to organize her day, jostling her into an hour of reading ballads, an hour of studying Shakespeare, an hour of reading history. But it was impossible to help in these ways without making her feel threatened by the encroachment on her new independence, and, like a rebellious pupil, she seized on moments when he contradicted himself or laid himself open to charges of fanaticism. Why was his neck stiff? It must mean the exercises he did were too strenuous. She also started to enjoy his absences.[3]

They both believed in spirits, but she may have been more ambivalent than he was. When they conducted séances together, using a homemade Ouija board and an inverted brandy glass, she was half skeptical, knowing their manipulative fingertips were liable to spell out semiconscious desires and intentions, but she went on hoping and half believing that she could make contact with her dead father. Spirits would regularly want to pass on instructions from Prince Otto, who sounded like a great power in the underworld. When she wanted to communicate with him directly, she was told he was unavailable because he was under orders from the Colossus. She would then ask for contact with the Colossus and be refused.[4] But she was to honor the Colossus in 1960 by using the name as the title for her collection. The Colossus of Rhodes was a gigantic statue of the sun-god Helius, over a hundred feet high. In Sylvia's work, as in her fantasies, her father kept reappearing, magnified to colossal and godlike dimensions.

The spirit they called up most was named Pan. He was capable, so they believed, in helping them to fill out coupons for football pools, but usually his communications were gloomy or macabre, though not humorless. They never ran out of questions, and she found their semiserious game more exciting than the movies. Pan said he was happy in America, where he'd been using his freedom to write poems, and he recited one called "Moist." They'd have two sons before they had a girl, he predicted, and her first collection would be published by Knopf. His favorite poem of hers was "Mussel Hunter at Rock Harbor." "Colossus likes it."

By-products of their séances, some of her poems incorporate words taken from the spirits they conjured. An example is the posthumously published "Dialogue over a Ouija Board," which was written in 1957 or 1958. When the woman in the poem asks the spirit about her father's health, his answer is "INPLUMAGE-OFRAWWORMS." But is the spirit, Pan, more than a puppet of their intuitions? Asked where he lives, he answers "INGODPIE," then changes this to "INGODHEAD" and later to "INCOREOF-NERVE," but when he calls them "APES," she smashes the glass.

Prompted to suggest subjects for poems, Pan gave her the idea of writing about the Lorelei, the sirens in German legend who lure boatmen to their death. The Lorelei, he said, were her own kin. As she now remembered, they featured in a German song her mother used to sing. In spite of their associations with the sea and the death wish, she had never thought of using them as a theme. Her poem "Lorelei," which she began the next day, links them with the underwater world Jacques Cousteau had described in a book she'd been reading. She borrows his phrase "drunkenness of the great depths" for the acute oxygen shortage that causes visionary euphoria in deep-sea divers, making them forget the need for caution.

"It is no night to drown in," she begins, going on to describe the river's blackness underneath the bland mirror sheen, with mists dropping scrims like fishnets. Reflections of castle turrets hint at an alternative world, fuller and clearer than is possible. The sirens' harmonious singing is like an attack on the ordinary world. Lodging on the "pitched reefs of nightmare," they promise safety. The goddesses of peace inhabit the river, and the speaker asks at the end of the poem to be ferried down there.

Sylvia knew that the contrast between her manic and her depressive moods was extreme, as if her life were controlled magically by two electric currents. Howard Moss, poetry editor of the *New Yorker*, who had rejected all her previous submissions, accepted both "Mussel Hunter at Rock Harbor," calling it a "marvelous" poem, and "Nocturne," which he rated "extremely fine." When his letter arrived, she ran upstairs to tell Hughes, shouting "Yippee," and jumping around "like a Mexican bean." The fee, she calculated, would cover the rent for nearly three months. Her next ambition, she decided, was to get a story into the *New Yorker*, even if it cost her ten years of work.

But the old pattern seemed inescapable: overexcitement led to sleeplessness, exhaustion, anxiety, deep depression. She felt no less suffocated, no less hysterical than she had when she was teaching. Once again her nerves were "razor-shaved." Instead of starting the novel, she was paralyzed with terror. Ideas offered themselves, but how could she structure them? She should be able, she told herself, to stockpile poems at the rate of one a day for her first collection, and she was furious when a day's work ended in twelve bad lines. She felt intermittently nauseous. She was distracted by noises from the street or workmen hammering in the house opposite. She knew she was making tyrannical demands on herself, but cool reasonableness was out of reach. Time was invaluable and she was wasting it.[5]

Nothing if not ambitious and competitive, she still had objectives, but they were less specific than the ones that had previously motivated her: win a scholarship to Smith, get a degree, win a Fulbright, travel to Europe, find a husband. Again and again she succumbed to panic, without knowing what was frightening her. Sometimes she talked hysterically; sometimes she thought she would explode. Life was full of opportunities, but she was caught in a vicious circle, doing nothing but roaming around, staring at other people who seemed enviable only because they were other people.

Somewhere beyond the terror she felt was the possibility of calmness. She pictured herself as steadily in control of her day-to-day thinking and mature enough to distance herself from nightmares and setbacks. The alternative Sylvia would be writing happily, reading, playing with her children, chatting with friends. None of this should be unattainable. She must take control of her life, recognize her terrors as figments. She felt all right when she was working; activity dissipated the rage that paralyzed her, but the anxiety always came back, gripping her like poison lodged in her gullet. The greatest danger was the stubborn belief that she could allay her fears only by plummeting to the bottom of nonexistence. If she could afterward rise to the top again, she would have proved she could survive.

In the morning she would wake up exhausted, as if coming out of a coma, or as if hostile electricity in her bloodstream were drying her out. Later in the day she still felt drugged. Objects were slipping out of reach, and when she sat down at her typewriter, she was no longer in charge of what she typed. Good lines presented themselves, but stopped dead before she could develop them. She looked back nostalgically on the teaching, which had given her week a structure and forced her to be articulate. Stultified by the sedentary life, she thought of applying to Harvard or Yale to see whether she could do a Ph.D. or a master's degree. Anything. Hughes produced a word—doldrums—as a name for her malaise. This temporarily made her feel better. Perhaps she could reorganize her life. Perhaps she should begin the novel with a girl's search for her dead father, for an outside authority she could develop from inside. Perhaps she should become a Catholic. This notion occurred abruptly at the beginning of August, but she was expecting to find much of the dogma unpalatable.[6]

For nearly a week their routine was disrupted by a baby bird that had fallen out of its nest. Her yearning for maternity and their decision to postpone it had set up such powerful tensions that Hughes was swept into uncharacteristic behavior. The man who had killed hundreds of healthy birds and animals sacrificed a week's work in a hopeless effort to save an injured fledgling. They'd found it in the street, apparently dying. It was on its back next to a tree, scrawny wings outstretched. Its pain made her feel sick. Hughes picked it up and carried it home, cradled in his hand. After making a nest by putting scraps of soft paper and a dish towel into a cardboard box, they tried to feed it morsels of bread soaked in milk, holding them on a toothpick. When it refused to swallow, they bought fresh ground steak, and when it accepted the worm-shaped bits of meat, Sylvia fed it at two-hour intervals. Sometimes they went out searching for worms. It looked like a young starling, with furry eyebrows. She stayed awake at night, listening for the sound of feeble claws and wings against the cardboard.

The bird survived for three days, but when it tried to run, it collapsed: one of its legs had started to stiffen. It became feebler, choking and chirping pathetically. On the third day, when they went out for a walk, they were reluctant to go back indoors, nervous of having to confront the dying creature. Hughes finished it off by gassing it. He attached a rubber bath hose to the stove, taping the other end into the artificial nest. But the bird was still alive when he lifted it out of the box. It lay in his hand, feebly opening and shutting its beak, waving its upturned claws. Five minutes later it was dead.

They took it to the park, and buried it under a big stone, leaving ferns and a green firefly on its grave. Ten days later Sylvia was still thinking about it obsessively.[7] She tried to cure the obsession by writing a story. A dying bird becomes a tormenting spirit, twisting the lives of the couple who take care of it.[8]

In addition to all her other work, Sylvia tried to teach herself German, studying a grammar lesson each day in a textbook. She widened her vocabulary by reading the Grimms' fairy tales in the edition Aurelia had given her, and listing all the unfamiliar words.[9] But this wasn't enough, and urgently wanting to make contact with other people, she thought of learning the Stenotype, a machine to transcribe speech, to qualify herself for a part-time job. If she could work as a court reporter, she would pick up material to use in her fiction.

At the beginning of October she went out to three agencies, and was interviewed the next day for a secretarial job in the psychiatric clinic of Massachusetts General Hospital. The pay was low and she would have to work more hours than she had intended, but she agreed to start at the beginning of the following week. She had to answer the telephone, type records and make arrangements for a staff of over twenty-five doctors and their patients.

She gained unexpected insights into the private anxieties of Bostonians. On the second day she met a fat woman who had nightmares about her own funeral; she was lying in a coffin but also weeping among the mourners. There was a lesbian cloakroom attendant who modeled in the nude for a photographer, a man who believed he'd called up a hurricane and was responsible for the programs he watched on television—he had created them like dreams. One woman had nightmares about her amputated head, which was hanging on by the skin. Another dreamed of finding her mother's head in a laundry bag, together with the heads of four children. There were so many kinds of fear, so many sources of terror. Snakebite, loneliness, the snapping of an elevator cable. Fear was the chief god. During attacks of panic over the past two years, Sylvia had sometimes thought she ought to get herself psychoanalyzed, but by the middle of October this impulse was evaporating. Daily contact with other neuroses seemed to be doing her good, making her more objective.[10]

Her story "Johnny Panic and the Bible of Dreams" centers on the idea of fear as a god. Typing reports on patients' complaints about their anxieties, the narrator regards herself as Johnny Panic's secretary, and in the context of patients' dreams she records her own dream about being suspended over a vast, semitransparent lake with dragons at its bottom. Developing the imagery she had used in "Lorelei," Sylvia transposes it. This time the lake represents the collective unconscious, a public reservoir of nightmares. When the narrator stays in her office overnight to copy out notes on nightmares, she's caught and punished with electroconvulsive therapy. Before the switch is pressed to operate the machine, the false priests in surgical masks and gowns sing a devotional chant in praise of fear. Nothing else deserves to be loved.[11]

The hospital experience—ever since her affair with Dick Norton Sylvia had had some of her scariest experiences in hospitals— also provided her with material for another story, "The Daughters of Blossom Street," which prefigures her own posthumous fame by featuring a messenger boy who's awarded a gold medal for breaking his neck while doing his job. He's lucky, says the narrator's cheerful friend, Dotty. It had been his only chance to become a hero.[12]

If daily contact with patients and psychiatrists had at first made Sylvia disinclined to believe she could benefit from psychoanalysis, it soon began to have the opposite effect. On December 12, 1958, she went to see Dr. Beuscher. Within two days Sylvia had decided to go back into therapy without telling either Hughes or Aurelia. Possibly she wanted an ally against both of them. Certainly she needed one against herself. During the year of teaching she had felt in no need of psychiatric help, but she wanted an approximation to the academic timetable. If she couldn't quite go back to writing weekly essays for a supervisor, she could at least feel her life would be supervised by the best surrogate mother she had ever found.[13] She would even have an opportunity to work hard, analyzing dreams and ransacking her mind for insights into her turbulent mood swings. Instead of having Hughes as her only mentor and confidant, she would have an advisor who was female and detached.

Until two years before, the discomfort of not having a long-term relationship had been compensated by the comforting assumption that everything in her life would be incomparably better as soon as she married: she would be just as capable as any fairy tale princess of living happily ever after. After two years of marriage, she was still gratefully certain that Ted Hughes was the right man. She loved his protectiveness, his looks, his bigness, his sexual demandingness, his poetry, his commitment to living creatively, his courage, his jokes, his independence, his male toughness, the comfort he offered when she was miserable, his way of responding to food she cooked and his willingness to share household chores. She was in no doubt about wanting to go on living with him, making love and eventually bearing children, cooking, sewing on buttons, blending her life as a writer into his.[14] She still believed she had found the one man in the world who was the right mate, but she wouldn't have sacrificed precious writing time for a part-time hospital job if she hadn't been desperate. It was characteristic of her that although the job had given her material for two stories, she chafed against it resentfully as an intrusion on time she could have used for writing. She had to check the dizzying alternation between onsets of shattering panic and bouts of optimism, when her smile seemed to reach inside her, making her feel "creamy as a cat."[15]

The analytical session on Wednesday, December 12, seemed like a watershed in her life. It was then that Dr. Beuscher uttered the liberating formula: "I give you permission to hate your mother." It felt to Sylvia as if a shot of brandy had gone home, or as if a sniff of cocaine had buzzed through the whole of her being.[16] But the new feeling lasted. It wasn't that she had consistently repressed all negative feelings toward Aurelia. At the beginning of August Sylvia had been reminding herself that she ought to be funny and tender, not a "desperate woman" like her mother. There had even been moments of admitting to herself that she hated Aurelia, but not without feeling ashamed. For at least seventeen years Sylvia had lived deviously, revealing only one side of herself when talking or writing to Aurelia, and feeling guilty about the dissimulation.

In the last year, when she and Hughes had jettisoned the teaching that offered financial security, they had incurred disapproval not only from Aurelia but from all the other mother figures. Perhaps even Dorothea Krook would have felt sad, as Mary Ellen Chase and Olive Higgins Prouty did, that their former protégée was rejecting academia in favor of a free-lance life. With their teaching jobs, she and Hughes were earning a steady six thousand dollars a year. Hadn't it been willful and dangerous to throw this away? Until now, her husband had been her only ally against all these powerful mother figures. Now, suddenly, Sylvia had an authoritative mother figure on her side, and had permission to stop feeling guilty over failing to reciprocate all the motherly love she had been offered. Responding lovingly to her charm, the mothers had been unstintingly generous. She had accepted all they had to offer with a convincing show of gratitude, but she had nothing to offer in return except words, and in withholding these, wholly or partially, she had been uncomfortable. Now she felt like a new woman. Dr. Beuscher had driven off the "Panic Bird" which had been perching on Sylvia's typewriter and keeping her awake at night. [17]

Though the ambivalence toward her mother was deep-seated, Sylvia had never previously used such savagely censorious words. Aurelia had forced herself to be "a man and a woman in one sweet ulcerous ball." With the father rotting in the grave he "barely paid for," the little white house on the corner stank of women. The prevailing odors had been Lysol, cologne, rose water, glycerine and cocoa butter used to stop nipples from cracking. [18]

Dr. Beuscher was having a noticeable effect on Sylvia's writing: licensed hatred souped up the old vernacular abrasiveness as she began to look back critically at the love Aurelia had offered. Had it really been adequate? There was no sacrifice she wouldn't willingly have made, but had this been as altruistic as it seemed, and did it justify her self-righteousness? Temperamentally, Aurelia had been ill qualified to give the help a daughter needs from her mother when she starts to pick her way among the snares and booby traps set by masculine desire. [19]

Dr. Beuscher helped Sylvia to differentiate between depression and dissatisfaction with herself. Ignorance of German or inadequate work on a poem was remediable. You could learn the language or rewrite the poem. Even when depressed, you weren't condemned to passivity. You could analyze what made you feel resentful. She resented all the mothers who had tried to make her into something she didn't want to be. [20] Admittedly, she and Hughes hadn't yet proved they could support themselves by writing. But Dr. Beuscher could reassure her even here. If they hadn't kicked over the traces to find out whether they could survive as free lances, they might have felt bitter for the rest of their lives, knowing they had missed the opportunity to discover their full creative potential. Besides, writing was a religious act which involved reshaping people and the world. Unlike teaching, it left a visible residue which could help other people to live with greater intensity. For the writer, the financial motive should be secondary. [21]

Thanks to the sessions with Dr. Beuscher, Sylvia's spirits quickly improved. She felt happier than she had for months, and when Aurelia called, hovering between tearfulness and brightness, to invite her daughter and son-in-law to come and live in her house for a while if they wanted a change, Sylvia refused without feeling either threatened or guilty. Again and again the words echoed through her mind: "I give you permission to hate your mother." Of all the comments Ruth Beuscher had made, this was the most crucial. It was like being given permission to feel happy. Unresolved feelings about her mother had been paralyzing her with fear and had stopped her from settling into a steady routine of work. She still hadn't weaned herself away from the habit of writing with the object of winning Aurelia's approval. What so often made it hard to get started—she procrastinated by sewing on buttons, making the bed, watering the plants—was nervousness about producing something that wasn't good enough.

She also feared that failure would prove Aurelia had been right about the imprudence of refusing to go on teaching. But alongside Sylvia's awareness of Aurelia's disapproval, there was still such a strong current of love that she was apprehensive about the overlap between her own feelings and her mother's.[22]

The therapy illuminated a variety of questions that had been troubling her for years, without ever goading her into confronting them directly. When she had thought about studying for a Ph.D., she hadn't asked herself what use it would be or why she wanted it. She already had two degrees. Why did she feel that a third would give her a greater sense of purpose? She also came to see how nervous she'd been of making premature choices which would reduce her options, and she now felt strong enough to bring her writing into intimate contact with her life, as she had in the Johnny Panic story.[23]

She even began to worry less about quarrels with Hughes when she understood the disparity between the pretext and the real cause. If they argued about buttons she hadn't sewn onto his jacket, the conflict was rooted in her attitude toward the conventionality of his ideas about a woman's role in the household, and all their disputes were exacerbated by anxiety about money. They could count on being able to pay their bills over the next nine months, but poetry was so unprofitable that they might be forced into other ways of earning a living. One possibility was to write books for children. Sylvia didn't want a succession of odd jobs, but she did think about switching into a well-paid profession. In her admiration for Dr. Beuscher, she talked to Hughes about whether they should both become psychologists. But when they checked up on the requirements for a Ph.D. in psychology, they found it would take six years.

They also needed to decide where they wanted to live. Hughes had never settled down in America. Dick Norton's mother had often said that the woman should supply the emotional power of faith and love, while the man supplied direction. Sylvia and Hughes were still directionless because they hadn't committed themselves wholeheartedly to living in a particular place.[24]

When he complained, in the presence of her Smith friend Marcia Brown and her husband, that Sylvia hid shirts, tore up socks with holes in them and never sewed on buttons, she felt he was trying to shame her into being more subservient. But his attempts to manipulate her, like hers to manipulate him, were often counterproductive. He could always get a strong emotional reaction by telling her she was just like her mother; this usually made her submissive. Psychoanalysis didn't provide her with an escape from the domestic bickering, but it did give her new insights. Though she was constantly tempted to confide in him, since he was always there, she could achieve greater independence if she became more selective about what she said.[25]

One night she dreamed he was with another woman, and she ran after him through a huge hospital, rushing into mental wards. She took the dream to Dr. Beuscher, who told her the husband she was pursuing was also her father and her mother. In the aftermath of Otto Plath's death, she had often dreamed about losing Aurelia: if one parent could abandon her, so could the other. When, on her last day of teaching, she had found Hughes with another woman, she identified him with the father who had rejected her by failing to stay alive. This was the root of her need to hug so much. She was so demonstrative about her affection, felt such a strong daily need to hug and be hugged and go on hugging, that she had never found a man who didn't grow impatient with her. Dr. Beuscher made her feel ashamed by saying she wouldn't want to be left on a limb with her love hanging out.[26]

Sylvia would often weep during sessions without understanding why and, having started, go on uncontrollably, as if it were an hour for mourning. Like a fanatical penitent, she castigated herself mercilessly, but this was partly to provoke Dr. Beuscher into correcting the balance by praising her. As soon as she received praise, she felt hungry for more. By the time she left the consulting room, she felt purged, clean, better equipped to organize her life. Sometimes she would go shopping as if to reward herself, partly as a reminder that there was no need to punish herself, as she so often did, in such diverse and devious ways. By not reading Yeats and Hopkins, for instance, she was punitively depriving herself of pleasure. [27]

Believing her sleepy reluctance to get up in the morning was rooted in a desire to creep back inside the womb, she set the alarm for 7:30 A.M. and forced herself to get up, however tired she felt, however badly she had slept. She prepared their breakfast of coffee and oatmeal, made the bed, washed the dishes, cleaned the apartment, laundered the dirty bedclothes and started writing before nine, even if she was only formulating misgivings about herself or animadversions on her face. It was aging too quickly, her nose was too pudgy, she disliked the brown mole under her chin and the big pores full of pus. She needed a bath, didn't know what to do with her hair, wished she had a firmer bone structure.

After she gave up the hospital work, her mind kept jerking back to the possibility of imposing another routine on herself by studying for a Ph.D. or finding another job. If she had a baby, she might begin to forget herself in the right way, but until they both felt ready to start a family, she needed to get out of the apartment and make contact with other people. Though there was no chance of converting Hughes, she could join a church if she wanted to make herself part of a community. Sometimes she still thought about suicide. She was afraid of choosing death prematurely, foreclosing on all the other possibilities, but she couldn't make any other choice without being nervous about the consequences. [28]

She went on having nightmares. In one a baby died inside her. In another she was in a corridor with decaying corpses being wheeled down it. They were wearing coats and hats but their faces were mottled and half falling away. When they were all pushed into a stream, the corpses began to grin and move. In another dream, men wearing white blouses and bright cumberbunds stood in a line while a man with a big sword hacked off their legs at the knee. The leg stumps scattered, and the men, who fell down like ninepins, had to dig their own graves. She had so many nightmares about death and deformity that it was hard to resist Dr. Beuscher's suggestion that she believed she was not only responsible for her father's death but had castrated him. Perhaps these dreams were guilty visions of him; perhaps they revealed fear of being punished for what she had done.[29]

Many of the sessions started with a long silence. Perhaps she was hoping she could force Dr. Beuscher into deciding how the fifty minutes should be spent, but it was always Sylvia who had to open the dialogue. She was coming more directly to grips with deep feelings about Aurelia, whom she irrationally blamed for the early loss of her father, while believing Aurelia blamed her.[30]

Toward the end of January 1959, when she and Hughes decided to settle in England, she became more optimistic. She would have to manage without help from Dr. Beuscher, but things would possibly be better and certainly different. Hughes would be more relaxed there, and they would start a new life. Perhaps she could work for a weekly paper and write in women's magazines. Everything, she told herself, would be easier in England: it was such a small country, and easy to digest.[31]

🎵 10 🎵

The Poetry of Death

After Sylvia killed herself, Robert Lowell wrote: "Maybe it's an irrelevant accident that she actually carried out the death she predicted... but somehow her death is part of the imaginative risk."[1] And in his review of her posthumous *Ariel,* which got its name from a horse she rode in Devon, he said she was herself rather like a racehorse—dangerous, more powerful than a man. Galloping recklessly and relentlessly, she'd been able to leap one death hurdle after another. "In her lines, I often hear the serpent whisper, 'Come, if only you, too, could have my rightness, audacity and ease of inspiration.'" But most readers would be too apprehensive to emulate her. "These poems are playing Russian roulette with six cartridges in the cylinder, a game of 'Chicken,' the wheels of both cars locked and unable to swerve."[2]

Introducing a reading of "Lady Lazarus," which is dated October 23–29, 1962, and is perhaps the most reckless of her *Ariel* poems, she described the speaker as a woman who has the "great and terrible gift of being reborn," but has to die first.[3]

The passage of time has made it more apparent that Sylvia's suicide was no irrelevant accident. Though she repeatedly used the imagery of death and rebirth, we can't infer that she had some crazy belief that she could survive suicide. The right question is whether the literary flirtation with death could—by serving as a safety valve—have saved her life.

"Her vision of death," writes Ted Hughes, "her muse of death in life and life in death, with its oppressive evidence, fought in her against a joy in life, and in every smallest pleasure, for which her

130

favorite word 'ecstasy' was simply accurate, as her poems prove."[4] The death wish wasn't separate from the joy in life. She was a gambler whose enjoyment of the game derived partly from knowing she'd once staked everything and could easily have lost. The 1953 suicide attempt would have succeeded if her groans from the cellar hadn't been audible in the dining room, or if she had been too drugged to groan. Afterward she took nothing for granted. She enjoyed the view from the windows of a train from which she could jump at any moment. Though the option of suicide is permanently open to everyone, she was in a special position. Having once screwed up her courage to the point of swallowing enough sleeping tablets to kill herself, she was making only a guest appearance in life. However much pleasure she got from having poems accepted by the *New Yorker* or making love or eating or touching furry animals, death was always winking at her from a dark corner.

This special status in life began to affect her poetry long before October 1962. The late *Ariel* poems are prefigured by the death-oriented poems of March 1961, such as "Tulips" and "I Am Vertical," while these are prefigured by such poems as "Suicide off Egg Rock," which she wrote in March 1959. Her reflections on death and suicide kept circling back on themselves. Before the man in "Suicide off Egg Rock" swims out to drown himself, his blood beats a tattoo: "I am, I am, I am." Contemptuous of his body and its processes, he tells himself that his bowels belong to the same "landscape of imperfections" as gas tanks, mongrels barking at seagulls and hot dogs being cooked at the beach on public grills. He looks forward to the moment when he'll be washed up on the beach with the other garbage. Here she was retrieving an image she'd used in her diary after she'd been lying under the maple coffee table weeping and thinking she could stay there till her body started to rot. In the end her body would be thrown out with the rubbish.[5] To commit suicide is to insist on having your body treated like garbage.

In other poems, such as "Last Words" and "Mirror," which she wrote in October 1960, Sylvia engages with death as if it were imminent. This was partly a literary device: she knew she was at her best, both in verse and in fiction, when, playful and serious at the same time, like the Metaphysical poets, she toyed with death. As in a flirtation which might at any moment become something more, she enjoyed finding out how far she could go. A committed diarist from the age of eleven, she liked to dramatize her day-to-day experience. Though the death-oriented poems aren't mere translations of what she might have written in a diary, they're intimately involved with current experiences and preoccupations. They also look into a future in which she's dying or dead. The hypothesis may have helped to build up the pressure that killed her, or may have relieved it. Probably it did both, at different times.

Struggling with the death wish, she could not struggle in a way that was purely literary. To write a poem or a story is to play an imaginative game with all its ingredients, and there's no water-tight separation between the imagination and the part of the brain that makes practical plans. Writing poetry is a practical activity, and Sylvia, both before and after working at "Suicide off Egg Rock," was having enormous trouble in articulating what she felt. When she began the poem, she set up such a strict verse form that it drained power out of the statement she wanted to make. Some inhibition seemed to be stopping her from speaking with her "true deep voice." Her feelings seemed to be trapped inside a "glass caul," and nothing could emerge except a "facade of stupid verbiage." The frustration was enough to make her feel violent. Maybe she could break out of the prison only by committing some "inner murder."[6] She was ready to fight against herself, but she often found herself siding with the part she wanted to suppress against the part she wanted to release.

Nietzsche said: "I want to make things *as hard* for myself as they have ever been for anybody; only under this pressure do I have a *clear* enough conscience to possess something few men have ever had—*wings,* so to speak." With her perfectionism and her ruthless zeal to excel in every activity, Sylvia had always put herself under the greatest possible pressure. When she was lashing herself forward, the idea of suicide could work as an extra goad. She was immensely strong and intensely vulnerable.

This often made her feel physically small. She talked "of being little, as if I were a homunculus." Like a small country with a history of being annexed by one or another of its large and powerful neighbors, she felt as if her identity could be invaded and overrun. This was advantageous in her verse when she empathized with small and fragile creatures, such as the dead crab, but in everyday life it was liable to make her overdependent on Hughes and uncertain whether she could impose her will on other people. At the end of January 1959, she wasn't even certain whether she could make her hairdresser do what she told him to do. She wanted another pageboy cut, thinking it would make her look more like she had as a student at Smith. But she canceled the appointment to have her hair cut and permed, partly because she wasn't sure whether it would cost more than they could afford, but also because she didn't trust herself to win the argument if he raised objections to her idea.

At the same time she was trying to reduce her dependence on Hughes. She stopped herself from saying everything that came into her mind and from showing him everything she wrote. When she finished "The Bull of Bendylaw" and kept it to herself, she felt she'd achieved a minor victory. Perhaps she could go on consolidating her separate identity, write regularly, work her way gradually toward a better life by reminding herself about the good things instead of letting herself be enveloped in negativity.[7]

Always competitive, she felt insecure when she measured her achievements against those of Adrienne Rich or Anne Sexton. She had met Anne Sexton in February 1959, after they both started attending Robert Lowell's poetry seminar at Boston University. Though Lowell struck Sylvia as ineffectual and mildly feminine, it was helpful to have his reactions to her work, which Ted could no longer criticize as an outsider. At the same time the personal contact with Lowell, slight though it was, prepared the ground for the impact he made on her with the volume he brought out the following year, *Life Studies*. It was no accident that she edged much further toward the confessional mode after *Life Studies* came out.

In his 1951 collection, *The Mills of the Kavanaughs,* Lowell had written recurrently about madness, incest and suicide. In "Her Dead Brother" the incestuous sister thinks at the moment of gassing herself: "The Lord is dark and holy is His name," only to have the vision of God fade as her breathing stops. The best of these suicide poems is "Thanksgiving's Over," in which a man feels guilty about the death of love between him and his wife, who killed herself by jumping out of a sanatorium window. Had their love survived, she would neither have tried to kill him or herself.

In the poems that would eventually be collected in *Life Studies,* Lowell began to use shorter lines and to make proselike statements which achieve a poetic resonance like casual remarks made quietly inside a powerful echo chamber. The resonance is achieved through a combination of precision, selection, rhythm, organization and literary allusion, which add richness to what looks like a very simple texture. Sylvia was particularly interested in the poems he wrote about his experiences in a mental hospital, and she made no secret of the excitement she felt at "this intense breakthrough into very serious, very personal emotional experience, which I feel has been partly taboo."

In the long run this breakthrough was enormously helpful to her, but the immediate effect of his classes in Boston was inhibiting. The poems read by other poets in the group made her feel like a hermit who had come back into the world with what he thought was a lifesaving gospel, only to find no one could understand him because people were speaking a new language.[8]

Lowell said after her death that he had "sensed her abashment and distinction," though none of the poetry she showed him "sank very deep into my awareness." She made friends with Anne Sexton. Four years older than Sylvia, she'd been through periods of depression and mental illness. Her first collection was called *To Bedlam and Part Way Back.* She eventually committed suicide, but not till 1972, though this wasn't her first attempt. Together with her lover, George Starbuck, Anne and Sylvia would squeeze into the front seat of her old Ford and drive to the Ritz-Carlton, where they discussed their suicide attempts "at length, in detail and in depth between the free potato chips. Suicide is, after all, the opposite of the poem.... We talked death with burned-up intensity, both of us drawn to it like moths to an electric light bulb. Sucking on it! She told the story of her first suicide in sweet and loving detail.... We talked death and this was life for us, lasting in spite of us."[10]

But if Sylvia was working her way toward death, she was simultaneously trying hard to cooperate with Dr. Beuscher. The sessions came to matter enormously to Sylvia. She would sometimes stay awake all night beforehand, planning what she wanted to discuss. She could ask how to handle anger. She could admit to lusting for praise, money and love, and to rage against anyone who competed with her. But what should she do when this rage became uncontrollable? Sometimes it felt as if Aurelia no longer mattered: her image had been dissolved into all the editors, publishers and critics from whom Sylvia wanted acceptance and praise. And in one dream, when some of her work appeared in the *New Yorker,* Dr. Beuscher praised it but Aurelia turned away, saying it didn't give her any feelings—a dream which suggested that Dr. Beuscher had replaced Aurelia as the critic whose praise was needed most.[11]

However much Sylvia wept, and however much pain she felt during a session, she felt more at peace with herself by the time it ended. She felt disproportionately resentful if Dr. Beuscher had to alter any of the appointments, and because Sylvia couldn't afford the normal fees, she was terrified of being discarded, passed on to a colleague. When the doctor finally asked for five dollars an hour, Sylvia felt deeply relieved and grateful.[12]

✎ 11 ✎

Pregnancy

It's doubtful whether motherhood, even under different circumstances, could have saved Sylvia Plath from self-destruction. After her first baby was born, she would announce that childbirth was "closer to the bone" than love or marriage, and that being "mountainous-pregnant" was her favorite experience.[1] But she often used superlatives to express a momentary elation, and throughout the pregnancy she suffered the same giddy ups and downs that made her hold on life so precarious. She tried, though, to warn herself not to expect maternity to transform her life magically. She mustn't delude herself as she had about matrimony. So much of her life had been spent looking impatiently forward—to being a Smith girl, to graduating, to marrying, to publishing her first collection. Whatever happened, she would still be the same woman, "the same old sourdough."[2]

In the spring of 1959 she was twenty-six. Wanting to become pregnant, she consulted a gynecologist and had her "tubes blown out," which apparently did more harm than good. For two months she didn't menstruate, and on June 19, when she went to the hospital for a cervical smear, the black chemical on the Q-tip failed to turn green, as it would have if she had ovulated. She should have conceived by now, the doctor said.

This provided new ammunition for her assaults against herself. Convinced she had been sentenced to remain barren for the rest of her life, she derided herself as "something from which nothing can grow." She wanted nothing more than a house full of children. With no chance of conceiving, she told herself, making love and having a literary career were both pointless. Though she couldn't

136

live without writing, literature would be a hollow substitute for living, and Hughes would soon lose interest in her.[3]

She conceived almost immediately after her visit to the hospital, but instead of submitting to another humiliating examination, she trusted her conviction that a new life had started inside her. In July she and Hughes moved out of their Boston apartment to drive around North America in Aurelia's car, camping. They drove north to Ontario and west to Wisconsin and the Dakota Badlands. After crossing Montana, they camped in Yellowstone Park, where a bear smashed a window of the car and helped itself to food for a midnight feast.

In the resultant story, "The Fifty-Ninth Bear," Sylvia gave sadistic traits to both the husband and the wife. He daydreams about himself as a widower and half believes he has magical powers. Praying to the genius of the place for a private miracle, he wills animals toward him. It may be coincidental when they appear, but that doesn't destroy his sense of power. This is what his wife is up against, and it's she, apparently, who calls up the bear that kills him. His dying consciousness fades on her ambiguous cry, which may be signaling either terror or triumph.[4]

Surviving the bear's raid, Sylvia and Hughes drove to Lake Tahoe and San Francisco. After driving south to Los Angeles, they crossed the Mojave Desert, passed the Grand Canyon on the way to New Orleans, and went on to Tennessee, Washington and Philadelphia before returning to Boston. Visiting Aurelia in Wellesley, Sylvia seemed exhausted and "tremulous."[5]

Between September and November she and Hughes were invited to spend two months at Yaddo, the colony that provides room and board for artists and writers in Saratoga Springs, New York. When they arrived, Sylvia's pregnancy was still unconfirmed, and though morning sickness began while she was there, she didn't have a medical checkup till she went back to Wellesley. By then she was five months into the pregnancy.[6] At Yaddo they were given an enormous ground-floor bedroom.[7] In addition, Hughes had a studio in the woods, while she had a workroom on the top floor of an annex to the main building. Never had they had so much space at their disposal. They had both almost forgotten what it was like to work in silence, without the sounds that act as constant reminders of a partner's presence. She enjoyed this luxury. "That is what we've really needed," she wrote.[8]

The books Sylvia chose from the well-stocked library at Yaddo were mostly by American women: Elizabeth Bishop, Eudora Welty, Jean Stafford, Katherine Anne Porter. She read Mavis Gallant's novel about a suicidal daughter's relationship with her mother, as well as Theodore Roethke, Jung, and Paul Radin's *African Folktales*.[9] Often she read out loud; this was the way she could "feel on my tongue what I admire."

She rarely spoke to the other guests, and one of them, Sonia Raiziss, noticed how she walked slightly behind Hughes, "content to be there and almost secretively pleased with the status and circumstance of their attention—like a double billing."[10] Sometimes Sylvia agonized about whether, at bottom, she was interested in other people. Her aim was to become a vehicle, "the pure vehicle of others, the outer world." If only she could learn how to start from herself and work outward, her life and her fiction would both become more interesting. Ted criticized her for being negative, but she went on using her journal to reprimand herself. She couldn't lose herself in characters and situations, she grumbled. "Always myself, myself." She tried to force her vision outward, encouraging herself to focus on other people for their own sake, not simply to compare herself with them.

For two days at the end of September she suffered from palpitations so violent that she felt as if a wild bird were trapped inside her rib cage. She kept holding her hand impatiently against her heart, wanting to hit it, pierce it, if only to stop the throbbing.[11] The palpitations made it impossible not to concentrate on herself; the desire to hit out was partly the wish to punish herself for doing so.

Her sleep, which Hughes sometimes induced by hypnosis,[12] was full of nightmares. In one she gave birth to a baby less than five months old, but normal-sized. The nurse told her it had "a nest of uterus" in its nose, though nothing was wrong with its heart. Wondering whether the dream referred to being smothered in the womb, Sylvia pictured her mother dead, with her eyes cut out by an eye bank. The next night she dreamed her father was making an iron statue of a deer, but there was a flaw in the casting of the metal, and the deer came alive, though its neck was broken and it had to be shot. It was her father's fault.

In another dream she was about to sail for Europe. Hurriedly packing, she stuffed sweaters and books into her typewriter case, but she couldn't find Hughes. The next night she dreamed she was living among Jews. Participating in a religious service, she was repeating a name and drinking milk from a golden chalice while the congregation drank from small cups. She was sitting with three other pregnant women when Aurelia mockingly produced a big wraparound skirt to demonstrate Sylvia's grossness. Then she was shaving her legs under a table with her Jewish father sitting at the head of it. In a less disturbing dream, Marilyn Monroe gave her an expert manicure.[13]

When Hughes dreamed about killing bears, donkeys and kittens, she wondered whether he felt aggressive toward her and the unborn baby, while her own dreams merged affection for the baby with aggression against other people. In one dream a heavy, sweet-smelling, blond, five-month-old baby, Dennis, was riding on her hips, facing her. Hughes told her this meant her deep soul had been reborn. But a few nights later she had a savage dream reminiscent of the murderous rage she had felt against the girls who were stealing rhododendrons. Two juvenile delinquents were on the lawn in front of her old home in Winthrop, throwing out a saucepan of milk. Furious, she jumped at one of them and started tearing him to pieces with her teeth and hands.

She was still suffering from palpitations when she used material from her nightmares in a story about a mummy, "Diatribe Against the Dark Mother." Afterward she was surprised to find in Jung a case history that contained some of the images she had used: the child dreaming of the beautiful, loving mother as a witch or animal, the mother later going mad and barking, grunting, growling in a fit of lycanthropy. Jung was writing about an ambitious mother who manipulated her child on the "chessboard of her egotism." Sylvia had used the phrase "chessboard of her desire." She had also used the image of the wolf, while Jung wrote about the devouring mother or grandmother, all mouth, as in Little Red Riding Hood. It was startling that she had approximated so closely to writing she hadn't yet read, and she wondered whether she was sufficiently in control of her material. Was the story any more than a naked recreation of what she had felt, ever since childhood, to be the truth?[14]

During her last weeks in America, according to Hughes, she was changing "at great speed and with steady effort."[15] But she still felt in need of someone to make decisions for her, telling her what to do and praising her for doing it well. Hughes kept having to take the initiative. He hypnotized her, took the lead in devising breathing exercises, invocations and incantations, edged her into meditating with him, and gave her subjects for poems and exercises. This doesn't mean he was playing Svengali to her Trilby. They were preparing together for verse they would write separately.

He extended his routine into her life, nudging her into the techniques he used to achieve concentration and stimulate his writing. By using an exercise he suggested, combining deep breathing with free association, she wrote "The Manor Garden" and "The Colossus."[16] But she was apprehensive about the dangers of being so close to him all the time: she was liable to "become a mere accessory." She also found that when they were with other people, she left all the talking to him, letting him become her "social self."[17]

His sense of vocation as a writer seemed to be stronger than hers. He worked harder, more regularly, more consistently, caring less about other people's expectations, or their reactions to what he wrote. At the same time he was achieving more success and recognition. After he won a Guggenheim award, the five thousand dollars liberated them both from financial anxiety for about a year. Sometimes he managed to give her all the reassurance and love she needed. When he held her, made love to her, her nerves seemed to melt and sleep. But she was nervous that the baby was coming before she had made enough headway in her writing. She might hate the child if it "substitutes itself for my own purpose."

Sometimes she enjoyed the feeling of being pregnant, and some of her dreams about the baby were happy. Others were anxious and confused. In some she died during childbirth in an unfamiliar hospital where she couldn't see Hughes, or had a blue baby, or one so deformed she wasn't even allowed to see it. In some dreams her father was alive again, and Aurelia was a rival mother with a baby son that was twin to Sylvia's son. In another dream she bit the arm of an Aurelia who was old, thin and endlessly vigilant. She and Warren were both puritanical and inquisitive. He found his sister on the point of going to bed with someone called "Partisan Review."[18]

In one of the poems she wrote at Yaddo, "Blue Moles," she is inspired, as she had been in "Mussel Hunter at Rock Harbor," by the sight of dead animals. Finding two moles on the road, about ten yards apart, Hughes said they had fought to the death. They had been chewed by a fox into "caskets" of shapeless smoke-blue fur. The white pointy noses were sticking up, while the white palms on the clawlike hands looked human.[19] The poem implicitly compares their duel with the nocturnal traffic between lovers; the phrase "fat children of root and rock" refers both to the small creatures for whom they're delving and to pregnancies resulting from blind amorous burrowing into the female passage.

Five days before her twenty-seventh birthday, October 27, 1959, Sylvia made what she called a "surgical" sketch of a stove in the greenhouse and a few flowerpots. The drawing acted as a catalyst on the interest she'd been taking in Theodore Roethke, who had found his father's greenhouse full of usable imagery. She too could make poetic use of watering cans, gourds, squash, pumpkins, cabbages dangling from rafters, the purple outer leaves worm-eaten, rakes, hoes, brooms, and shovels. Pregnancy had accentuated her interest in the process of growth and sharpened her responsiveness to the utensils of fertility. Perhaps she could find a new way of steeping objects in emotion without depriving them of their objective identity. She sees the greenhouse as the gateway to a mad underworld, and although she had said she would prefer death to a return of the madness that had preceded her suicide attempt of 1953, she deliberately loosens her hold on reality, using memories of recent nightmares as a passport to the underworld. "Poem for a Birthday," really a sequence of seven poems, ends with the confident if ironic assertion that in emerging from the mental hospital she will be good as new. The birth of the child will also be the rebirth of the mother.

Her reading of Jung had given her "All mouth," which becomes "All-mouth," who seems to be male, but also to be connected with the devouring Mother, the one mouth she "would be a tongue to," but she identifies simultaneously with small, vulnerable and even inanimate things. As in "Blue Moles" she connects cellular growth with subterranean movements, but instead of giving birth to a child, she may produce puppies or a horse. The dreams merge with the memories of madness as she remembers being unloved by "the mother of mouths" and recalls the old man who shrank to the size of a doll. The temptation is to regress, but she's too big for that, and the mother is warned to keep out of her territory. She also derides the "cupboard of rubbish" she has married. With harsh monosyllables and vicious nicknames such as "Hairtusk," she stabs out in protest at having to keep house in "Time's gut-end."

One of the poems recalls the slothful submarine otherworld which seems to represent something akin to death but safer, and in another she identifies with a witch and with a grain of rice expanding painfully as it's cooked. In the phrase "mother of pestles," the last poem, "The Stones," again associates the maternal with the male, while the jewelmaster who chisels open the poet's stone eye recalls the process of recovering consciousness after the suicide attempt.

According to Ted Hughes, this last poem "ends the first phase of her development": the self, which had been shattered in 1953, is whole again after six years of hard work. Two years later, he says, she consolidated her hold on the second phase and dismissed everything she'd written before "The Stones" as juvenilia, "produced in the days before she became herself." She had arrived at "her own center of gravity" and with the birth of her first child on April 1, 1960, "she received herself."[20]

This is too rigid a separation between the first twenty-seven years of her life and the last two and a half; it's misleading to say she wasn't herself until she reached a specific turning point in a development that was full of turning points. Undeniably, it took her a long time to achieve the urgent demotic directness which is characteristic of her late work, and Hughes, undeniably, helped her. At Yaddo, according to Grace Schulman, who was there, he was working with Sylvia on devising exercises in incantation to "change the tone of her earlier descriptive poems... to a more immediate diction."[21] But the only abrupt change was in the speed at which she wrote. She surprised herself by turning out these seven poems so fast—in time for her birthday—and after writing "Tulips" shortly before her baby was born, she never went back to her old hesitant way of writing poems, pausing frequently to consult her thesaurus. She stopped being what she called "Roget's trollop."[22]

In December 1959 they left for England, and arrived in time to spend Christmas with the Hughes family in Heptonstall. Olwyn was surprised to find her sister-in-law no longer blond. "You look different," she said, and when Sylvia stepped back "like an animal at bay," Olwyn quickly went on to say the darker hair suited her. She had brought tarot cards with her, and in the evenings they played the game tarok for sixpences until she found that gambling enervated her too much for her to sleep afterward.[23]

Early in January 1960 Sylvia and Hughes went to London, where they stayed with his Cambridge friend Daniel Huws and his wife, Helga. Though she was in her seventh month of pregnancy, Sylvia spent the days house hunting, returning in the evening exhausted and despondent, but in addition to sending Aurelia long letters and writing assiduously in her notebooks, she often did the cooking, teaching Helga recipes she had learned from Grammy.[24] There was no bath in the Huws' apartment, and they shared the basement lavatory with other tenants.[25]

It was thanks to the American poet W. S. Merwin and his English wife, Dido, who lived in a spacious apartment overlooking Primrose Hill, that Sylvia and Hughes found an unfurnished apartment on the first floor of a very small house in a nearby square. It cost only six guineas a week, and they took it on a three-year lease which allowed them to sublet it or assign the lease.[26] Today Chalcot Square is fashionable and well kept. At the beginning of the sixties it was dirty and dilapidated, still occupied by the working-class families who were ousted when developers seized on the area and raised rents.

The critic and poetry editor A. Alvarez has described the apartment. Once inside the front door of the house you had to squeeze past a pram and a bicycle. The flat was "so small that everything seemed sideways on. You inserted yourself into a hallway so narrow and jammed that you could scarcely take off your coat."[27] The bedroom was just big enough to accommodate a double bed. The small living room overlooked the neglected garden in the square and the small houses, which nearly all had flaking paint.

Hughes and Sylvia bought a big bed, an oven and a fridge; the Merwins lent them tables and chairs. After going back to collect books and other possessions from Yorkshire, they both worked extremely hard to get their new home ready. Sylvia got less rest than she needed, but, apart from tiredness, the only symptoms of pregnancy were occasional heartburn and backache after standing too long or typing. Before they had even moved in, Hughes had constructed a bird feeder outside the window, with scraps of bacon rind on a clothesline.[28]

They moved in at the beginning of February. On the sitting-room wall they put a poster-sized print of Isis, mother goddess of the underworld and fertility. The apartment was so small that

Hughes had to do his writing on a borrowed card table in the narrow hallway near the front door. It was windowless and barely big enough to accommodate table and chair, but he was to look back on it as one of the best spaces he ever had for writing.[29]

From mid-November to the end of June Sylvia wrote virtually no poetry, but she worked hard at preparing the flat while doing a great deal of secretarial work for Hughes. After winning a Somerset Maugham award—a literary prize which provides money for travel—and getting enthusiastic reviews for his second collection, *Lupercal,* he was receiving floods of letters, including requests for readings and for submissions. Sylvia typed answers to all these letters.[30] In her last month of pregnancy she found it hard to behave politely when visitors came to the flat. Tiring easily, she needed undisturbed peace for cooking, reading, writing and resting without adjusting to other people's needs. It seemed to her that Hughes was being too nice to relatives and friends. Why should she have to sit for eight hours at a stretch in a smoke-filled room waiting for them to leave?[31]

The baby was born in their apartment on April 1, 1960. Hughes hypnotized Sylvia to minimize the pain. They named the baby Frieda after Sylvia's aunt, her father's sister.

❧ 12 ❧

Close Quarters

The two years in America had produced no conclusive proof that Sylvia and Ted Hughes were compatible in the long term. He could never have settled down to live in America, while she never settled for any great length of time into any of her English homes. In Massachusetts they soon realized that neither of them would want to do more than a brief stint of teaching, and soon after they moved to Boston, Ted became restless. He didn't like living in a city, especially an American one.

But if they were going to settle in England, it was natural to opt for London when they were both trying to build careers that would depend largely on contacts—with publishers, editors of literary magazines, poetry editors of newspapers and BBC producers. Looking back on the period after their return from the States, Ted Hughes said London had been "death" to him,[1] and Sylvia too found she was much happier in the country.

In January 1960, after they moved to London, they were soon under financial strain. Though rents and prices were low in comparison with today's, they seemed high to Hughes and Sylvia, who would have been under less emotional and nervous pressure if they could have afforded a bigger home. Though Hughes had often had to live in a confined space, Sylvia, much as she had suffered from restrictions on the family budget, had always had plenty of living space until she married him. Both in Winthrop and in Wellesley, the family had owned a fair-sized house. She had never lived in an apartment until she shared one with him, first in Cambridge and then in Boston. At Yaddo she enjoyed the spell of not having to live with him at such close quarters. But their new home in London was the smallest of the three they had shared.

When A. Alvarez visited them, he had the impression that Hughes "was in command. . . . Sylvia seemed effaced, the poet taking a back seat to the young mother and housewife." She appeared to be absorbed in the baby, "subdued," and "friendly only in that rather formal, shallow, transatlantic way that keeps you at a distance." Alvarez had published one of her poems in the *Observer*—an untitled poem which she later called "Night Shift"—but he had come to interview Hughes, who was wearing his usual black corduroy jacket, black trousers and black shoes, with his dark hair in his eyes. Alvarez portrays him as tall and strong-looking, with a long witty mouth, while she's described as having a long, rather flat body and a longish face, alert and sensitive, with a lively mouth and fine eyes. She was wearing jeans, with her hair in a bun. She struck him as being briskly American—competent, bright and clean, "like a young woman in a cookery advertisement."

The three of them decided to go out for a walk on Primrose Hill. Sylvia dressed the baby while Hughes went downstairs to get the pram ready. When she told Alvarez the poem he'd picked was one of her favorites, he didn't know what she was talking about. She had to explain. He was embarrassed at not having realized who she was, while she seemed "embarrassed. . . and also depressed." It's strange that Hughes hadn't made it clear when he introduced them that his wife was Sylvia Plath. He knew how eager she was to start writing again, and how hard she was finding it to concentrate. She needed a specific incentive, and Alvarez, having once responded to her work, might publish more of it.

Later, reading *The Colossus,* he found it fitted the image he had of her: "serious, gifted, withheld and still partly under the massive shadow of her husband." What gave her work its distinction, he said in his *Observer* review, was a sense of threat, "as if she were continually menaced by something she could see only out of the corners of her eyes." At a party given by his publishers, Faber and Faber, in June, when Hughes posed for a photograph with T. S. Eliot, W. H. Auden, Louis MacNeice and Stephen Spender, Sylvia was no more than the admiring wife, invited to watch from the sidelines. Though there's a bitter irony in her account of the evening, she felt genuinely privileged to be drinking champagne while on leave of absence from the smell of sour milk and diapers.[2]

Considerable tension developed in the tiny flat when Hughes was writing in the vestibule and she was trying, often unsuccessfully, to suppress her desire for conversation while nursing the baby, cooking and cleaning the flat. In May, after the Merwins left to stay at a farmhouse they owned in France, Hughes took advantage of their invitation to write in Bill Merwin's study, which eased the tension.[3] During the second half of May, Hughes was working there in the mornings and afternoons while Sylvia, still writing nothing of her own except letters about the baby, dealt with telephone calls and with his "voluminous" correspondence—invitations to give readings and talks, as well as letters from schoolgirls and other readers posing questions about his poems and the stories he had been writing. By the end of May he had decided not to give any more unpaid readings, and Sylvia asked Aurelia not to pass on their address or telephone number to any more of her friends. Visitors had become a strain.

Hughes was good at sharing household chores, and in early June, preparing for a visit from his mother and his Aunt Hilda, they cleaned the apartment thoroughly, scrubbing bookshelves and cupboards. He painted the hallway and one wall of the kitchen vermilion. Describing for Aurelia's benefit the "superb" red, the "black-marbled" linoleum, the white woodwork and the dark green cord curtains, Sylvia might have been writing a feature for *House and Garden*. The two Yorkshirewomen stayed at a hotel, coming to the tiny flat on Saturday evening and again on Sunday afternoon.[4]

The visit left Sylvia exhausted. Hughes started to give her three or four hours of freedom every day when he looked after Frieda and took responsibility for all the chores. She read a good deal and, wanting to improve her French, translated Sartre's play *Le Diable et le bon Dieu* into English, but found it hard to get started on any original writing. She felt oppressed by the lack of space, and on the last day in June, after taking the baby to the doctor for an injection, she was walking down Fitzroy Road, the street where Yeats had lived, when she saw a "Freehold for sale" sign being put up outside Number Forty-one. Pushing the pram, she ran excitedly home, and called Hughes at the Merwins' flat. He came to look at the house, which had a walled garden and enough rooms to give them separate studies, a nursery for the baby and a spare room. The asking price was £9,250. They had $5,000 in the bank at Wellesley, accumulated from earnings and prizes.

The income from Hughes's Guggenheim had stopped at the end of May, but, by economizing, they hoped to go on living on it till September. They were committed by the terms of the Somerset Maugham award to spend three months abroad, and they were planning that one of them would take a job in the fall if they couldn't afford to live any longer on their savings and their earnings from writing. Sylvia was prepared to be the one who worked; if Hughes would feed the baby her noon meal, he would be free to write whenever she was asleep.

All the same, Sylvia would willingly have gambled on buying the house by taking a mortgage. Hughes was more cautious, and his hesitation was complicated by a half-formed intention to take an extramural degree in zoology. But when she told Aurelia, Sylvia asked her not to make it obvious in any reply that she'd been let into the secret.[5]

Hughes raised four hundred fifty dollars by selling the manuscripts of his two poetry collections to Indiana University, and they saved baby-sitting money by going out separately. Sylvia went without him to see Laurence Olivier in *The Entertainer*. They also paid separate visits to the Picasso exhibition, but by leaving the baby with one of the lodgers at the Merwins' flat, they went back to it together. Hughes was feeling homesick for the Yorkshire moors, and during the third week of August they traveled up to Heptonstall, where they relaxed and did little but eat, sleep and go for walks. When a cousin of Hughes's drove them to Whitby, Sylvia found the beach muddy and dirty in comparison with the beaches of Cape Cod. She wrote scathingly to Aurelia about the tinted plastic raincoats and the untidy habits of the British working class.

When they returned to London after two weeks, Sylvia decided it was essential to spend more time outside the flat. If only she could work somewhere else, she believed, for three or four hours a day, she could produce some good stories. In the apartment, even when Hughes was on duty, she was distracted by the baby's sounds. The Merwins had returned from their summer in France, but Hughes found himself an alternative working space by asking the upstairs neighbor, an amiable woman who worked for the telephone company, whether he might use her attic flat while she was out. She agreed readily, and, except on weekends, she was out most of the time, leaving at seven-thirty in the morning and returning at five-thirty in the evening. But not feeling at home in the apartment, he used it only a few times.[6]

He was trying to write for the theater, and a fantasy they shared was that he would earn enough money for them to own a big car, tour Devon and Cornwall, and buy a property there with spacious grounds and a house in Hampstead, overlooking the heath. They were also planning a long stay in Italy during the spring, and in late September Sylvia enrolled in an Italian course at the Berlitz School, hoping to take the German and French courses later.[7]

Her twenty-eighth birthday, October 27, 1960, was unproblematically happy. When she woke up, she was facing a German coffee cake with a lit candle in the middle of it. Supported by Hughes, the seven-month-old Frieda was sitting at her side, holding a bar of German chocolate. Her presents included a pair of red plush slippers, two pairs of plastic galoshes, a Fortnum and Mason chicken pie, a bottle of pink champagne, Tolkien's *Lord of the Rings* and three slabs of cheese.[8] But in the middle of November, when Frieda was teething, it was hard to get enough sleep, and Sylvia's depression is reflected in the poem "A Life." The woman, who seems to have suffered "a sort of private blitzkrieg," is living without attachments, quietly, like a fetus in a bottle. The future is compared to a gray seagull whose squawking sounds a note reminiscent of separation, and the drowned man who crawls up out of the sea is probably Sylvia's father.

She felt full of energy, but uncertain how to direct it, not knowing whether to look for a part-time job, start another baby or concentrate on writing stories for women's magazines. By the end of November she had finished one and written half of another. She was hoping to make enough money from them to pay for someone to help regularly on a half-day basis with the baby and the housework.[9]

Just over a week before Christmas, they went up to Yorkshire, where, half seriously, they worked out plots for a romance to be set on the moors and for two suspense stories, one about an art gallery and the other about a lady astrologer. Hughes could work out the horoscopes. Sylvia also began an ambitious story about a woman who falls in love with a beautiful old house and eventually gains possession of it.[10]

After Olwyn arrived on Christmas Eve, she and Sylvia quarreled bitterly. Their relationship had been difficult from the start. Sylvia wrote about it to her mother on January 1, 1961. The published version of the letter starts with three dots. The omitted sentences describe a quarrel with Olwyn and call her relationship with Hughes pathological. According to Sylvia, Olwyn found it hard to accept that another woman should have ideas and opinions he respected. She turned on Sylvia, insulting her in the presence of her husband and her mother-in-law. This outburst was followed by a tirade in which Olwyn gave vent to resentment which had accumulated since the marriage. She accused Sylvia of being intolerant, selfish, inhospitable and immature. Hughes didn't step in to stop the tirade, but afterward, alone with Sylvia, he agreed that the situation was intolerable.

To Sylvia, it seemed that Olwyn still felt possessive and resentful that another woman had come to matter so much to him. Although it had been planned that Olwyn would be Frieda's godmother, Hughes now agreed to drop the idea, and they left Yorkshire earlier than they had intended. Olwyn and Sylvia never saw each other again. [11]

Sylvia had been suffering spasms of pain around her appendix, which still felt tender when she probed with her fingers after the pain had receded. When she consulted Dr. John Horder, the local doctor, she was told she would need an appendectomy, though there was no urgency as yet. Wanting to get the operation over before they left for Italy, she made an appointment to meet a surgeon. She felt as if she had a time bomb inside her. Persistent rain and a series of winter colds had combined to lower her morale, and in January, finding that she was pregnant again, she tried to build up her resistance by taking vitamin and iron pills, drinking the cream from the top of the milk, eating steaks, salads, and cooked breakfasts with a lot of fruit juice. [12]

Her decision to start part-time work was motivated by the same needs which had led her to the job at Massachusetts General Hospital: she needed to escape from the flat and involve herself with other people's activities. She also needed something to distract her from her fears of hospitals, anesthetics and surgery. She worked for some months from one o'clock till five-thirty every day at the offices of the *Bookseller,* a weekly trade paper. Her work involved copy editing, page layout, rewriting picture captions and sorting through biographical material sent out by the publicity departments of various publishers. When she was found to be one of the fastest typists in the office, she was also given rush typing jobs.[13]

In January 1961 she and Hughes recorded a twenty-minute radio interview under the title "Poets in Partnership" for the series *Two of a Kind*. Half-jokingly, they talked about their poverty, and Sylvia revealed that in addition to writing, bringing up a baby and working as a housewife, she was holding a part-time job. Their dream, she said, was to have a house big enough for them to yell from one end to the other without hearing each other. The mail that flooded in included a letter from a woman in Devon, Elizabeth Compton, who lived in a farmhouse with her writer husband, David. She invited Sylvia and Hughes to come and share it with them.[14]

In late January or early February they had their worst quarrel since the one on the day Sylvia finished teaching at Smith. Hughes was doing a lot of radio work—they had bought a car, a Morris Traveller, with his BBC earnings—and after submitting an outline for a series of children's programs, he was invited to meet Moira Doolan, the head of Schools Broadcasting. According to Dido Merwin, who heard the story much later from Ted Hughes, Sylvia answered a telephone call from Ms. Doolan and decided "that the timbre and lilt of the voice on the line boded Shared Experience beyond the call of duty," and when Ted Hughes returned from a meeting with her half an hour late for lunch, he found that Sylvia had torn up all his work on hand—manuscripts, drafts and notebooks. She had also destroyed his complete Shakespeare. Only the spine and endboards survived; the rest had been reduced to fluff.[15]

This account of what happened sounds implausible and incomplete, but a few additional clues are to be found in "Day of Success," a story reprinted in *Johnny Panic and the Bible of Dreams*. The story is dated 1960, though it's more likely to have been written after this incident. Ellen, who has a six-month old daughter, puts down a pile of diapers to answer a telephone call from Denise, a television producer, an elegantly groomed woman with red hair. Instead of fetching her writer-husband, Jacob, who's working in the flat above, Ellen offers to take a message, and when Denise says his play has been accepted, Ellen pictures the smooth-sheened coppery head bent over a script next to

Jacob's dark head. This, Ellen tells herself, is the beginning of the end. Denise, who has a confident musical voice, can offer success as casually as a bunch of hothouse grapes.

Before passing on the good news, Ellen broods about the way success can destroy a writer's marriage. One writer she knows discarded the wife who couldn't compete with the charming blond actress starring in his first West End play. After Jacob has left for lunch with Denise, Ellen convinces herself that she's homespun, "obsolete as last year's hemline." In the afternoon, taking the baby to the doctor for a checkup and sitting in the waiting room, Ellen looks enviously at the immaculate models pictured in the magazines.

Later on in the afternoon, when Jacob still hasn't come home, the ex-wife of the successful writer calls and deliberately sows seeds of suspicion: she saw Jacob in the Rainbow Room, tête-à-tête with the redheaded producer. After inviting herself to tea, the bitchy ex-wife plays maliciously on Ellen's incipient suspicions, describing Denise as a professional homewrecker who specializes in family men. But as soon as Jacob comes home, all her suspicions are dispelled; it's obvious that he doesn't even like Denise. [16]

Whatever reasons Sylvia had for feeling jealous, she was soon reconciled with Hughes. On Sunday, February 5, writing to Anne Sexton, she said he and Frieda were both wonderful, and her next letter to Aurelia calls him the "most blessed kind person in the world." This was written after she had suffered a miscarriage earlier in the morning. She was staying in bed, and he was taking care of her.

She told her mother she had been looking forward to "sharing a new little baby with you." She was as sorry, she said, about disappointing her as about anything else, and, writing again three days later, she promised to "make sure I can produce a new baby for you." [17] Before Frieda was born, Sylvia had nightmares that Aurelia was liable to dispossess her of the baby; now she was volunteering, as if in appeasement, to share the new baby with her.

The clearest evidence of her grief after the miscarriage is the poem "Parliament Hill Fields," which addresses the dead fetus as "you." Your absence is inconspicuous. Nobody can tell what is lacking from my life. It's pointless to think about you. "Already your doll grip lets go." The speaker reproaches herself for being too happy. Your cry is fading like the cry of a gnat, and at home on the nursery wall the blues in your sister's birthday picture start to glow. The poem is dated February 11. In one of the most cryptic lines the speaker says the old dregs and difficulties take her to wife. This may imply rivalry between the husband and old problems that had led to the suicide attempt, or it could mean that within the marriage she feels wedded to disagreements which have created friction.

A poem written three days later, "Zoo Keeper's Wife," refers to old problems while expressing violent female revulsion against male desire. The mouth opened by the husband's two-horned rhinoceros is as dirty as a boot sole and as big as a hospital sink. Lying sleepless but motionless in bed, with darkness enveloping her like a dead lake, the wife knows that if she moves, old grievances will jostle each other in her gut like loose teeth, making a noise like a rattle. Hughes had once worked in a zoo, and while the references to the armadillo and the mammal house match the poem's title, the bloodied chicks and the quartered rabbits seems more relevant to his past then to the average zookeeper's.

The apology to her mother and the promise about the next baby are both at odds with the hostile attitude she was adopting in *The Bell Jar,* which she'd already started. Narrating in the first person, Esther Greenwood tells the story of events before and after a suicide attempt very much like the one Sylvia made in 1953. When the story starts, Esther is in New York, working as guest editor on a magazine closely modeled on *Mademoiselle,* but the laconically chatty style allows her to move freely backward and forward in time. By the age of nine Esther had developed a taste for vichyssoise and caviar, thanks to her grandfather, who worked—as Sylvia's grandfather did—as headwaiter at a country club. Though the affair with Dick Norton was over before she worked for *Mademoiselle,* he served as the model for Buddy Willard, the most important of the boys who fall in love with Esther. But she loses her virginity to a twenty-six-year-old professor of mathematics, a character based on the balding lecturer.

The novel can be read as an anecdotal alternative to an analytical account of events surrounding the suicide attempt. In a series of semicomic episodes, we see how the strain on Esther increases as she has to cope with the boys who want to seduce her, the girls who are competing with her, the mother and the older women who want to control her. After the suicide attempt, the novelist Philomena Guinea pays for a private clinic where Esther recovers and prepares to face the world again.

Though the act of writing this autobiographical novel may have been intended as an attempt to work through old problems in an approximation to self-analysis, Sylvia couldn't have been expecting its therapeutic value to equal that of the help Ruth Beuscher had been giving her in Boston. By the time Sylvia started on the later novel she was going to call *Double Exposure,* she'd given herself permission to hate Hughes, and the hatred apparently helped to fuel the fiction; there's no husband figure in *The Bell Jar,* which sets its sights on the events of 1953, events that had been thoroughly discussed in her sessions with Dr. Beuscher both at McLean and later from 1958 to 1959. Whereas most of her poems deal with the present and the recent past, her one surviving novel focuses on experiences that were eight years old. Esther Greenwood's relationship with her mother is given a lot of emphasis, as if Sylvia were still struggling with the hatred, still feeling uncomfortable with the dichotomy between the loving letters and the hate-filled fiction.

It would have been depressing for anyone to go into the hospital for an operation so soon after a miscarriage, and Sylvia's experiences had given her an abnormally strong aversion to hospitals. There is a strongly suicidal tone in the poems she wrote in the ward after the appendectomy she underwent later in February, and the depression may have been exacerbated by conflicting emotions toward both Ted and Aurelia.

On Sunday, February 26, 1961, leaving him to look after Frieda, she set out on her own for the St. Pancras Hospital, where she was kept "under observation" until Monday evening. When he appeared among the visitors at 7:30 P.M. his face struck her as the kindest and most beautiful in the world. For him, she told herself, she could go through anything with fortitude. She had the appendectomy at eleven on Tuesday morning, and for the rest of the day felt so drugged that nothing troubled her. The next day she was sick and resentful that everyone else in the twenty-eight-bed ward could be so healthy and lively. On Thursday she was still exhausted, but on Friday she felt more like her normal self. By Sunday she was planning a story about the rhythms of the ordered ward society she had involuntarily joined. She felt fond of the young nurses in their black and white pin-striped dresses, their white aprons and hats, their black stockings. She liked their starched cleanliness and the way they kept straightening things up.

She enjoyed passivity: doing for her what she'd been doing for Frieda, other people were taking charge of all the necessary actions. Her poem "Tulips" shows how the death wish becomes inseparable from the regressive desire to abdicate responsibility for routine tasks. She has given her name and clothes to the nurses, her history to the anesthetist, her body to the surgeons. She's at peace; she's nobody. Between the pillow and the sheet, her head's like an eye between two lids that won't shut. She welcomes the numbness brought by the nurses in their needles; the photograph of husband and child reminds her of needs she must dutifully gratify. Their smiles are hooks that catch onto her skin. All she wants is to be empty, to lie with her hands upturned, enjoying the peacefulness, which is what the dead shut their mouths on, like a Communion wafer.

The red tulips quarrel with the peaceful whiteness of walls and sheets. The air was calmer before the flowers arrived: they're eating her oxygen. The flowers had been sent by her friend Helga Huws,[18] and though Sylvia didn't throw them into the wastepaper basket, like the roses her mother brought after her suicide attempt, the tulips act as a provocation. They may even have contributed to her recreation of the earlier hospital experience in *The Bell Jar.*

The same death wish is expressed in "I Am Vertical," which she wrote ten days later. The first line states a preference for the horizontal position, and the ending suggests she'll be more useful after lying down for the last time. The trees will touch her, and the flowers have time for her.

While Sylvia was working on a story about the suicide attempt she had made eight years before at the age of twenty, the effort of remembering and reconstructing the events may have given her a sense of gaining control over them and therefore being able to resist the new surge of suicidal depression. She wrote amiable letters to Aurelia and, after tearing up so many of her husband's papers, worked at repairing her relationship with him. They decided to postpone their Italian trip till autumn, and he applied to the Royal Literary Fund for money to cover the cost of a fortnight's holiday for the three of them in the Scilly Isles.

They could seldom afford theater tickets, but to cheer Sylvia up before she went into the hospital, he had taken her to the Royal Shakespeare Company's production of *The Duchess of Malfi.*[19] Before she was discharged from the hospital, she was allowed, both on Saturday, March 4, and Sunday, to sit outside on a park bench with him and Frieda. As she wrote in her journal, his stint of washing diapers and emptying the pot had made him more appreciative of how hard she'd been working in the apartment.[20]

Her stitches were taken out on Tuesday, March 7, but by then she felt so at home in the ward that she was making a daily tour around the twenty-seven other beds, chatting to the patients. The next day she was discharged, with strict orders not to do any lifting or heavy work for a fortnight. Frieda was teething again, which made it impossible to get any uninterrupted sleep. Sylvia took her out on Primrose Hill every day, to lie in the sun on a blanket, and on Saturday, March 18, she resumed the routine of working for four or five hours every morning in the Merwins' flat, determined to make as much headway as she could with the novel before they returned at the end of May.[21]

It had been harder in America than in England to find a publisher for her first collection, *The Colossus,* and when Knopf finally accepted it, the fifty poems had to be cut to forty. This not only boosted her confidence but made her aware of a theme which ran through the book: someone is broken and repaired. The collection started with the shattered colossus and ended with "Flute Notes from a Reedy Pond" and "The Stones." The last two lines of this poem contain three short sentences. "My mendings itch. There is nothing to do. / I shall be good as new." This seems to have helped her toward structuring *The Bell Jar,* which starts with a thinly fictionalized account of the week as guest editor at *Mademoiselle* and the other events that led up to the suicide attempt. At the end, after all the episodes reproducing Sylvia's period in clinics, the heroine, Esther Greenwood, is on the point of being discharged. There should be a ritual, she tells herself, for being born twice—"patched, retreaded and approved for the road."[22] She may feel like a used tire, but she has reasonable confidence that the retreading process has made her tough enough for the mileage ahead, while the choice of her grandmother's name, Greenwood, acts as a pointer to the theme of rebirth.

Throughout April and May Sylvia worked intensively on the novel, but had the opportunity to go away with Hughes in June. Aurelia, who was coming to England, had offered to stay in their flat and look after Frieda for two weeks while they went off to the south of France, where they would spend a week with Bill and Dido Merwin at their farmhouse at Lacan de Loubressac. Sylvia was already pregnant again when Aurelia arrived in the middle of June, and now that she had a daughter of her own, Sylvia found it harder to be nice to her mother. Aurelia often returned to the Merwins' flat in tears. "Everything I do is wrong," she told Molly Raybould, an Australian friend of theirs who stayed at the flat when they were away. "I can't seem to do anything right."[23]

Aurelia moved into the small Chalcot Square flat when Sylvia and Hughes left for France in their car on the last day of June. Driving along the Normandy coast on their leisurely way to the south, they stopped at Berck-Plage, which is near Le Touquet, and saw inmates from a hospital for mutilated war veterans and accident victims taking their exercise on the beach. Sylvia was reminded of her father's amputated leg and the beach at Winthrop, but her long poem "Berck-Plage" wasn't written until a year later.

Writing to Aurelia was easier than talking to her, and from the farmhouse Sylvia described the joys of sunbathing on the geranium-lined terrace and luxuriating in freedom from letters and telephone calls. Saying Dido Merwin was the world's best cook, Sylvia was equally enthusiastic about the view, the tinkling cowbells, the billion stars overhead and the satin finish on the waxed antique furniture in the house. But the holiday was far from peaceful. According to Dido Merwin, Sylvia behaved rudely to the other houseguest, Margot Pitt-Rivers, wife of the anthropologist Julian Pitt-Rivers and owner of a chateau not far away. Earlier she had been the wife of the Spanish ambassador to England and had twice faced a firing squad in the Spanish Civil War.[24] On the first night, when Hughes stayed with the others, listening to music instead of going to bed when she did, Sylvia stormed out into the night with a raincoat over her nightgown. He had to set out in pursuit.

The next day, after being left alone when Hughes drove Bill Merwin to rescue Dido and Margot Pitt-Rivers from a car accident, Sylvia lapsed into a sulky silence, and went on behaving inconsiderately throughout the rest of the week, using up all the hot water, helping herself greedily to food from the fridge, rear-ranging furniture in their bedroom, and generally being high-handed and bad-tempered. In the evenings she became more friendly when, by playing with verve and finesse, she usually won at their favorite card-game, *Ascenseur.* It was Hughes who decided to cut the stay short. In the memoir published as an appendix to Anne Stevenson's biography, Dido Merwin sums up the visit as "a kind of macabre marathon for all concerned." "Apart from when she was sleeping, eating, sunbathing or playing cards, to a greater or lesser degree their stay at Lacan had been one long scene." Sylvia never saw either of the Merwins again.[25]

Dido Merwin's narrative hinges on the assumption that the "catalyst and Spanish fly in the ointment" was Margot Pitt-Rivers. It seems more likely that Sylvia was behaving badly because she was nervous about Hughes's feelings toward the dangerously attractive and enviably accomplished Dido, who was older than Merwin, her third husband, who was only three years older than Hughes.

Sylvia wrote two poems about Dido, "Face Lift" and "The Rival." Both are vindictive. In "Face Lift" the cosmetic surgery makes the years drain into the woman's pillow while for five days her best friend thinks she's in the country. The skin peels away as easily as paper, and when she grins, the stitches tighten. She grows backward to the age of twenty, lying on her first husband's sofa. The surgery gets rid of the lined, dewlapped lady she'd seen in the mirror; mother to herself, she wakes up swaddled in gauze, as pink and smooth as a baby.

In "The Rival"—the title is significant—the other woman is accused of giving the same impression as the moon: of something beautiful but annihilating. She borrows light, turns everything into stone and loves to make remarks that are unanswerable. The version of the poem published in *Ariel* discards the two final sections, one of which calls the woman an "angel of coldness."

After returning to London in mid-July and taking Aurelia up to Heptonstall, Sylvia and Hughes again left her in charge of Frieda and the Chalcot Square flat while they drove to Devon and Cornwall in search of a house. Living in the country would not only be less expensive than living in London but healthier for Frieda and the new baby. They could move back later if they could afford to.

Of the eight houses they saw, the only one they liked belonged to Sir Robert and Lady Arundell. Prejudiced against titles, Hughes had been reluctant to see it, but Court Green turned out to be an old thatched rectory which had once been a manor house. It had nine rooms, an attic and a cellar, while the grounds, which spread over three acres, contained a big lawn, an apple orchard, a cobblestone court, a derelict tennis court, a two-room cottage and a stable that could be used as a garage. The house was sinking into the earth. In many places the plaster was being held up only by wallpaper, while the birds had held the thatched roof together by nesting in it. The Arundells agreed to have the house treated by a woodworm company and guaranteed for twenty years.

With their savings and a little help from both mothers Sylvia and Ted Hughes were able to pay the thirty-six hundred pounds needed to buy the house without a mortgage. With the move to organize and the baby coming, they abandoned the idea of going to Italy. Hughes offered to return the five-hundred-pound Maugham award he had received, but he was told to keep the money for future travel.[26]

When they advertised the London flat, two couples arrived simultaneously and both wanted it. One of the men immediately sat down to write out a check, but Sylvia and Hughes preferred the other couple, David Wevill, a young Canadian poet, and his German-Russian wife, Assia. The excitement and the preparations for moving to the country didn't prevent Sylvia from finishing her novel, *The Bell Jar,* on August 22.

✿ 13 ✿

In Devon

When the batteries of a marital relationship are running down, a move to a new home can provide a powerful boost. Husband and wife are working as partners, sharing decisions and collaborating to reorganize and redecorate a home they'll share. Excited, optimistic and full of family plans for the future, Sylvia and Hughes worked hard at unpacking, scrubbing and painting. He made bookshelves and dug at the vegetable garden which would eventually, they told themselves, make them self-sufficient. She was happy in Devon, she told a friend; London hadn't been good for her.

The contrast with the Chalcot Square flat could hardly have been greater. Jerked, as if by a magic carpet, from a cramped and humble two-room apartment to a house of seigneurial size, derelict though it was, Sylvia was exhilarated and almost incredulous. The house was white with black trim. It had plenty of large rooms. In the back part, which dated from the eleventh century, the walls were "castle-thick," and the hill behind it had been the site of a prehistoric moated fort. Growing from the summit of this moated mound were three giant wych-elms so close together their foliage formed a single mass.

After they moved on August 31, 1961, Sylvia picked the largest bedroom as her study. Like the room they chose as their bedroom, it looked out on the adjoining church and the old graveyard, which was separated from their garden by a high retaining wall.[1] Together with the age of the house, the graveyard, which had a big, ancient yew tree in it, and the old elms seemed to put them in touch with the distant past, while the abundance of space made it

160

seem natural to make long-term plans for the future. In fact Sylvia had only eighteen months to live.

They had so little furniture that it could all be fitted into a small van when they moved. They had to put deck chairs around the trestle table in the playroom, but David and Assia Wevill, who had too much furniture for the small two-room apartment, lent them a round table, from which they ate in what Sylvia called the "heart room" of the house, a large back room with pale green linoleum on the floor. Its walls consisted of cream wood paneling to shoulder height and pink paint above. In London the Wevills had made friends with the couple who were to be Hughes and Sylvia's first houseguests. The Portuguese poet Helder Macedo and his wife, Suzette, had come to England as exiles from the Salazar regime. Hughes and Sylvia had met them at a dinner party during the summer. At Court Green, when they talked to the Macedos about the Wevills, Sylvia was glad they'd given the flat to a couple they liked.

In September Warren came to stay for a week and helped them with the work that had to be done on the house and garden. He also took turns looking after Frieda. Warren and Hughes made an enormous elm plank into a new writing table for Sylvia, and taking picnic meals, the three of them explored Tintagel, Exeter and the north Devon coast.

Once the visits from Warren and the Macedos were over, Sylvia and Hughes resumed the routine that left her free to write during the mornings. He gave Frieda her lunch before putting her to bed at about noon, and Sylvia then made lunch for him and her, taking over the household duties so that he could write in the afternoons. In order to plunge immediately into writing every morning, she even left Frieda's pot unemptied and the bed unmade. But she now had regular help. Nancy Axworthy, who for the last eleven years had been working for the Arundells, came twice a week to help with the cleaning and ironing. She was married to a local carpenter who also worked as a bellringer and assistant head of the fire brigade. The Arundells had let stinging nettles take over most of the grounds, but there were petunias, zinnias and two good rosebushes in the front garden, while daffodils and narcissi were growing thickly in the orchard.[2]

Galvanized into poetic activity, Sylvia finished four long poems by the end of September. Despite her exhilaration, her death wish is clearly audible in the undertone, and instead of focusing wholeheartedly on the landscape around her new home, she uses a Proustian device, trawling for memories between two points, separated in both space and time. In "Wuthering Heights" Devon is linked with the Yorkshire moors. The first phrase in "Finisterre" contains the words "land's end," but the reference is not to the westernmost tip of Cornwall and England but to the same area of north Devon coast which features in "Blackberrying." This is linked to the cape that forms the westernmost tip of Brittany. In "Wuthering Heights," comparing the horizons to faggots that could be ignited, she's implicitly comparing herself to a witch about to be burned, but the ironic suggestion that death would be welcome (the flames "might warm me") is reminiscent of the lines in "I Am Vertical" which looked forward to the horizontal time in which the trees would touch her with their roots. Now, if she pays too much attention to the roots of the heather, she thinks they'll invite her to whiten her bones among them. Beyond the admonitory black cliffs at the end of the land in "Finisterre," the faces of the drowned are whitening the unbounded sea, while in "Blackberrying" the blue-red juice on her fingers tells her the berries must love her, but she hadn't asked for a blood-sisterhood.

The most sinister of the four poems is "The Surgeon at 2 A.M.," which looks back at her last hospital experience. Disconnected from any real landscape, the poem creates a surreal one by taking a scenic view of the bodies cut up by the surgeon. The sheet is a snowfield, while the opened body is a garden with a lung-tree in it and orchids that coil like snakes. The heart is a red-bell-bloom; the blood is a sunset, and, later, a hot spring he has to seal off. His rubber-gloved assistants hook back the tubers and fruits that ooze jammy substances. The man feels small in comparison with the purple wilderness he's hacking. The anesthetized body has shut its mouth on the stone pill of repose, an image reminiscent of "Tulips," in which the dead shut their mouths on peacefulness like a Communion tablet. In this poem the body is a statue, a work of art perfected by the sculptor; the amputated limbs are entombed in an icebox and replaced by clean plastic limbs. One dead patient is floating below the ceiling, borne up by angels of morphia. The white-coated surgeon feels like a sun. Red night lights are moons, and gray faces of anesthetized patients are flowers.

The battle between the life force and the death wish had become more violent than ever. She was so keen to meet the villagers and "grow into" the community that she decided to start attending services at the church, which was Anglican, and to join its mothers' group, which held monthly meetings. She wrote to the rector, who called to see her. An Irishman who had worked in Africa and Chicago, he offered to take her through the creed and the order of the service. Her Unitarian past made it impossible for her to accept the idea of the Trinity, but he said she was welcome to come in the spirit of her beliefs. Attending her first service in October, she enjoyed the organ music, the hymn singing, the psalms and the prayers, but, bored by the platitudinous sermon, she tried to concentrate on the three illuminated stained glass windows. She decided to attend Evensong occasionally and send Frieda to Sunday school.[3]

Continuing to think of herself as a pagan Unitarian, she partly defined the limits of her faith in three death-oriented poems written between October 21 and 23, when the moon was full. She still found it easier to perform tasks that were set for her by someone else, and Ted Hughes explains that "The Moon and the Yew Tree" was written as a verse exercise he "assigned" to her when, just before dawn, the full moon was setting behind the yew. The poem tells us that though the grass around her ankles is murmuring humbly as if she were God, and though the Gothic-shaped tree is pointing upward, she simply can't feel any sense of direction. She needs to feel she's going somewhere, needs comfort, needs to believe in tenderness, but, far from being a door, and far from being sweet, like Mary, the moon is a face, white and desperate, bald and wild, while the comfortless message of the yew is blackness and silence.

In both the other poems, "Last Words" and "Mirror," the looking glass measures the movement toward death. "Last Words" personifies the forces which will eventually gather her into death. Her spirit is escaping like steam, and when there's none left, she'll be dead, but objects, which have no spirit, retain their luster. She wants, when bound in a winding cloth, to be surrounded by things she once owned—her turquoise, her copper saucepans, her rouge pots. Soon her mirror will reflect nothing; she should be preserving her days like fruit.

She does this in the poems, and in "Mirror" she empathizes

164 / *The Death and Life of Sylvia Plath*

with the looking glass that always swallows what it sees, but tells the truth, unlike the moon and the candles, which are both romantic. The woman who looks in the mirror every day has drowned a young girl in it and sees an old woman rising toward her like a terrible fish.

"Mirror" was written four days before Sylvia's twenty-ninth birthday, which she and Hughes celebrated more luxuriously than the previous one: he bought cans of caviar and octopus from a delicatessen. Now in the final months of her pregnancy—the baby was due in mid-January—she paid fewer visits to London than he did, but she attended a dinner at the Goldsmiths' Hall, where she received the seventy-five-pound Guinness Award, a literary prize she had won. She stayed overnight with the novelist Alan Sillitoe and his poet wife, Ruth Fainlight, who had met Sylvia during the summer at the presentation of the Hawthornden Prize to Ted.

As the winter grew colder, life in the drafty, uncarpeted house became more uncomfortable. It was too cold for a new baby, said the midwife, Winifred Davies, a short, round, gray-haired Lancashire woman with a wise, moral face and a blue nurse's uniform under a round blue hat. Nothing could be done about the drafty halls, but Sylvia and Hughes bought heaters for the rooms they were using. To write in the mornings Sylvia dressed in her fluffy pink bathrobe over layers of maternity clothes, and they both wore so many sweaters indoors that they looked, she said, as fat as bears. At the end of December, taking Mrs. Davies's advice, Sylvia bought a thermometer to check room temperatures, and then wrote to tell her mother that the unheated rooms varied between thirty-eight and forty degrees while the heated rooms were between fifty and fifty-five.[4]

Sylvia had applied to the Eugene Saxton Fund, a charitable foundation, for a grant to write prose fiction, and on November 9 the news arrived that she had been awarded two thousand dollars, to be paid in four installments as she submitted evidence of progress. Though she had already finished *The Bell Jar* and exchanged contracts with Heinemann, her advance had been only a hundred pounds. By delaying publication and feeding the typescript to the Saxton administrators in four installments, she could appear to be complying with their requirements. Aurelia, who knew nothing about the contents of the novel, was told Sylvia had finished "a batch of stuff" and already tied it up in four parcels, which she was ready to submit as required.[5]

Obligingly, Heinemann postponed publication until January 1963, when authorship was attributed to Victoria Lucas, the idea being to keep Aurelia in ignorance of the hurtful characterization of the mother. All Sylvia said was that thanks to the Saxton money, she and Hughes could make annual payments of a hundred pounds to his parents and to Aurelia until they'd repaid the loan that had saved them from taking out a mortgage.[6] But they sent Christmas cards in lieu of presents, which they couldn't afford after spending so much on electricians, plumbers, lawyers, electric heaters, taxes and health insurance. Of the presents they received, the most useful was the box of tools Warren sent Hughes, who immediately set to work fitting clips for the staircase carpet.[7]

According to the doctor's latest forecast, the baby was due on January 11, 1962, but it wasn't till six days later, at four in the morning, that the twenty-nine-year-old Sylvia was awakened by contractions which persisted intermittently through the day while she gallantly went on cooking to stockpile food for Hughes. She was expecting the baby to be a boy because it felt bigger and heavier than Frieda had. The doctor and Mrs. Davies both called at the house, but the contractions didn't become violent till five in the afternoon, and at eight-thirty, when they were coming at five-minute intervals, Hughes called Mrs. Davies, who brought a cylinder of gas. She and Hughes stayed with Sylvia, who inhaled through the mask whenever she felt a strong contraction. Frieda's delivery had been effortless, but Sylvia had used up the whole cylinder and was just beginning to bear down when the baby got stuck and the water failed to break. A few minutes before midnight, just as the doctor arrived, the baby, yelling lustily, was precipitated onto the bed in a flood of water.

Frieda had weighed only seven pounds four ounces, Nicholas weighed nine pounds eleven ounces. He looked swarthy, with dents in his head where he'd pushed his way out. He reminded Sylvia of a bad-tempered and wrinkled boxer, but the dents soon disappeared, while he gradually became pinker and more translucent. In the morning when the excited Frieda met her brother, Mrs. Davies suggested she should be allowed to share the various tasks, even if they took longer. Not yet two, Frieda immediately proved herself capable of doing everything she was told to do, holding safety pins, kissing Nicholas and helping to wrap him up. She then held him, unaided.[8]

For the next week Sylvia spent part of each day in bed, but at night, because the baby kept crying, she was getting so little sleep that the doctor gave her tranquilizers. When she developed milk fever, with a temperature of a hundred and three for over two nights, he prescribed penicillin. Hughes, who had to look after Frieda all day, fed Sylvia chicken soup, salads and mushrooms on toast. The neighbors were helpful, too. The friendliest of them, Percy and Rose Key, brought over a roast beef and gravy dinner. But it was a strenuous time for Sylvia and Hughes. By the end of January she was suggesting that if Aurelia came over in the summer, they should join forces to give him a six-week holiday from child minding.[9]

Sylvia had been hoping she could go back to the pre-Christmas routine, but though Nicholas settled into a rhythm of waking her only twice during the night, at two and six, she afterward needed to sleep till nine, and most of the day disappeared into a "whirlwind" of baths, washing clothes and preparing food. Frieda became more mischievous, peeling off wallpaper where the plasterwork was cracked, throwing objects down the lavatory, uprooting bulbs from flowerpots and tearing up paper to sprinkle over the carpet. Normally efficient at both secretarial and household tasks, Sylvia was functioning badly, especially when she had little sleep. She grew impatient with herself when, in spite of help from the hardworking Nancy Axworthy, she fell behind with both typing and domestic chores. Still in the habit Ruth Beuscher had inculcated of scheduling tasks for each day, she crossed off only two of the jobs she listed for February 12. She typed a story for Hughes and cleaned the playroom, but didn't do the mending, vacuum her study, type his latest radio script, write her diary or bring the abandoned scrapbooks up to date.[10]

If the move to Court Green had brought Sylvia closer to him, the birth of Nicholas seemed to be having the opposite effect. Their friend Suzette Macedo thought he was less happy about having a boy than a girl. A daughter was not threat to him, but a son could grow into a usurper.[11] There was a growing awkwardness in his relationship with Sylvia, who became jealous of his friendship with a sixteen-year-old girl, Nicola Tyrer. Her parents were neighbors who tried to foist her on him, expecting him to give her educational help. One day, after he had tea with the Tyrers, Nicola wandered back with him to Court Green, and when Sylvia saw them standing at opposite sides of the path under the bare laburnum, she thought the girl looked posed and coy. They reminded her of kids back from a date. Nicola said she was returning some phonograph records Hughes had lent her father, and asked whether she could come over later in the week to hear Sylvia's German Linguaphone records. Immediately fetching them from the house, Sylvia thrust them into the girl's hands. Afterward she seriously thought of "smashing our old and ridiculous box Victrola with an axe," and resolved to be "omnipresent" whenever Nicola paid one of her visits. [12]

In March Sylvia managed to write a 378-line poem for three voices, modeled partly on Ingmar Bergman's 1952 film about pregnant women, *Women Waiting*, and partly on Dylan Thomas's "play for voices," *Under Milk Wood*, which had been directed, in its original radio production, by Douglas Cleverdon. He had worked a great deal with Hughes and would eventually produce *Three Women* on the radio. The action is set mainly in a maternity ward, and while Sylvia doesn't try to give the women three different ways of speaking, she contrasts their experiences of childbirth. One has a son, one has had a miscarriage, and one has an illegitimate daughter. The first is positive, fulfilled and healthy, but the speeches given to the second suggest that Sylvia had been scarred by the miscarriage she'd had in February 1961. The second woman sees death in the winter trees. She asks herself whether death is her lover, whether the death of her unborn baby is a penalty for loving a name on a tombstone when she was a child, whether it is her own death she's been carrying in her womb. Unlike other children, who are too noisy and full of life, the unborn baby remained quiet, holy and perfect.

The third woman is the most frightened. Not ready for motherhood, she wishes she'd murdered the child who is murdering her, while the first woman is full of love for the shiny blue baby boy, who arrived as if he had hurtled from a star. After giving birth, she has to be stitched up as if she were a fabric, but she can no longer remember what her fingers did before she held him. The third woman resents the demands her baby daughter makes. Though they're separated in the maternity ward by glass, her cries are like hooks—a recurrent image in Sylvia's work of this period—that catch and grate like the claws of a cat. Finally discharged from the hospital, she feels like a walking wound.

In Sylvia's tired state, it must have taken tremendous willpower to write *Three Women* in March, but she went on to produce five poems during the first week of April. The first, "Little Fugue," reflects her new interest in Beethoven's late quartets and especially in the *Grosse Fuge*.[13] Remembering a blind pianist she'd seen on the boat that brought her to England in 1955—when he groped for his food, his fingers looked like weasels—she associates the horrific complications of Beethoven's music with black statements and the black wagging fingers of the yew tree, while she connects Beethoven's deafness with her father's voice at the end of a dark tunnel. The amputation of Otto Plath's leg has lamed her memory.

The best of her April poems, and the most death-oriented, was "Elm," written on April 19. The tree expects her to be scared of the bottom which it knows with its great tap root, but she says she isn't frightened, she has already been there. The memory of electroconvulsive therapy helps her to empathize with the great tree, which has suffered the atrocity of sunsets and has been scorched to the root. The first person singular refers to both her and the tree when she speaks of being terrified of the malign dark thing that is sleeping in her. She can feel its soft feathery turnings all day, and in the strangle of branches is a murderous face that petrifies the will.

Developing a theme stated only briefly in "Zoo Keeper's Wife," one of the April poems, "Pheasant," and "The Rabbit Catcher" (dated May 21), protest against Hughes's predatoriness toward animals and birds. Feeling privileged to be visited by the majestic pheasant which was pacing through the uncut grass by the elm on the hill, she pleads with him not to kill it. In the first draft of the poem about the rabbit catcher, his young wife dreams of a marriage which will give her enough freedom to become herself. In the event, she has too little, but it's the man who gets angry, threatening to do whatever he feels like doing. In the final version the speaker finds herself in a hostile landscape. Tasting the malignity of the gorse, she associates its yellow flowers with candles and extreme unction. The inescapable snares are zeros, closing on nothing. This image is reminiscent of the sly world's hinges that shut against the mussel hunter at Rock Harbor.

In the first draft of "The Rabbit Catcher" the husband's hands muffle the wife like gloves. In the final draft she identifies more subtly with his victims. Looking at his blunt hands as they encircle a teacup, she tells herself how excited he is by the little deaths that wait for him like sweethearts, and she compares the marriage with a snare. There are tight wires between them, and she's being killed by the constriction as a ringlike mind slides shut on her.

As the poems show, death was again beckoning seductively, but superficially Sylvia was still vivacious and full of plans for the future. When Elizabeth Compton, the woman who had offered accommodation after the *Two of a Kind* broadcast, visited Court Green with her husband, David, Sylvia impressed her as lively and tremendously energetic. She had painted the trestle table white, decorating it with little enameled flowers. She had also painted hearts and flowers on her sewing machine, on a doll's cradle, even on some of the door trim. Questioning Mrs. Compton eagerly about her children, her home, her interests and her politics, Sylvia kept getting up and running out to look at Nick, who was sleeping in his pram under the laburnum tree. Their intention, she said, was to have five children. She'd made whole-meal banana bread, which she gave the Comptons with their tea, and Frieda was being given dates and nuts instead of sweets. Though she talked with pride about Hughes's writing, Sylvia never mentioned her own. When Mrs. Compton asked whether the sponge cake had been made from a mix, Sylvia turned on her angrily: "I separated and whipped those eggs for twenty minutes."[14]

The Sillitoes came to stay at the beginning of May with their month-old son, and Sylvia was looking forward to having the Wevills for the middle weekend in the month—"a nice young Canadian poet and his very attractive, intelligent wife" she called them in a letter to Aurelia.[15] The Wevills arrived on Friday, May 18. Born in Japan in 1937, David had been a nineteen-year-old Cambridge undergraduate when he met Assia in 1956 on the boat from Canada to England. Ten years his senior, she was born in Germany. Her mother was a Protestant and her father, Dr. Gutmann, was an orthopedic surgeon of Russian-Jewish extraction. Unsafe in Nazi Germany, they escaped to Palestine in the late thirties with their two daughters, Assia and Gilli. They lived in Tel Aviv until 1948, when they moved to Canada, and Assia married a Royal Air Force sergeant she had met in Palestine. She had divorced him and married again by the time she met David. In 1958 David began a two-year teaching stint in Burma at the University of Mandalay, where she joined him in 1959, divorcing her second husband. She married David in 1960 before returning to London, where they took over the Hughes's small apartment in Chalcot Square.

By May 1961 Assia's passion for David had cooled sufficiently for her to make up her mind before she left London that she intended to seduce Ted Hughes. Half-jokingly, she confided this intention to at least three women friends.[16] She was now thirty-four. She had big greenish eyes, a rich, deep voice, a tendency to be mischievous and a relish for unconventional behavior. She was rumored to have attacked her first husband with a knife and slashed up the inside of his car. She still sounded angry when she spoke about her second husband, and one day she announced that she was going to send roses to his wife. The florist was instructed to send him the bill.

Assia was working in London as a copywriter for Coleman, Prentice and Varley, an advertising agency which had once handled the Tory party account. An office colleague describes her as "exceptionally attractive, very good company, and full of outrageous ideas, which unlike most of humanity, she did not tremble to fulfill."[17]

Though Assia's immediate superior at the agency had the impression that she had lied about her previous experience in order to get the job, she did it well, writing imaginative copy. As an office colleague she was lively and amusing. She appeared to be egoistic, untamed, impulsive and unscrupulous, but she didn't give the impression of being promiscuous. She had considerable panache, and she dressed stylishly.[18]

The weekend in Devon began promisingly. The four of them got along well. Hughes was friendly and encouraging to the diffident, soft-voiced poet, who thought he was going to be helpful. David described the weekend as "cordial, exploratory, gracious.... Sylvia could be good company—intelligent, witty, interested, good in conversation." He couldn't tell whether the friendliness was costing her an effort, and he sometimes sensed "something like terror—a look in her face—breaking through ordinary conversation, as though she were looking inward." The marriage hadn't genuinely been under threat on her last day of teaching at

Smith when she saw Hughes with the student, or during the holiday with the Merwins, or when Nicola Tyrer followed him back to Court Green. But the marital relationship had become more difficult since Nick's birth. Sylvia was now more vulnerable than ever before, tethered more firmly to the home, and the provocative Assia was potentially the most formidable rival she had yet had.

On Friday night Sylvia went to bed early and called down to Hughes, telling him to come up, but he stayed downstairs with the Wevills. On Saturday morning he drove David and Frieda up on the moor, while Assia worked with Sylvia in the vegetable garden. When tapestry came up as a topic, Assia said she had done some; Sylvia, who was always planning new activities, intended to start. She described what she wanted to do—the pattern involved roses and ribbon.[19]

Though she wasn't at her best in the kitchen, Assia offered to make a potato salad for lunch on Sunday. She was peeling potatoes when Sylvia, who was with David in the front room, heard Hughes come in through the back door. Taking off her shoes in the corridor, Sylvia crept around to the kitchen where Hughes was with Assia, but found they were only talking. Afterward, Sylvia made her anxiety so apparent that there was no alternative to cutting the weekend short. When they had finished lunch, she drove Assia and David to the station.

On Tuesday, May 22, Assia wrote a friendly letter to Sylvia, sending materials she had bought at Harrods for a tapestry, including wool, canvas and a diagram. She had taken considerable trouble to identify the rose pattern Sylvia had described. It had been published about two years previously in the *Sunday Times* and, according to the shop assistant, was still available from the newspaper. After giving Sylvia some advice about "tramming"—a technique of stretching the thread across five or six inches of canvas and then working over it diagonally—Assia warned her that tapestry could become addictive. She might find herself staying up all night, or might "stop eating, or mending and baking and working. Please, please don't let it possess you.... But I hope you'll enjoy it. Much love, Assia."[20]

❧ 14 ❧

Infidelity

"A pprehensions," the poem Sylvia wrote on May 28, mingled her own fears with what she imagined to be those of her kindly neighbor, Percy Key, who was dying. Writing in the first person, she finds it easy to identify with a dying man. The color of the wall changes from white to gray to red to black. The sky is green, fertile but unreachable and irrelevant. She's scared of being wheeled away under crosses and a rain of pietàs. The heart is opening and closing like a red fist. The lungs are gray, papery bags, and she expects a negative answer to the question of whether there's any escape from the mind. For him there's no prospect that his consciousness will survive; for her there's no solution to the problems that have been dogging her.

In May, when Hughes's parents and his uncle Walt came to Devon for six days, only his mother stayed at Court Green. The two men slept at the hotel in town on the hill. "Sylvia is a lovely wife and mother," wrote Mrs. Hughes to Aurelia, who was due to arrive in mid-June.[1] In letters to Wellesley, Sylvia was saying this was the richest and happiest time of her life. She wanted to go on having babies, loved owning flowers and trees. They were picking between six hundred and a thousand daffodils every week and selling most of them—very cheaply—at the market. She had become a beekeeper, she enjoyed gardening, she was making a new effort to learn French and German, she was considering whether to take riding lessons on Dartmoor. Life begins at thirty, she declared.[2]

A. Alvarez, who called in to see them when he was on his way to Cornwall for the Whitsun weekend, noticed a change in the balance of power between them. No longer a quiet, reticent housewifely appendage to a powerful husband, "she seemed made solid and complete, her own woman again.... There was a sharpness and clarity about her." While Hughes sat back, playing with Frieda, Sylvia showed Alvarez around the house and garden, taking proprietary pride in everything, including the mound with the yew tree on it.[3]

Aurelia arrived during the third week of June to find a welcoming enamel heart on the door of the guest room, painted with a garland of flowers. Inside the room was a trunk, similarly painted, for use as a wardrobe. Though there were some oppressive silences between Hughes and Sylvia, she seemed cheerful for much of the time. The long poem, "Berck-Plage," which she finished on June 30, the day after Percy Key's funeral, links his death with her father's and, implicitly, with her own hopelessness. But much of her behavior with Aurelia contradicted that hopelessness. On July 9, leaving Hughes to look after the children, they went shopping in Exeter and had lunch there; Sylvia claimed to have everything she had ever wanted—a wonderful husband, two adorable children, a beautiful home and her writing. But after they got back to the house, the telephone rang and a male-sounding voice asked for Hughes. Assia, who had a deep voice, was pretending to be a man, and she kept up the pretense even after Sylvia said she knew who it was.

Her face had paled. She called shrilly for Hughes, who rushed down the stairs to take the call. Sylvia disappeared upstairs, but when the telephone conversation was over, she pulled the wires out of the wall. With her mother, after this, she was oddly bright, but in the morning it was Aurelia who got the children up and gave them breakfast. When Sylvia appeared, she made herself a mug of coffee and sat down on a high stool in the kitchen. When her eyes met her mother's, the hand holding the mug was trembling and her lips quivering. She had to put down the mug and retreat upstairs. When she reappeared, it was with Hughes. They wandered to the far end of the vegetable garden, deep in conversation. Frieda, who ran to them, ran back to tell her grandmother that Mummy and Daddy were both crying.

It was six years since they had married. In spite of all the tensions, the disagreements and the exorbitant demands they had made on each other, the relationship had been extraordinarily close. They had seldom been separated for more than ten or twelve hours at a stretch, and in spite of all their temperamental dissimilarities, the partnership had been beneficial to both of them. There may have been moments of emotional betrayal in Hughes's letters to Olwyn and in flirtations, such as the one with the girl at Northampton, but Sylvia appears to have taken no interest in any other man. Hughes's only rival was death.

In the evening, when he left for London, he drove the car to the station, accompanied by Aurelia and Sylvia, who brought it back. She said she'd been suspicious about his frequent trips to London, ostensibly for BBC work. In the evening, not wanting to sleep alone in their bedroom, Sylvia dressed Nick, bundled him into his car bed and took him to the car. Leaving Frieda with Aurelia, she drove the twenty-five miles to Elizabeth and David Compton's house.

She had come to like the Comptons so much that she dedicated *The Bell Jar* to them. In July, for Elizabeth's birthday, she had made a cake, iced it, put candles on it and, together with Hughes, delivered it wrapped in a shawl. Neither of them had given any sign that anything was wrong. Now, arriving with Nick, and during the next weeks, when Hughes was often in London, Sylvia confided in Elizabeth, who was appalled by the change in her. She wept and, holding Elizabeth's hands, begged for help. Her milk had dried up, she said. She could no longer feed Nick. "Ted lies to me," she said. "He lies all the time, he has become a little man. . . . When you give someone your whole heart, and he doesn't want it, you cannot take it back, it's gone forever."[4]

Sylvia stayed with the Comptons overnight, refusing their bed, which they offered her, and sleeping instead on the sofa. Elizabeth has described how she found Sylvia in the morning, bending over the litter of new kittens. "I see her now, wearing a pink woolly dressing gown with a long plait of hair falling into the box, turning her head and saying 'I never saw anything so small and new and vulnerable. They are blind.'"[5]

It was probably on the evening of the same day that, after returning to Court Green, she performed a sad ceremony in the moonlight. She went to Hughes's desk and, with a knife, skimmed from the surface what she called "Ted's scum," the residue of dandruff, dead skin, fingernail parings—whatever had fallen from him. She took letters and papers from the wastepaper basket, and she may have taken some from the desk. Without reading them, she made a pile in the garden. Aurelia was holding Nick and trying to keep Frieda inside the house. In spite of everything her mother did to dissuade her, Sylvia set light to the pile and stepped back, saying a magical incantation. A charred piece of paper landed at her feet, a fragment of a letter with the signature legible in the moonlight. "The truth always comes to me," Sylvia afterward told Elizabeth. "The truth loves me."

The poem "Burning the Letters" (August 13) tells the story of this forlorn ritual. As she pokes at the carbon birds, they console her, rising and flying blindly, like coal angels, but they have nothing to say. With the butt of a rake, she flakes up papers and fans them out. A name with black edges wilts at her foot. The phrase "Pale eyes, patent leather gutturals!" is incomprehensible unless you know that Assia was of partly German extraction, and that, although she normally wore brogues, Sylvia had got it into her head that in Devon Assia had been wearing inappropriately high-heeled shoes.

It's hard to be sure what motivated this bizarrely improvised ritual. Improvisation assorts oddly with the kind of ritual which involves the repetition of actions and utterances in a prescribed order. Sylvia was behaving as if she believed her actions had a religious or mystical dimension and a specific objective. In an unnervingly precise way, the poem documents what she did, but this doesn't mean it offers a precise record of what happened. Whether the papers had been in the attic or whether she was actually wearing a "housedress" matters no more than whether Assia had been wearing patent leather shoes. It's the emotional truth that counts, and the poem makes her emotional experience so vivid that it's worth asking whether she burned the letters in order to give herself material for the poem, having it—in some undeveloped state—in her mind from the moment she went into Hughes's room, or earlier. Instead of being a by-product of the experience, the poem, though it existed only as a vague idea, may have guided her actions.

One big difference, though, between the poem and the experience is that Aurelia, who's absent from the poem, witnessed the bonfire. Sylvia was turning her normal habits upside down. Only once before had she stripped herself emotionally naked in her mother's presence, and that was in 1953, when she suggested a suicide pact: "Let's die together." In the nine years since then, Sylvia had played the role of dutiful and grateful daughter. If she hadn't been quite consistent in her behavior, she had in her letters, while in verse she had never yet unleashed as much aggression against Aurelia as she did in the novel, which she never intended to publish under her own name. But what Sylvia now burned, besides the letters, was the persona of the loving, dutiful daughter. Signing her letters with her childhood nickname, "Sivvy," she had been trying to preserve an identity that had started in the nursery. The bonfire and the poem constitute a turning point in the development of her art and in two relationships—with her mother and with death—which had always been intertwined, but never so tightly.

In lighting the bonfire she lit a fuse that would burn slowly toward the Ariel poems and toward suicide. At first the grief was so overpowering that she wrote little; in July she produced only three poems, all aimed at Assia: "The Other," "Words heard, by accident, over the phone" and "Poppies in July." What was the bad smell in her handbag? The knitting was hooking itself to itself, like sticky sweets. Her adulteries were sulfurous, her fornications circling a womb made of marble. It would be hard to clean the telephone table after her words had plopped like mud out of the many-holed earpiece, the muck-funnel. In "Poppies in July" Assia's presence can be felt only indirectly, but it seems to be contributing to the appearance of the poppies, which are like little hell flames, wrinkly and clear red, or like the skin of a bloodied mouth.

At this time, journeying between Devon and London, between Sylvia and Assia, Ted Hughes was under great emotional strain. Though temperamentally disinclined to write autobiographically either in verse or prose, some of his feelings may have filtered into a play for the BBC's Third Programme, *Difficulties of a Bridegroom*. Sullivan is driving toward London, whistling and thinking about the beautiful, seductive, sensual woman he's going to meet. Somehow she managed to reach "the secret switch" in his brain. In his fantasy she says he can have her, but demands a top-floor flat in Soho, a red convertible Cadillac and an unlimited allowance for clothes and sundries. If she's to own him, she says, he must describe to her every least girl he has so much as kissed.

When he sees a hare in the road, he accelerates, wanting to kill it. As he accuses himself of brutality, he has the illusion that distant wedding bells are ringing. He picks up the dead hare and, after arriving in London, sells it for five shillings to buy flowers for the irresistible woman. If Sylvia, who was a keen listener to the Third Programme, heard the play, she would have been forcefully reminded of Assia by the character's provocative way of talking and by the line "Here she comes, her perfumes before her." Hughes, as she knew, was strongly aware of the scent Assia used. At the same time, Sylvia identified with the hare that the husband wanted to kill. She told Elizabeth Compton that Hughes had talked to her about a dream of his in which he deliberately killed a hare.[6] The play was repeated on Saturday, February 9, two days before Sylvia committed suicide, but she's more likely to have tuned in to the first broadcast.

Hughes's ambivalence toward Aurelia was almost as extreme as Sylvia's. Afterward he gave his mother-in-law's presence at Court Green as one of his reasons for moving out, but that summer he pressed her to stay on until August 4, the day she was due to leave for the States. Though Sylvia seemed to have some irrational faith in her mother as someone who could heal the rift, Aurelia knew she could do nothing useful. She moved out, and from July 16 stayed with the midwife, Winifred Davies. But on July 26 Aurelia looked after the children while Sylvia and Hughes went to Bangor in North Wales, where they were to give a joint reading organized by the editors of *Critical Quarterly*.

A few weeks later they put on a less public performance, behaving as if nothing had gone wrong when Mrs. Prouty and her sister-in-law arrived in London and stayed at the Connaught Hotel. Hughes and Sylvia, who accepted an invitation to see *The Mousetrap* with them, were treated to cocktails, dinner and overnight accommodation at the hotel, which Sylvia called the loveliest she had ever stayed in.[7] Soon after Aurelia left, on August 4, Sylvia started her riding lessons, on a gentle, reddish-brown horse called Ariel, not at all like "God's lioness," which is what she's called in the poem.

On August 27, in a letter to Aurelia, Sylvia announced her intention to get a legal separation from Hughes. She didn't believe in divorce, she said, but couldn't bear the degradation and agony that were interfering with her health, her sleep and her work. She and Hughes apparently agreed to a trial separation of about six months from November. Hughes wanted to spend time in Spain, presumably with Assia; Sylvia wanted to spend the winter, or part of it, in Ireland.

The poet Richard Murphy lived in Cleggan, a small village on the Connemara coast, where he earned a living by taking tourists sailing and fishing in a renovated Galway fishing boat. When he invited Hughes and Sylvia to stay, they accepted. Possibly Hughes's main reason for going was to help Sylvia find a cottage.[8]

Traveling by train and ferry, they left Devon on September 11, leaving the children with a nanny from an agency. Two days later, when Murphy took them in his boat to Inishbofin, Sylvia "lay prone on the foredeck," he says, "leaning out over the prow like a triumphal figurehead, inhaling the sea air ecstatically."[9] The next morning, he drove them to Yeats's Tower at Ballylee and Lady Gregory's Coole Park. At Coole Sylvia egged Hughes on to climb the spiked iron fence and carve his initials in the copper beech tree next to those of Yeats. His deserved to be there, she said, more than those of other poets who had left their mark. They had taken with them Seamus, the fifteen-year-old boy who helped Murphy sail the boat, and at Ballylee, wanting to steal apples from a tree Yeats had planted, Hughes and Sylvia made Seamus shake the branches. They then gathered over two bushels.

When she talked to Murphy about separation, he argued that it was a cruel alternative to divorce. His wife had threatened suicide, and his marriage had begun to break up five years earlier, after she had been unfaithful. Sylvia was so enthusiastic about Connemara that she offered to rent the cottage, which he let to tourists who chartered his boat, and to let him stay in it. Taking this to mean she had designs on him, he quickly rejected the idea. At dinner the same evening, when he felt her leg rubbing against his under the table, his suspicion seemed to be confirmed. When he introduced her to Kitty Marriott, a woman who had a house only a mile and a half from Cleggan, Sylvia immediately made a rental agreement with her, starting on November 1.

The poet Thomas Kinsella came to spend the evening at the cottage, and took part with Sylvia and Hughes in a session at the Ouija board, which the two men continued long after Sylvia—and, later, Murphy—had gone to bed. The next day, a Sunday, Murphy had to go out in the morning, and when he came back, he found Sylvia alone in the cottage. Without thanking him or saying good-bye, Hughes had left to go fishing with a painter in County Clare. Sylvia said she had her return ticket and would meet Hughes in the train on Wednesday. He had previously walked out on her in this way, she said, but Murphy suspected she had got rid of Hughes in order to be alone with him. Not wanting an affair with her and eager to avoid gossip in the village, he asked her to leave the next day with Kinsella. She was furious, and wrote to him from Devon, canceling the invitation for him to stay there. She also canceled the rental agreement with Mrs. Marriott.[10]

Informed of the breakup with Hughes, Ruth Beuscher wrote to Sylvia twice in September, advising her to sue for divorce. This tallied with the advice she was getting from her mother and from Mrs. Prouty.[11] On September 24 she still wanted only a legal separation,[12] but a day after, when she went to see a lawyer in London, she decided to sue for divorce. She wrote to Aurelia again the next day, explaining that a wife was allowed a third of her husband's income, but that litigation would be protracted and expensive if he didn't pay up. At the beginning of October she wrote a friendlier letter to Murphy saying he had been right: divorce was liberating.[13] A letter of October 9 to Aurelia confirms that she had decided on divorce.[14]

Sylvia insisted—probably at the end of September—that Hughes should move out of the house. If she hadn't, he'd almost certainly have stayed on much longer. She was soon aware how much difference his absence would make to the children. "For a Fatherless Son" is dated September 26. Absence will grow beside the child like a colorless tree, a death tree. But she took comfort from having her nose grabbed by the little boy and from his amused reaction when she stared into the features that seemed to mirror her own.

The poem she completed four days later, "A Birthday Present," was closer to being suicidal. The present waiting for her is either a veiled person or a wrapped thing, but being alive only by accident after trying to kill herself, she doesn't especially want a present. Perhaps they should sit down, the giver and she, on either side of the gift, and eat their last supper. Hating the uncertainty, she would prefer to have the gift unwrapped. The veils are killing her days, like armies of carbon monoxide clouds. But the poison is sweet. Inhaling it, she fills her veins with invisible particles that tick the years off her life. If death is under the veils, she will admire its deep gravity. The knife that enters will be as clean and pure as a baby's cry, and the universe will slide away from her.

This is the first of twenty-six poems she completed in thirty days, from September 30 to October 29. She was taking sleeping pills every night, but when the effect wore off at about five in the morning, she couldn't get back to sleep. One of the turning points in her writing career came during a three-hour conversation with Winifred Davies, the invaluable midwife, who suggested she should use the early morning wakefulness on her new novel. She did write three pages of it in the early morning of September 28.[15] On most days the edge of her savage indignation was too sharp for her to concentrate on constructing plot and writing narrative prose, though she could pour out emotion in the verse she was now creating so fluently. Alone in the big house with the children, she found it hard to get through the day. She drank a lot of coffee as soon as she woke up, but she was too depressed to feel hungry. She made herself eat by sitting down with Frieda at mealtimes. She made tea in the nursery at four, and she tried to see the Comptons or other friends every day, either visiting them or inviting them to the house.[16]

The uncompromising vindictiveness of the October poems is sometimes partially redeemed—and always elegantly veneered—by knowing playfulness, technical mastery and rhythmic subtlety. Some of the aggression is aimed at Hughes and Assia, much of it at herself, some at her mother. There's a reference in "The Tour" to coal gas, while "Poppies in October" mentions carbon monoxide. In "Ariel" the suicidal dew is at one with the drive into the rising sun, the "cauldron of morning." The speaker in "Lady Lazarus" is only thirty but has to make a suicide attempt every ten years. Sylvia must already have had her end in mind, but she may not yet have made a firm decision about using the escape route which for ten years had been available as the one remedy that couldn't fail.

These poems also contain references to electroconvulsive therapy, and one of the questions posed in "The Detective" suggests that the death he's investigating was rooted in this experience, though there may also be oblique allusions to Hughes's affair with Assia in some of the phrases. Lies shake out their moist silks in a woman's garden, and deceits are tacked up in a kitchen like family photographs.

The sequence of poems about beekeeping shows how defenseless Sylvia now felt in the village. Throughout more than six years of marriage she'd been protected by Hughes's powerful and imposing presence. It wasn't only at Yaddo that she tended to walk slightly behind him. Now she was the one who had to protect infants even more vulnerable than she was. In "The Bee Meeting," wearing only a sleeveless summer dress, she feels unloved and naked as a chicken neck, while potentially hostile villagers, wearing protective clothes and masks, nod their square black heads like knights in visors. Red flowers, which, thanks to the bees, will eventually be edible, remind her of blood clots. She can't run away but she's scared. She's a magician's girl who mustn't flinch even if she doesn't trust the device meant to save her from being sawn in half, and the long white box in the grove seems to confirm her fears that someone is going to be sacrificed.

In "Stings" she dissociates herself from the bees who pay with their lives for the aggression of a sting. She has a self to recover, a queen, and she visualizes herself as alive and dead at the same time, a queen bee with glass wings and a lion-red body, flying like a comet above the hive that killed her.

The idea that Hughes had been a replacement for her father is never suggested more forcefully or explicitly than in "Daddy," where the mask, the girl with an Electra complex, soon becomes transparent. After being stuck together with glue—repaired after the suicide attempt which had been intended to put her in contact with her dead father—she made a model of him, going through the wedding ceremony with a sadistic man who wore black and had "a Meinkampf look." He was a vampire who claimed to be her father and drank her blood for seven years. There is even a mention of the black telephone which is "off at the root": voices can no longer "worm through." But this man is now dead, and the villagers, who never liked him, are dancing and stamping on him.

"Daddy" was written on October 12, to be followed four days later by a spitefully abusive attack on Aurelia in "Medusa." Medusa was one of the three Gorgon sisters who had snakes on their head instead of hair; their gaze was enough to turn people into stone. But the name Medusa is also used, as Aurelia knew, for a species of jellyfish, *aurela*. In the poem the medusa is described as an old barnacled umbilicus, Atlantic cable, keeping itself, apparently, in a state of miraculous repair. (Aurelia was fifty-six, and Sylvia still didn't know about the gastrectomy.) The medusa was always there, tremulous breath "at the end of my line," which has the double meaning of fishing line and telephone line. The poem goes on to describe her as dazzling and grateful, touching and sucking, a fat red placenta which paralyzes the kicking lovers. She's an eely tentacle, whose wishes, green as eunuchs, hiss at the speaker's sins.

In the letter she wrote to Aurelia the same day, Sylvia was exuberant. Hughes had agreed to the divorce, and she was now a "famous poetess." She'd been mentioned in the *Listener*, alongside Marianne Moore and the Brontës, as one of the half-dozen women who would survive. She described herself as joyous, happier than she had been for a long time. The poems she was now writing were terrific, as if domesticity had choked her.[17] Ten days later she made almost the same point in a letter to Ruth Fainlight, Alan Sillitoe's wife; she had been effectively gagged by domestic happiness, but now she was producing "free stuff" that had been locked in her for years. Hughes had moved out, and the muse had moved in.[18] She had consistently said that if she married a poet, she would want him to be more successful than she was, and during the marriage, Hughes, though he'd helped her enormously, may also have unintentionally been an inhibiting influence. There's no evidence to suggest she had ever felt she was being held back by fear of outpacing him, but now, finally free, she was writing more aggressively and incisively than ever before.

Hughes is the object of the attack in "The Jailer," which voices a wife's resentment against her husband. The edge is strongly personal, even if the details don't correspond with the biographical facts. The poem elaborates a fiction in which the husband has been torturing the wife with his cigarettes, pretending she is a negress with pink paws. His breakfast plate is greased with sweat she has exuded overnight. For seven hours she has been drugged and raped, knocked out of her right mind into a sack where she at last relaxes, the inspiration of his wet dreams. He hurts her with his deceitfulness and his pretense of forgetfulness. She wishes him to be dead or absent.

The imagery in "Lesbos" (October 18) is equally violent, though the man is absent. The fluorescent light winces on and off like a migraine; the smiling baby is like a fat snail; the other child is like a little unstrung puppet. The man has put her kittens into a sort of cement well, where they puke and crap and cry, out of her earshot. Though still doped by her last sleeping pill, the speaker knows there's a stink of fat and baby crap.

In her depressed state, Sylvia was unable to shake off a flu that kept her temperature permanently high. She had lost twenty pounds over the summer. Nancy Axworthy had left, and Sylvia was so desperate for help in the house that she pleaded with

Aurelia to sound out Warren's new wife, Margaret. Would she come to England for a couple of months? Instead, Aurelia sent a telegram to Winifred Davies, offering to pay the salary if she could find someone to help Sylvia. The ever-helpful midwife found Susan O'Neill-Roe, a local nurse of twenty-two, who was to start work at the Great Ormond Street children's hospital in mid-December but would be free in the interim to work for Sylvia. She came in every day from eight-thirty in the morning till six at night. The children liked her, and with someone to share the burden of looking after them, Sylvia was not only under less pressure, she was also free to visit London. When she wanted to stay there overnight, the Macedos put her up and Susan slept at Court Green with the children.

Sylvia's high temperature continued mysteriously, but she made use of it in "Fever 103°." She's astoundingly hot, glowing like a camellia. Too pure for anyone, she floats high into the air, rising like pure acetylene and her selves dissolving, like "old whore petticoats" as she ascends to Paradise.

On her trips to London Sylvia took to dropping in on Alvarez, who had recently been divorced from his first wife. He had published Sylvia's poem "Crossing the Water" in the *Observer* at the end of September, and not long afterward she arrived unannounced, "smartly dressed, determinedly bright and cheerful." She said she had been passing by. Hughes had stayed in Alvarez's spare room for a few nights after he moved out of Court Green, and one of Alvarez's first thoughts was that Sylvia had come to look for signs of her husband's presence.

When Sylvia said she had brought new poems with her and pulled a sheaf of paper out of her shoulder bag, Alvarez held out his hand, expecting her to hand them over, but she insisted on reading to him. These were poems that had to be *heard*. She read "Berck-Plage" fast, "in a hard, slightly nasal accent, rapping it out as if she were angry." He had "a vague impression of something injurious and slightly obscene," but didn't understand much. She read six or eight poems. Each time she came to London, she dropped in on him, always with a batch of poems to read. On one of these visits, saying she wanted him to hear some light verse, she read "Daddy" and "Lady Lazarus." Her voice, as she read, "was hot and full of venom... the things seemed to be not so much poetry as assault and battery." But he recognized that they were entirely successful.[19]

When he asked why she was in town, she replied "with a kind of polished cheerfulness" that she was apartment hunting.[20] On October 12, before Susan came, Sylvia had already written to Warren and his wife about wanting an apartment in London, where she would be able to earn money from free-lance writing and broadcasting. She also relished the idea of running a salon for a circle of intellectual friends. In this fantasy she may have been giving Alvarez a costarring role, imagining that through him she would meet important writers, artists and intellectuals. He was the editor of a well-received anthology published by Penguin, *The New Poetry*. As a critic he was so influential at this time that she described him as "*the* opinion-maker in poetry over here."

She needed a champion, or thought she did, and she had jumped far too quickly to the conclusion that Murphy was the man. Perhaps Alvarez, despite his shortness, was a better candidate for the role, and she began to take more trouble over her appearance. She found a cheap local hairdresser, the wife of Dr. Webb, the local doctor, who cut her bangs high on top, curling down around the ears, leaving her long hair in a bun at the back.[21] And after a long period of wearing only clothes bought before the two pregnancies, she began to spend money on new outfits. At the Jaeger shop in Exeter she chose a camel-hair suit with a matching sweater, a red skirt, a green cardigan, a blue tweed skirt and a black sweater; at St. Ives she bought an enameled necklace and pewter jewelry.[22]

She had a lot in common with Alvarez. He had attempted suicide, which made it easier to confide in him. Telling him about a June incident in which she drove her car off the road, she described it as a suicide attempt. He was a poet in his own right, and he read poems to her. She told him she liked his work. In his introduction to *The New Poetry* he had attacked the restraint of contemporary English verse, the nervous gentility and the avoidance of negative emotions. The only American poets he had included were Robert Lowell and John Berryman, but Sylvia couldn't take offense at being left out when he said she was the only woman he had taken seriously as a poet since Emily Dickinson.[23] In later editions he included her. Already, he was more responsive than anyone else to her work, and, like Hughes, he could make constructive suggestions. She cut a line from "Lady Lazarus" because he criticized it, thinking she had put it in for the sake of an extra rhyme and as a gratuitous reference to the Japanese victims of the first atom bombs. [24]

The love poem dated November 11, "Letter in November," was probably written with him in mind, and she sent him a copy with a rose petal enclosed. After the bitter savagery of the October poems, the change of mood is startling. The speaker feels cushioned by the delectable soft green in the air, and as her Wellingtons squelch through the "beautiful red" she feels "stupidly" happy. She wanted to dedicate the poem "Ariel" to him, and when he praised it as the best thing she had done, she sent him a manuscript copy illuminated with a hand-drawn flower. [25]

Just after Susan had started working for her, Sylvia had an accident in the kitchen, cutting off the tip of her thumb. She went to Dr. Webb, who not only failed to stick it on again, but didn't even take off the bandage to inspect the damage. She immediately turned the experience into a poem, which is reminiscent of the one she had written about her leg when it was broken and in a cast after the skiing accident in 1953. Again a part of herself had become almost unrecognizable, and she could describe her thumb as if it were an object. The tip was still attached to the thumb by a sort of skin hinge, a dead white flap, while the flow of blood made her think of redcoat soldiers running out of a gap, and the stump resembled a trepanned veteran. But she could also address it as "dirty girl."

On November 4 she went to meet Hughes in London, where he helped her to look for an apartment, but they found nothing suitable. She made another trip to London a few days later to consult Dr. Horder about her thumb, which was beginning to look deformed and to smell dangerously bad. His office is close to the corner of Regent's Park Road and Fitzroy Road. The fact that Yeats once lived there had been part of the road's attraction in 1960, when she had tried to persuade Hughes they ought to buy Number Forty-one. Yeats's house, Number Twenty-three, has a blue plaque on it, and walking past it on her way back from the doctor she saw contractors working on it, and a real estate agent's sign saying FLATS TO LET. The contractors let her in. The top part of the house was a maisonette with three bedrooms on the upper floor, a sitting room, kitchen and bathroom on the lower floor and a balcony garden. Sylvia hurried to the real estate agent and immediately started negotiating for a five-year lease. Back in

Devon, when she half playfully opened a volume of Yeats at random in the hope of receiving a personal message, she hit on the sentence: "Get wine and food to give you strength and courage and I will get the house ready."

Partly because of the arrangements she had to make in preparation for the move, and partly perhaps because she no longer felt an urgent need to vent her spleen, she wrote less poetry in November. Death is still an obsessive theme, but the emphasis is on survival. In "Getting There," which is dated November 6, she has to cross Russia on a nightmarish train, dragging her body through the straw of the boxcars. She passes wounded men, nurses in nunlike veils, piles of amputated limbs, but in the end she emerges from the black car of Lethe pure and intact, stepping out from the skin of old bandages, boredoms and old faces. But she resumed the attack on Hughes and Assia in such poems as "Gulliver" (November 6), "The Fearful" (November 16) and "Childless Woman" (December 1). Imprisoned by Lilliputian spidermen who hate him, the man is on his back, entwined in silken bribes. "The Fearful" harks back to the telephone conversation in which the woman had said she was a man, and, like "Childless Woman," it comments abrasively on Assia's barrenness. She detests the idea of a baby, which would steal cells and beauty from her.

The October poems had been desperate. Sylvia had been lonely and pessimistic, unable to see how she could escape from isolation at Court Green. Now she was looking forward to a new life in Yeats's house.

❧ 15 ❧

Cul-de-sac

On December 12, 1962, Sylvia moved out of Court Green, driving to London with Susan and the two children. She needed all her strength and courage; Neither Yeats nor anyone else had got the house ready. The gas stove hadn't been installed or the electricity connected. Both were fixed later in the day, but she still had no telephone, and as in Court Green, she would have to live without central heating. The flat was still undecorated and only sparsely furnished. But this time she would have to do all the work single-handed. Many of the local shopkeepers remembered her, but she didn't have many friends in London, and of the few she had, the Sillitoes were away. Nor had she been getting encouraging reactions to her new poems: although she'd been sending them out, most were being rejected.

Her relationship with her downstairs neighbour, Trevor Thomas, was uneasy. When Sylvia arrived, he hadn't yet moved into the ground-floor apartment, and because the real estate agents had broken their promise to keep the upstairs maisonette for him, he was suspicious that she might have gained possession of it by unfair means. She met him on the evening of her first day in London, when, in her nervous excitement, she locked herself out of the maisonette while the children were inside. He couldn't help her, and didn't sympathize.

After Thomas moved in, about a week later, they had altercations whenever they met in the hallway. When she left her bulky old-fashioned pram in the entrance passage, he had trouble squeezing past, but she reacted to his protests as if he were being

187

unreasonable. She had to have a pram for the children. How could she wheel it up and down the stairs each time she came in and went out?

Instead of buying a garbage can, she went on using his, which regularly overflowed. She struck him as selfish and humorless: after her death he had no memory of hearing her laugh or seeing her smile. She asked for help if she had to go out and needed someone to listen out for her children, but he was fearful of becoming friendly. In the process of divorcing his wife, and wanting to keep "care and control" of their two sons, Thomas took care not to compromise himself.

Sylvia's most urgent problem was to find an au pair. With nobody to help her with either the children or the work to be done on the maisonette, she put herself under constant strain. With prose pieces to write for the BBC and for *Punch*, she failed to keep up with the domestic schedule she set herself. She started using the part-time maid who worked for Trevor Thomas, but when they found out the woman was stealing, they both fired her.

Sylvia still used a weekly calendar pad to list jobs that had to be done. At the top of the page for December 23–29, 1962, she noted three painting jobs: she intended to paint three bureaus, the floor of the au pair's room and the downstairs hall. On Sunday, December 23, she wanted to paint the bureau, do the ironing, make some pancakes and bake banana bread, but she postponed the first three jobs till Christmas Eve, when she also needed to go shopping, wash her hair and wash the kitchen floor. On Christmas Day she was invited to lunch with the Macedos, but the bureaus were still unpainted, and her note for December 25 reminds her to do that during the day as well as painting the au pair's room and the hall.

At about six o'clock in the evening on December 24, she invited Alvarez to dinner. Only someone as lonely as she was would have been free to accept, but he came for a drink on his way to dinner with friends. She struck him as having driven herself much closer to the verge of insanity. Her vitality and her resistance had been eroded; she even looked different. Her hair was loose, hanging to her waist "like a tent, giving her pale face and gaunt figure a curiously desolate air." When she walked in front of him down the hall passage and up the stairs, her hair "gave off a strong smell— sharp as an animal's."

The flat was bare and very cold. The walls were freshly painted white, but there were no carpets and only rush matting on the floor. The makeshift decoration only emphasized the desolation of the Christmas ahead of her. "I had never seen her so strained," he writes. They drank wine, and she read some poems, including "Death and Company," a suicidal poem, with references to funeral bells and dead babies. Written on November 16, it was the latest of the poems she'd selected for *Ariel*.

Today we view all this poetry of death in the perspective of her suicide, but until she killed herself, it had a different meaning. When she read it to Alvarez, he couldn't fail to notice how the technical mastery gave an air of emotional detachment to the statements she was making. She had talked about suicide "with a wry detachment, and without any mention of the drama or suffering of the act." There was seomthing of the same detachment and control in her writing, and according to him, when she read the poems, there was neither hysteria in her voice, nor any appeal for sympathy. Yet she had been writing about what she might do to herself and to the children. Suspended weightlessly in the poems and in the act of reading them was an appeal for help, which doesn't mean she was expecting to get it, or that anyone could have given as much as she needed. Suicide is an impossible appeal for unavailable help.

When Alvarez left the bleak maisonette at about eight o'clock, it was with the feeling, he says, of having let her down by refusing to accept responsibilities he didn't want. He was too depressed, anyway, after the breakup of his marriage, to cope with them. However much he admired her poetry, he can't be blamed for refusing to give up a major part of his life to looking after a demanding woman he didn't love. But irrationally, after her death, he felt uncomfortable enough to destroy all the letters she had written to him.[1]

On December 26 it began to snow. This was the first snow she had seen in England, and she was pleased because it reminded her of thick snow during her Massachusetts childhood, and of the fun she had had with snowball fights and sledding. But the cold maisonette became colder, and the snow went on falling. She expected to see snowplows in the street, but London was unaccustomed to deep snow, and unprepared for it. By New Year's, parked cars were thickly blanketed.

Without liking Thomas, she kept turning to him for help. He was there, and she had no one else. She summoned him by opening the front door of the house to ring his bell and then waiting outside the door of his flat. One day, when traffic was moving slowly over the rutted snow, he found her standing there with a heavy, old-fashioned handle for cranking a car. The engine wouldn't start. Would he help her? He refused. He wasn't used to cranking cars, and he was afraid he might break his thumb or his wrist. When she became agitated—she was due to make a recording for the BBC—he said she could use his telephone. She was told a car would be sent for her, and while she was waiting for it in his living room, she told him how she just loved all his old English things.

When she again locked herself out, one of his sons, Giles, helped her by clambering across the glass roof to her half-open kitchen window. Thomas afterward grumbled that she was a nuisance, but the boy said: "Can't you see, Daddy? She's very sad. It's in her eyes."

London's generating system was vulnerable to the freeze, and when power cuts started, she appeared at his door in her bathrobe, muffled up with scarves, looking frightened and tearful. All her lights had gone out and so had her fire. The children were crying. He explained what power cuts were, filled two hot water bottles for her, gave her candles and advised her to make hot drinks for the children.

Another day she appeared at his door and tearfully complained that her bath was half full of dirty water with tea leaves in it. When he went up to inspect it, he thought she had blocked the pipe by emptying tea leaves down the kitchen sink. But the freshly painted ceiling was oozing drops of liquid, and the wallpaper was bulging at the seams. Eventually she called the real estate agent from a telephone booth with a black puddle on the floor. So many pipes were bursting all over London that plumbers were in enormous demand, but the agent sent workmen, who found that snow was leaking through the roof. The waste pipe was frozen, and not being properly insulated, the pipes for the inflow of water had frozen too.

Standpipes with taps were soon being installed in the streets to provide drinking water for the many people who were in the same predicament. Frieda, who was now two years and nine months old, and Nick, who was not quite twelve months, had both caught colds which developed into flu, and Sylvia followed suit. Another neighbor gave her night lights, but the lonely ordeal continued.

Six years before, the coldness of the Cambridge winter had been profoundly depressing, although Hughes had been there to look after her, and she'd had neither children nor frozen pipes. Incomparably worse, the cold spell of 1963 lasted for about a month.[2]

At the end of January, after the thaw had begun, she went to a party at the house of her friends Jillian and Gerry Becker. Douglas Cleverdon, who had directed *Difficulties of a Bridegroom*, arrived with Richard Murphy, who reports that Sylvia's "face looked feverish, and she seemed ecstatic." She seemed to bear him no grudge and said she was glad to be in London.[3] Doris Lessing, who met her at about this time, noticed an "incandescent desperation" in her.[4]

In later January or early February, when she finally got a German au pair, Sylvia was free to work in the mornings and go out sometimes in the evening, but she found the girl difficult to handle. She wrote little verse during December and January, but in a final flurry of creativity between January 28 and February 5, she devised a new ending for a poem written in early December and produced ten new poems—less turbulent, more resigned than the Devon poems, more stoically suicidal.

"Sheep in Fog" draws a sad contrast between the white hills and the blackening morning. At the end she feels afraid the distant fields will admit her to a starless, fatherless heaven, a dark water. "Munich Mannequins," written the same day, goes back to the theme of childlessness. With Assia, no doubt, in mind, Sylvia characterizes perfection as incompatible with childbirth. Like shop-window mannequins, naked and bald, the two lovers want no idols but themselves. "Totem" equates the future with a long railway track that will be killed by the engine. Human existence is circular; no terminus is to be found in this blood-hot personal world, only suitcases from which the same self is unfolded like a worn suit with tickets, folding mirrors, ideas and wishes in its pockets.

Her frustrated yearning for domestic happiness is tenderly expressed in "Child," which juxtaposes darkness and lamentation with beautiful young eyes which ought to be feasted on colors and ducks. In "Paralytic" she identifies first with the magnolia tree, which asks nothing from life, and then, as all desires fall away from her, with a buddha. Like a paralytic, she feels as cut off from the forces that govern her movements as she is from nurses in starched uniforms and from acquaintances who offer perfunctory sympathy.

"Mystic" reaffirms the conviction that life has lost its significance: meaning has leaked out of the molecules. There is no remedy once one has been seized up and used utterly. Rodent faces invalidate the equation of bread with Christ's flesh, and the sea has no memory of the miracle he performed by walking on it.

It seems likely she did not decide until Sunday afternoon that she would do it during the night. In 1953 seven weeks had elapsed between the decision and the action, but in 1963, though she could be seen as acting on a decision taken ten years earlier, the interval seems to have been shorter. The last three poems, written on Monday, February 4, and Tuesday, February 5, suggest she had recently passed the death sentence on herself, but it is impossible to be sure whether writing the poems helped her toward the decision.

In some ways they are reminiscent of Genet's 1957 play *The Balcony*, in which every living element seems to lust after its own absence, its replacement by an image, a monument, a costume. To the Chief of Police nothing matters so much as to feature in other men's fantasies. He wants his image to detach itself from him. His function is weighing him down, but in the brothel, the palace of symbols where nothing is real, his image will "bask in the terrible sunshine of pleasure and death." Another client discards a bowler hat and gloves to dress in a general's cocked hat and resplendent uniform. Admiring his image in the mirror, he prides himself on being there in his pure appearance, with nothing contingent in tow. He daydreams of being "close to death...where I shall be nothing, but reflected *ad infinitum* in these mirrors, merely an image."

For Sylvia Plath the fantasy had nothing to do with a resplendent costume. The idea of her naked body was enough, but nine years earlier, Nancy Hunter had noticed her tendency to engineer crises in her life for the sake of the creative stimulation they gave her. Many writers have done this. Strindberg created experiences and pressured situations in order to write about them; he became almost suicidal when fiction and reality were interpenetrating so deeply that he was scared of finding out which was which. In the first week of February the dead Sylvia Plath was still a fiction in the poetry that Sylvia Plath was writing, but by the end of the second week the poet was dead.

The mask had never been thinner or more transparent than it was in these last poems. In "Contusion" the bruise is the only part of the body that isn't already washed out and colorless, like a pearl. The doom mark is crawling down the wall and the heart closes as the sea slides back. The sheeted mirrors of the final line are unmistakably emblematic of death.

Though less explicitly suicidal, "Balloons" says a reluctant farewell to the children, to the flat, with its straw mats and white walls, to the brightly colored balloons which have been hanging there since the Christmas that was so lacking in brightness.

In the last poem, "Edge," as in "Death and Co.," the implication is that she had been intending to kill the children when she killed herself. The woman is perfected, it says, and her dead body wears the smile of accomplishment, while her bare feet seem to be saying they have come so far, but this is the end. Like little white serpents, the dead children are coiled at her empty breasts, folded back into her body like the petals of a rose that has closed. Sylvia may have changed her mind at the last minute about killing them. And it may be that she was still hoping for a stay of execution. Perhaps she would give herself a reprieve if she had a satisfactory meeting with the man on the Friday night before she died. But the poems suggest she held out little hope, and the edge is the edge of death.

The pressures that made her kill herself came partly from her deep-seated death wish and partly from her immediate circumstances. The poems show that within a week of killing herself she was still capable of thinking with great lucidity, but at the end she was also drugged, exhausted, deeply depressed and confused. No one will ever be able to say with any certainty what was in her mind when she made the decision, or later, when it became irrevocable, but she knew she couldn't go on. She was up against more formidable pressures than the ones that had driven her to attempt suicide in 1953.

Alone with two demanding young children, in an underheated and underfurnished maisonette, she had been living through a ferocious winter which wasn't yet over. It would have been hard to survive the discomfort, the extreme cold, the isolation and the exhaustion even if she hadn't felt so much acrimony against the "scarlet" woman and against the man who had once seemed to be the ideal mate—handsome, almost perfect, the kindest man in the world. Sylvia couldn't know that Assia would emulate her suicide, but she could know her death would be overwhelmingly important to both Assia and Hughes as long as they lived.

Drugs had apparently played no significant role in the depression of 1953—there's no reference to them in her diaries—and it's hard to assess their importance now. Was the balance of her mind upset? Anne Stevenson, author of the biography *Bitter Fame*, has used the phrase "mental handicap"—not in the book but in subsequent newspaper correspondence. According to Dr. Horder there were no symptoms of psychosis, but he also said her changes of moods were "so excessive that a doctor inevitably thinks in terms of brain chemistry." This phrase blurs the difference between organic mental illness and the temporary effects of the pills he had prescribed. These may well have been the cause of the slurred vowels, the faraway look and the seraphic expression. She was obviously exceeding the dosage he had recommended, and the reactions of both Jillian Becker and Alvarez suggest that she was dangerously unbalanced by the drugs.

Her stamina was at its lowest, and the cumulative exhaustion had entered into a deadly alliance with the stimulants, the sedatives and the other medication. For weeks the drugged sleep had probably been little more than a prelude to her early morning stint of feverish writing. If once she had willed herself into having dreams she could take to Ruth Beuscher, she was now dreaming her way toward the next poem. But the writing was strenuously separated from the rest of the day. Once the children woke, she had to be available.

Even if her thinking had been consistently lucid, it would have been harder to sustain her faith in the future than it had been ten years before, when instability had been tolerable only because she could look forward to stable monogamy. Now that she knew what it was like to be happily married, there could have been no question of reverting to the raunchy bachelor life she had led during her late teens and early twenties. However unrealistic she had recently been about Murphy and Alvarez, basing hopes on insufficient knowledge of either man, she was realistic about the impossibility of going backward. Even if her freedom hadn't been restricted by the children, she was too much of a perfectionist to be capable of starting all over again.

Nor was it only in her sexual life that she saw herself as a failure. The woman who had set such high standards of efficiency in everything she did—looking after the children, cooking, housekeeping, writing—was no longer efficient as a mother or as the employer of an au pair. Without domestic help she had no lifeline to survival as a writer. It had been hard to find the German girl and impossible to get along with her. Would Sylvia ever be able to find another girl, or to keep her if she did?

At the same time, she had a strong sense of being alive only by accident. The critic Helen Vendler puts this well. Like the writer Cesare Pavese, Sylvia "continually needed to find reasons *not* to kill herself rather than a reason to do so."[5] Pavese said literature was one form of defense against the attacks of life and silence was the other. "But we must choose that silence for ourselves, not have it imposed on us, not even by death. . . . Those who by their very nature can suffer completely, utterly, have an advantage. This is how we can disarm the power of suffering, make it our own creation, our own choice, submit to it. A justification for suicide." This was written in a 1938 diary. Twelve years later Pavese killed himself.

When Sylvia died, she had had ten bonus years of a life she had rejected when she was twenty. In conversation with friends she sometimes used the word *resurrected*, and in spite of the happiness she had, suffering was the staple of her existence. She was one of those who by their very nature can suffer completely, but she couldn't disarm the power of suffering.

This is not to deny that she had moments of euphoria during the last days of her life. The last poems illuminate the feelings that led to the smile which Thomas described as seraphic, feelings that gave her the same pleasure as a beautiful dream or vision. We think of suicide as an attack on the self, but to fall in love with it is to want it as something you can use, to attack obstacles in the way of peace and harmony and to join yourself with the force which seems to have been working through you. You feel you have been used, and you want to be used more fully. Writing at high speed is like listening to a voice and taking dictation, or working as a medium who lets the spirit take over her voice.

This point can be made in terms of images that appear in poems Sylvia wrote between January 28 and February 1. (Was it then that she made the decision?) "Totem" separates the engine from the track, which can't run away but is being killed or eaten. In the evening the drowned fields are beautiful, but morning light reveals the connection between animal breeding and slaughter-houses. The reference to the aborted hare and the bowl would be impenetrably obscure but for the note which discloses that the same Pyrex bowl had been used for her son's afterbirth and for the cleaned body of a hare.[6] In the poem the bowl links the hare she had eaten with the baby she had borne and with the idea of eating God's flesh. The terminus and the tickets are small details in the perspective of death and circularity. Flies destined to be eaten by the spider are buzzing like blue children.

In "Paralytic" she produces a variation on the theme of the engine and the track by distinguishing between the iron god who lovingly makes her go on breathing and the lungs which are dustbags, reminiscent of the two gray papery bags in "Apprehensions." But how long will the breathing go on? The lines about the rock and the fingers are ambiguous. We don't know whether her mind is a rock with no fingers or a rock her fingers can't grip. She's lying like a dead egg on a world she can't touch. The dead egg suggests miscarriage, while the paradox is another image of circularity, linking death with the nonexistence that comes before birth. Other people have no more reality than photographs. She's beyond their reach. Wants and desires have fallen from her.

In "Tulips," a hospital poem of March 1961, the smiles in the photographs of husband and child were hooks that could catch on to her skin. Now magnolias have claws, while photographs are flat. Photographs are mentioned again in "Gigolo," but they're absent. In this cul-de-sac, where windows are mirrors, there are no rings through the nose, and the smiles of women, which are bright fishhooks, gulp at the bulk of the speaker, the gigolo, who fondles breasts and manipulates female sexuality as a source of cash. The circularity of regeneration (new oysters shrieking in the sea) parallels the circularity of his narcissistic attraction to his own image.

Hooks feature again in "Mystic," proliferating, like unanswerable questions. Depressively, she contrasts the hardy continuity of vegetable existence with the insecurity of the heart that hasn't stopped, yet.

The poetry offers no clues about whether Sylvia found out that Assia had become pregnant. A few weeks after Sylvia died, Assia had an abortion. In the vindictive poetry she wrote during December, Sylvia had been trying to cheer herself up by commenting on her rival's sterility. In the poem "Childless Woman," the speaker exults over a barren womb that rattles its pod, while the moon had nowhere to go. It would have been in character for Assia, who was not only unscrupulous but felt insecure about her hold over Hughes, to inflict the triumphant news of her pregnancy on her defeated rival, and if she did, this may have been a factor in Sylvia's decision to die.

She didn't kill herself till the early morning of Monday, February 11, but there may have been as many stages in the decision as there had been in the suicide attempt of 1953, when she made up her mind to kill herself without knowing when. Even when she'd given herself a deadline, the decision still hadn't become irrevocable, and even when she broke the lock on the steel case where her mother kept the bottle of sleeping tablets, it still wasn't inevitable that Sylvia would swallow them.

In February 1963, it seems likely she didn't decide until the afternoon of Sunday the tenth that she'd do it during the night. During her four days with the Beckers, their assumption was that she'd stay over Sunday night, returning in time to meet the nurse when she arrived on Monday morning. It's impossible to be certain when she made up her mind to return to the maisonette early on Sunday evening. We can't even be sure that she knew then she was going to kill herself that night. Throughout the conversation with Gerry Becker she was lucid and was talking about the future, and when Dr. Horder called, he was confident that she'd be all right until the morning. But by the time she saw Trevor Thomas she no longer seemed self-possessed. It may be that nothing specific happened to alter her state of mind. It's possible that no one called to see her, that she took no more pills, that the balance was so precarious that without any stimulus the seesaw tilted against her. By the morning she was dead.

In the 1959 story "The Daughters of Blossom Street," the boy who falls down a flight of stairs had been an unheroic stammerer with a bad complexion, but death had crowned him with a martyr's halo. Without wanting a halo, Sylvia may have wanted to create a legend centered on poems which had, as she knew, the stuff of greatness in them. Unlike her Lady Lazarus, she wouldn't find it "easy enough to do it and stay put." Sylvia Plath wouldn't survive the suicide, but "Sylvia Plath" would.

❧ 16 ❧

Posthumous Life

When Sylvia Plath died, she wasn't yet "Sylvia Plath." The name had none of the reverberations it has today. She has gained more of her fame in the years since her death than in the thirty years of her life. She had entertained fantasies of becoming a great writer, but to the people who met her in London during her last three months, she was a depressed single mother, American and alone in the vicious London winter with two children and few friends.

The one book of poems she had published, *The Colossus* (October 1960), had made only a minor impact. In the *London Magazine* Roy Fuller praised her cleverness,[1] while the *Times Literary Supplement* awarded the book only 120 words in which the anonymous reviewer complained that Miss Plath tended to be elusive and private. Reviews of the pseudonymous *The Bell Jar* were appearing just before and just after her death. In the *New Statesman* Robert Taubman was perceptive enough to call it "the first feminine novel in a Salinger mood,"[2] and L. D. Lerner praised it in the *Listener* for making brilliant criticisms of America.[3] But the novel would soon have sunk into oblivion if it hadn't been revealed that Victoria Lucas was the poet Sylvia Plath, who had just committed suicide.

Without mentioning the word *suicide* A. Alvarez paid tribute to her in the *Observer* on February 17, the Sunday after she died. In her last poems, he said, she had made "a totally new breakthrough in modern verse," which had established her "as the most gifted woman poet of our time.... The loss to literature is inestimable." Four of her last poems were printed on the same page as this obituary, and this provoked a flood of letters from readers. The cult of Sylvia Plath had already begun.

It was Alvarez who leaked the secret of the pseudonym. In a broadcast on the Third Programme he said she didn't consider *The Bell Jar* a serious work and that too many people would have been hurt if she had used her own name. But he rated it more highly than she did. He also talked about some of the late poems, which had been appearing in newspapers and magazines— "Daddy," "Lady Lazarus," "Fever 103°" and "Poppies in October." For the first time, a connection was being made between these poems and Esther Greenwood's nervous breakdown. The foundations were being laid for the cult and the legend which had already begun to grow before the poems were published in book form. In the autumn Alvarez's talk was reprinted in *The Review*.[4]

If she had already been a cult figure in February 1963, the suicide would have created a tremendous hullaballoo. Photographs of Ted Hughes and Assia Wevill would have appeared in the papers, and journalists would have probed into all the unsolved mysteries. Had there been a suicide note? What had it said? Who was the man she dressed up for on the last Friday evening of her life? Was it true that a doll had been found on the mantelpiece with pins stuck into it? What happened to the Morris station wagon? Had it reappeared in the street on the night of the suicide? The neighbor who saw it or thought she saw it would have become a star witness. Why had Aurelia Plath renounced her right to see the last letter Sylvia wrote to her? What was it that Hughes didn't want her to see? Who was the man in the dark suit at the inquest? Did she meet someone on the last night of her life?

But it was fairly easy to avoid a scandal. The local newspaper, the *Hampstead and Highgate Express*, reported the death as if it had been the result of a long illness, and there was little coverage in the national papers. The identity of the "other woman" was hushed up, only to be disclosed thirteen years later by Edward Butscher in the first book-length biography of Sylvia. Assia Wevill was then unavailable to answer questions. She too had gassed herself, and killed the daughter she had borne Ted Hughes.

Hughes was left, as Sylvia had possibly intended, in a highly unenviable position. His presence made the children seem more acutely aware of her absence, while other people apparently expected him either to be stricken with remorse or at least give the impression of living more in the past than the present. Although the scandal had been minimal, his parents reprimanded him about the damage he must have done to his reputation, and they disapproved of his living with a woman not yet divorced from her third husband.

After a period in which his Aunt Hilda looked after the children in the Fitzroy Road flat, Assia came to live there with him. He was hesitating about whether to sell Court Green, but Elizabeth and David Compton accepted his invitation to stay there temporarily, and they were in residence when he took Assia to have another look at the house. Elizabeth was asked to show her around it. "Don't you feel like a traitor?" Assia asked when they were on the threshold of Sylvia's room. Elizabeth said she did, and refused to go on with the tour. On another visit to the house, Assia asked for Elizabeth's opinion on whether she and Ted could be happy together. No, said Elizabeth, because Sylvia's ghost would always be between them.[5]

In the immediate aftermath of her death, many people felt her absence as if it were a presence. Assia was trying in several ways to take Sylvia's place. She wanted to make friends with people, such as the Sillitoes, who had befriended Sylvia. Assia was turned down when she asked Dr. Horder to take her on as a patient, but she lived with Ted Hughes at places where Sylvia had lived. They settled together into the Fitzroy Road maisonette, and later, when they moved in together to Court Green, she used things Sylvia had used, including a hand-painted pot on the bedside table.

Hughes was simultaneously under pressure to make decisions about the mass of poetry and prose Sylvia had left behind. His copyright control extended even to letters she had written to other people. In a black spring binder he found the forty-one poems she had collected under the title *Ariel*. They were arranged in a careful sequence. Except for juvenilia, he'd read most of her work, but of the poems written since he moved out, he'd seen only the few published in newspapers and magazines. If he published *Ariel* exactly as she'd left it, it would obviously make a great impact, but it would let readers in on secrets about the breakup of their marriage. Twenty-three of the poems had been written in October 1962, when Sylvia had been using verse to articulate rage, pain and anxiety.

Hughes would have been within his legal rights if he had

stopped the poems from appearing in book form, but her reputation was already growing, and there was increasing demand for
her work in newspapers and magazines. He had several options.
He could delay publication of the collection or publish only part of
it. He could provide commentary on passages that would otherwise be obscure, or he could leave them unexplained.

He used *Ariel* as the title of the book he prepared for publication, but it was substantially different from the *Ariel* Sylvia had
collected. Though it begins in the same way, Hughes's *Ariel* omits
fourteen of her forty-one poems, and he added thirteen, ten of
them written later than the one she'd intended to print last. *The
Bell Jar* is listed as a book "by the same author," but his *Ariel*
contained no introduction, no notes, no explanation of how it
differed from Sylvia's *Ariel*, which remained unpublished, while
only minimal biographical information was given in the blurb on
the dust jacket.

In his introduction to the *Collected Poems* Hughes acknowledges that the 1965 *Ariel* is "a somewhat different volume" from
the one she had planned, incorporating "most of the dozen or so"
poems she had gone on to write after finishing her *Ariel*, although
she regarded these as "the beginnings of a third book." He
"omitted some of the more personally aggressive poems from
1962," and, as he says, he might have omitted one or two more if
she hadn't already published them in magazines. The 1965
volume was, he says, his "compromise" between publishing a
large collection of the verse she'd written since *The Colossus* and
introducing her late work "more cautiously."

The *Ariel* Sylvia intended to publish would, as the critic
Marjorie Perloff pointed out, have had a clear narrative structure.
Opening with the birth of Frieda in "Morning Song," which
begins with the word *Love*, the story moves through Sylvia's
desperation after she found out about the infidelity; at the end
comes a ritual death and a strong hint of rebirth in the five
beekeeping poems written between October 3 and 9. Before
settling on *Ariel* as a title, Sylvia considered calling the collection
"Poem for a Birthday," which would have highlighted the theme of
rebirth. In the last line of the last poem, "Wintering," the bees,
flying, taste the spring.[6] Instead of ending with a hint of rebirth,
the book now ends with a drift toward death.

Perloff is overstating her case when she argues that "the
arrangement of *Ariel 2* implies that Plath's suicide was inevita-

ble... that it was brought on, not by her actual circumstances, but by her essential and seemingly incurable schizophrenia." Insofar as the sequence of poems constitutes a narrative, the two *Ariels* tell different stories. It doesn't, of course, follow that the story of Sylvia's life could have had a different ending.

Ted Hughes made few public statements about Sylvia, and some of his private statements have given rise to controversy. Alvarez wrote an account of the events leading up to her death as the first chapter of his book on suicide, *The Savage God*. In late October 1971, the first part of this chapter was published in the *Observer* under the title "Sylvia Plath's Road to Suicide." But the promised second part didn't appear, because Hughes brought an injunction and tried to discount what Alvarez had written: "I told him only a few details, and what I told him I distorted, as I was trying to work out many explanations for myself. He has misremembered even what I told him." We don't know whether the first distortion occurred in the story told to Alvarez or in this attempt to make his retelling of it seem unreliable, but facts, in either case, were already being tangled with fiction. Ted Hughes also tried—unsuccessfully—to persuade Weidenfeld and Nicolson not to publish the chapter in the book, which came out before Christmas.

Even some of Hughes's commentary on Sylvia's poetry can be misleading. "The Rival," which dates from July 1961, the month of their stay at the Merwins' farmhouse, is described in his 1970 "Notes on the Chronological Order of Sylvia Plath's Poems"[7] as "left over from a series specifically about that woman in the moon, the disquieting muse." In the perspective of the 1962 poems aimed at Assia, it's impossible not to read "The Rival" as a poem aimed at Dido Merwin. Why would the woman in the moon be portrayed as tapping her fingers on a marble tabletop, looking for cigarettes? The poem, which addresses the rival as "you," compares her not with a woman in the moon but with the moon itself. Both leave the impression of something beautiful but annihilating; both are great borrowers of light. Both abase their subjects, but while the moon is ridiculous during daytime, news of Dido's latest dissatisfactions arrives regularly in the mail.

Most of the verse invective against Assia is to be found among the fourteen poems Ted Hughes held back from the British edition of *Ariel*. He published nine of them in 1971—eight in *Winter Trees* and one in *Crossing the Water*—but the other five remained unread until his annotated collection of her poetry appeared in 1981, eighteen years after her death. It contains a list of the poems she had collected for *Ariel*, showing the order she planned to arrange them in, and the notes include excerpts from the commentary she recorded on poems she was reading for the BBC's Third Programme. These explanations and many of Ted Hughes's other notes are illuminating, but some of the most cryptic passages remain obscure because the book provides no information about Assia or the breakup of the marriage.

It looks as though all Sylvia's verse has now been published, but not all her prose. Two volumes of her journals have vanished, ledgers covering the period from late 1959 onward. Ted Hughes says that one of these volumes "disappeared," and that he destroyed the other, which covered the last few months of her life. "I did not want her children to have to read it."[8] Olwyn Hughes, whom he appointed as agent of the Plath estate, has dismissed the later journals as "mostly obsessed with her inner psychic states—private notes, anguishings, records of dreams, self-questionings. It's hard to see how such subjective documents can much help a biographer—other than to confirm her inner turmoil."

There is also some mystery surrounding the unpublished novel, which was provisionally titled *Double Exposure*, and which Sylvia rated more highly than *The Bell Jar*. It was about a marriage that had appeared to be happy but had been flawed with deceit. The author of *Chapters in a Mythology: The Poetry of Sylvia Plath*, Judith Kroll, who saw the outline, reports that the main characters were a married couple, a rival woman and her husband. On October 18, 1962, Sylvia told Aurelia that far from wanting to forget what she'd had to suffer, she intended to "commemorate" it in her next novel.[9] In her letters she wrote as if the novel were almost complete. She told her brother, Warren, that she was ready to finish it the minute she had a live-in nanny.[10] Ted Hughes says she had typed "some 130 pages" of it, but, using the same word, *disappeared*, he explains that these pages had "disappeared somewhere around 1970."[11]

Equally hard to explain is his decision to put Olwyn Hughes in charge of the literary estate. Even if he believed that consciousness is extinguished by death—and his use of Ouija boards suggests that he didn't—it would have been odd to put his dead wife's work in the hands of a woman Sylvia had disliked so strongly. Nor had the dislike been one-sided. To Sylvia's friend Clarissa Roche, Olwyn Hughes said: "You liked her. I thought she was pretty straight poison. God preserve me from mixed up kids." And in a letter of March 1986, Olwyn called her "a famous poetess Grace Kelly dream who descended on Yorkshire. Bloody cheek. A little American student with a couple of poems in magazines." Olwyn admitted that she earned her living from Sylvia, but talking to a dancer from the Heidelberg ballet, she denounced her dead client as "selfish, sick, neurotic, egotistical and a manic-depressive." Olwyn went on working as agent for the Plath estate until 1989, when Faber and Faber, the publishers, took over.

In 1969 Assia Wevill copied Sylvia's suicide, gassing herself, but also killing the child she had borne Ted Hughes. If he was expecting, just before Sylvia died, to be reunited with her in six months, he wasn't yet deeply committed to the relationship with Assia Wevill. But they lived together for longish periods, first in London and then in Devon, though in between she went back to her husband. Assia had the impression that Ted Hughes's parents were putting pressure on him to end the affair, and she seemed deeply depressed when the Comptons paid a visit to Court Green. Hughes invited them in to taste a Russian Christmas cake Assia had made, but she stayed in the shadows of the kitchen and hardly spoke.[12]

She became pregnant again with the child who was born in 1967, Alexandra Tatiana Eloise Wevill, nicknamed Shura. According to Fay Weldon, who was a friend of Assia's, "Sylvia's children moved back to Devon, and Assia looked after them as well as the new baby. Then Ted's parents joined the family. Assia felt they disliked her, and that they blamed her for Sylvia's death, as indeed, increasingly, did Ted; that they used her as a servant, punished her perpetually, and that her situation in the household was untenable. She left with Shura to live in London, hoping that Ted would escape his family's influence and join her, and that they would eventually be married."[13] Alvarez, who didn't like Assia Wevill, formed the same impression at Court Green of how badly she was being treated.

In London, after renting a flat for herself and Shura, she tried to earn money as a translator. Ted had encouraged the idea of translation when an Israeli poet, Yehuda Amichai, visited them in Devon. Why shouldn't Assia use her knowledge of Hebrew to translate some of his verse? Later on, in 1968, she met another Israeli writer, Eda Zoritte, the author of a play about a middle-aged woman who commits suicide after being abandoned by her husband. Identifying with the woman, Assia became enthusiastic about the play and started working on it, but by now she was in a deeply depressed state. Some people in London, blaming her for Sylvia's suicide, were going out of their way to humiliate her both privately and in public places. She had the impression that Ted didn't love Shura, and by now he was involved with another woman, Brenda Hedden.

A blond social worker, married to a drama teacher by whom she had two young daughters, Brenda Hedden had been introduced to Ted Hughes by Elizabeth Compton. She later said: "For the first few years I got to know him as a friend, with my husband. I can understand why his friends now appear to rally round and protect him—we did the same.... I have also realized recently that my involvement was in fact about as long as Sylvia's or Assia's."[14] Flattered by the interest he was taking in her, Brenda Hedden was astonished by his attractiveness to women who hadn't even met him. She remembers that he used to receive propositions in the mail from strangers who claimed to admire his poetry. She met Assia, who struck her as beautiful but fragile and excessively worried about losing her looks as she aged. Brenda's relationship with her husband was deteriorating. After Assia moved out of Court Green, Hughes told Brenda she was his one chance for happiness.

Assia went to live in northwest London and later in Clapham Common. Her life, as Fay Weldon remembers it, revolved around Hughes's visits: "Assia told me that Ted had said they'd live together if only she could find the 'right' house somewhere in the wild North; she would find houses but they'd never be the 'right' one. She was tired. The position of an unmarried woman alone with a child was difficult, practically; and painful, socially. She had, moreover, been sent to Coventry by the London literary community, who saw her as being to blame for Sylvia's suicide.... and she suffered greatly from this. Assia became despondent, feeling Ted would never marry her, and hurt because he was not prepared to at least share with her the responsibility for Sylvia's tragedy.... It seemed to Assia that her only way out was to find a man who would marry her and support her and the child. She went to a dating agency, but felt humiliated and gave up."[15]

According to a friend who had traveled to England on the same boat from Palestine, Assia was threatening to kill herself if Hughes didn't marry her. When she tried to telephone him at Court Green or the Merwins' flat, she wasn't always allowed to speak with him. In March 1969 Assia and Ted planned a trip to Scotland, where they intended to search for a lonely cliff house, but the trip was canceled. Assia had asked Fay Weldon whether she'd be willing to look after Shura if "anything happened" to her, but on March 25 she killed the two-year old child when she gassed herself in the kitchen of their flat.

Ted Hughes's 1970 volume *Crow* is dedicated "In Memory of Assia and Shura." In January 1987, cornered in Boston by Iain Walker, a journalist, who asked whether he was Shura's father, he didn't answer. Back in England, Walker went to St. Catherine's House, where the child's birth certificate names Hughes as her father.

Since the 1963 suicide, many attempts have been made to bring the facts of Sylvia's life authoritatively together, but biographical work was made more difficult by Ted and Olwyn Hughes's control over the copyright. Writers who wanted to quote from the poetry have been required to submit their work for approval, and have been told—so they say—to cut material that reflects unfavorably on the Hughes family. The Hugheses have sometimes litigated and sometimes threatened litigation. When George Melly and Jill Neville, reviewing Lynda Wagner-Martin's 1988 biography of Sylvia on a BBC television program, spoke about censorship and suppression of material by the estate, they were told a letter of complaint would be sent to the director general. After an informal discussion of Sylvia Plath and Ted Hughes on the radio program *Woman's Hour* on February 9, 1988, lawyers acting for the estate asked for a tape of the program, threatening libel action. In 1990 Ted Hughes issued a writ against the eighty-two-year-old Trevor Thomas, who had privately published a memoir giving details of his meetings with Sylvia and of events in the maisonette after the funeral. In the High Court on December 18, 1990, Hughes accepted an apology in settlement of the libel suit.

One of the first serious attempts to discuss the suicide in a book was made by David Holbrook, whose approach was based partly on theories evolved by the psychoanalyst Harry Guntrip. Holbrook completed a book called *Dylan Thomas and Sylvia Plath and the Symbolism of Schizoid Suicide*, but Olwyn Hughes refused him permission to quote from Plath's work. When he protested about being victimized by censorship, she argued in the correspondence columns of the *Times Literary Supplement* that Plath was likely to be "seriously misrepresented" by his book.

In 1969, Lois Ames was appointed the official biographer. She was to have access not only to Sylvia Plath's diaries, notebooks and correspondence, but also to Hughes's own records and memories. The contract with the publisher stipulated that the book was to be delivered by 1975, but though Ms. Ames contributed a long biographical essay to the periodical *Tri-Quarterly*, she subsequently abandoned the book.

The promise of exclusivity to Lois Ames meant that Hughes felt unable to help other writers. In 1972 Edward Butscher asked for Olwyn's help in the critical biography he wanted to write. Later, he says, she asked him to eliminate "any negative reference to the Hughes family," threatening to withhold permission to quote from Plath's work unless he submitted to this demand. Ignoring her request he published the book in 1976.

Sylvia Plath's mother had a similar problem. She had kept her daughter's letters, but couldn't publish them without permission from Hughes, who agreed in principle to give her copyright to the material, but reserved the right of final approval of the text. When the American publisher, Harper and Row, sent him the text Aurelia had prepared, he cut a great deal. Their legal department subsequently restored some of the material, which clearly couldn't be called libelous. Of the 700 letters Aurelia Plath wanted to publish, the volume contains 384, with internal cuts. The last year of Sylvia Plath's life is whittled down to forty-nine pages of text. And in 1982, when Sylvia Plath's *Journals* were published in the United States—there is still no British edition— the material was subjected to a similar process of censorship.

The next large-scale attempt at a biography was made by an American academic, Linda Wagner-Martin, who had difficulties when she approached the Hugheses. According to her account of what happened, Ted Hughes was unwilling to grant an interview or to help with her research, while Olwyn Hughes made it clear that permission to quote from copyrighted material would be granted only if a full text of the book were submitted for approval. In April 1987 Wagner-Martin received an enormous letter— twenty-six single-spaced pages—demanding deletions. She had shown too much sympathy for Plath, given too much prominence to her complaints about Ted, been too ready to believe the evidence of witnesses in Devon who had supported Sylvia when she was left alone with two children. Finally, in 1987 and 1988, different versions of the text were published in America and England. There are at least eleven major discrepancies between the Simon and Schuster text and the one published by Chatto and Windus. In both, quotation from copyrighted material had to be scaled down so that it fell within the category of "fair use." In the preface to the American edition, Wagner-Martin said she would have been given permission to quote at length only if she changed the manuscript to reflect the estate's point of view.

According to Ted Hughes, Wagner-Martin's book had incorporated "sensational fabrications" by two women who claimed to have known Sylvia better than they really did. Olwyn Hughes subsequently complained that Wagner-Martin hadn't been writing a biography but a feminist thesis on "Plath-as-the-libbers-wish-to-iconise-her," and that the book contained about five thousand words of Sylvia's work, including two thousand words of previously unpublished prose, all quoted without permission.

Ted Hughes maintains that he has never tried to stop the facts of Sylvia's life from being known or discouraged friends from giving interviews on the subject, and that he has always recommended people to follow their own instincts when approached by researchers. But it would be impossible for him to comply with all the demands made on him for information about Sylvia's life. His view of the Wagner-Martin book was clear from a letter he wrote to an editor at Chatto and Windus: "She's so insensitive that she's evidently escaped the usual effects of undertaking this particular job—i.e. mental breakdown, neurotic collapse, domestic catastrophe—which in the past have saved us from several travesties of this kind being completed."[16]

The next biography, *Bitter Fame*, was published in 1989. The original intention was that Anne Stevenson should be the sole author, but as she worked on the book, Olwyn Hughes's interventions became more strenuous. In a January 1987 letter to Trevor Thomas, Anne Stevenson wrote: "I have spent ten hours a day for the whole of the Christmas holiday 'de-olwynizing' my book." She had "fought Olwyn every step of the way," she says, "to establish my own tone." In October 1987 she wrote: "The only way to deal with O is to back away and never say a word. The disappearing act I've mastered has got me this far; I hope my luck lasts." It didn't.

In a December letter she claims her book "gives a fair and rounded picture of Sylvia until, in the last two chapters, Olwyn steps in with her insistence on revising out everything and anything that might cast a cold light on her or Ted's behavior." Gradually Olwyn Hughes came to play an increasingly dominant role, and the resultant book contains the acknowledgment: "Ms. Hughes's contributions to the text have made it almost a work of dual authorship."

As Ian Hamilton objected when he reviewed the book in the *Observer*,[17] "With Olwyn Hughes's influence omnipresent, it is hard for us ever to know whose version we are reading—the biographer's or the estate's. . . . Now, it must be wondered, will we ever see a biography of Plath that is not dictated either by feminist dogmatism or by private rage?"

In the *Independent* (March 12, 1988), Ian Thompson revealed that Anne Stevenson had agreed to pay Olwyn forty percent of her British and thirty percent of her American royalties.

After the book was published, Anne Stevenson defended herself at a public meeting held in the Arts Center at Exeter. Not knowing that Carol Hughes, Ted's second wife, was in the audience, Anne Stevenson spoke critically about him and Olwyn for being obstructive. Ms. Stevenson said she was in agreement with many of the reviewers, because the book had been spoiled. Asked why she had put her name to it, she said she had wanted to put material into the public domain.

In the last two chapters of the book it seems that the main effect of Olwyn Hughes's interventions was to exculpate her brother from any share in responsibility for the death. The emphasis had to fall on Sylvia Plath's self-destructiveness, and he was not to look like an accomplice or emerge as evil or destructive or unsympathetic. His infidelity must appear to have been forced on him by Sylvia's pathological and insufferable behavior. According to *Bitter Fame*, Assia told Olwyn Hughes "that she doubted whether the attraction between Ted and herself would ever have developed into an affair, as it later did, had Sylvia behaved differently."

In London Anne Stevenson was guarded and diplomatic in her public statements about the book. In Exeter she was less discreet, and in the United States she was still more outspoken when she gave an interview to *Michigan Today*, saying Olwyn Hughes "did want control" of the book, which "doesn't represent my complete idea of Sylvia Plath." The interviewer, Madeline Strong Diehl, was told about the book's origins. In 1985 Anne Stevenson had been approached by Penguin to write a short book on Sylvia for a series on contemporary women. When Olwyn Hughes read a draft, she suggested it should be expanded into a longer book, saying Anne Stevenson was "the first biographer who picked up something of the terrorist in Sylvia's extreme personality."

In this interview Anne Stevenson talks about the warfare between the "pro-Sylvia witnesses" and "the Hugheses' side," saying she was "repelled by the nastiness of the tactics used by both sides." In working on the last four chapters of the book, she was in conflict with Olwyn, who "would not allow me permission to quote anything if I did not use her contributions verbatim." This made Anne Stevenson eager to have Olwyn's name on the book as co-author, but Olwyn vetoed this, agreeing only to an author's note that acknowledged the importance of her "contributions." "She insisted on writing the author's note herself—on pain of withdrawing permission for the quotations." Since publication "Olwyn has been defending the book vehemently from attacks, but the attacks have mostly been on passages that Olwyn forced me to include."[18]

After *Bitter Fame* was published, Hughes said in a letter to a newspaper: "I do not approve of the book and dissociate myself from any responsibility for the opinions and conclusions contained in it."[19] But according to Anne Stevenson, he did have a significant role in relation to the book. When she contacted him in 1986, he "sent me one very good letter at that time and criticized what I had to say. A very long, seven- or eight-page letter. He then asked me to work with Olwyn, and he saw two complete drafts before publication."[20]

In 1989, after the book was published, a row blew up about the unmarked grave in which Sylvia was buried. Many people were journeying to Heptonstall to visit the grave, but failing to find it. There was a notice in the entrance of the church saying which row her grave was in, but the rows were unnumbered, and there was no name on the grave and no way of identifying it. On April 9 the *Guardian* published a letter from Julia Parnaby and Rachel Wingfield, who complained that their "pilgrimage to the memory of a great woman poet" had ended in frustration.

In a letter to the *Independent* (April 22, 1989), Hughes gave an account of what had happened. Over the years, everything had been stripped from the grave. He had planted daffodil bulbs there, covered the grave with shells and decorated it with pebbles from a North Devon beach, but everything had disappeared. The headstone had to go back to the stonemason's workshop four times after being vandalized in attempts to remove the raised lead lettering spelling out the name Hughes in the inscription "Sylvia Plath Hughes." After the fourth assault, he asked the mason to keep the headstone while he decided what to do next. In November 1988 he visited the mason, intending to order a less vulnerable headstone, but the old one had been repaired, and Hughes told him to set it up. At the beginning of April 1989, it still wasn't there.

After Sylvia's death Hughes published nothing, apart from books for children, until 1967, when his collection *Wodwo* appeared, followed in 1970 by *Crow*. After Assia's suicide he married again; his second wife, Carol, was formerly a nurse. He was appointed poet laureate of England in 1984.

His son, Nick, stayed out of the limelight, becoming a scientist in Alaska, but Frieda, who could read and write before she was four, soon knew she wanted to be a writer and artist. Like her mother, she had accumulated a collection of rejection slips by the age of thirteen. Dyslexia and anorexia helped to stop her from doing well at the school Bedales, where she passed in only one subject when she took her A-Level examination—English. Ever since leaving school, Frieda says, she has supported herself. She soon married, but the marriage was a brief one. She was employed as a waitress, as a tax collector in the Civil Service, where she was promoted to the grade of clerical officer, and worked for several years as sales manager for a greeting card publishing company in Devon. After this she went on to St. Martin's School of Art, and she was still there when, in 1986, at the age of twenty-seven, she published the first of her books for children, *Getting Rid of Edna*, which she dedicated to Olwyn. It's about a witch whose spells are always going wrong.[21]

Frieda knows little about Sylvia. She remembers being aware during childhood of her mother's absence and of the silence that was being maintained about it. Concluding that something painful was being held at bay, she didn't try to break the silence, and twenty-six years after the suicide, Frieda had still read only a handful of her mother's poems.

The most important of the unsolved mysteries hinge on the last few days of Sylvia's life. It would be useful to know more about the contents of her last letter to her mother, and of the suicide note, if there was one. If she saw someone at the house apart from Jerry Becker, Trevor Thomas and Dr. Horder, it would be good to know who it was and what happened. It would also be helpful to establish the identity of the man who appeared at the inquest, and to know more about the movements of the car. But what matters most of all is the triple convergence of the deep-seated death drive, the demoralizing circumstances in which she was living, and the effects of the drugs.

It can be argued that to raise these questions is to trespass on the privacy of people who are still alive, but when the poems were published—first without annotation and then with—personal material was being launched into public orbit. Since then, attempts have been made to define a frontier between what can be discussed and what can't, but no one has been able to arbitrate authoritatively about where this line should be drawn.

The argument of this book has centered on an effort to make new connections between Sylvia Plath's appetite for life and her death wish, between her poetry, her fiction and her private experience, between the diary habit she acquired at the age of eleven and the diarylike writing in her late verse. To do this is to raise the question of how much access the reading public should have to biographical facts when the writer is dead while her husband and children are still alive. Sylvia Plath is a special case, and it is she who effectively argues through her writing that the old conventions need to be reassessed. Since her poetry relays personal experience in a different way from virtually all the poetry written before Robert Lowell's *Life Studies*, it has to be read in a different way. Inevitably drawn into making connections between the words on the page and the texture of her daily life, readers need more help than they have been given.

Notes

Abbreviations

AA   Paul Alexander, ed., *Ariel Ascending*
AS   Anne Stevenson, *Bitter Fame*
BJ   *The Bell Jar*
CP   *Collected Poems*
EB   Edward Butscher, ed., *Sylvia Plath: The Woman and the Work*
J   *The Journals of Sylvia Plath*
JP   *Johnny Panic and the Bible of Dreams*
LH   *Letters Home*
LWM   Linda Wagner-Martin
NHS   Nancy Hunter Steiner
TH   Ted Hughes

Foreword

1. George Steiner. *Language and Silence*, London. 1969, p. 189.
2. *Michigan Today,* vol. 22, no. 2, April 1990.

Chapter 1. The End of a Short Life

1. Conversation with Gerry Becker, Jan. 18, 1991.
2. Letter from Catherine Frankfort to A. Alvarez, Dec. 7, 1981.
3. Conversation with Jillian Becker, Oct. 18, 1990.
4. "Plath–Hughes: One of Us Had to Die." Unpublished memoir by Gerry Becker.
5. Statement by Constable 567D/145526 John Jones, Feb. 14, 1963.
6. Catherine Frankfort letter.
7. Report by pathologist at University College Hospital.
8. Alvarez p. 56.
9. Conversation with A. Alvarez, Nov. 8, 1990.
10. TH in the *Independent,* April 22, 1989.
11. Conversation with Jillian Becker.
12. Conversations with Gerry and Jillian Becker.
13. Conversation with Jillian Becker.

14. TH in the *Guardian,* April 20, 1989.
15. Ibid.
16. Conversation with Suzette Macedo, Jan. 15, 1991.
17. AS p. 296.
18. Telephone conversation on Oct. 21, 1990, with Dr. Richard Larschan, who spoke on my behalf to Mrs. Plath on Oct. 12.

Chapter 2. *My Colossal Father*

1. Television program on Sylvia Plath in the series "Voices and Visions," New York Center for the Visual Arts.
2. J p. 298.
3. BJ pp. 174–77.
4. J p. 25.
5. J p. 26.
6. BJ pp. 174–77.
7. LH p. 18.
8. Ibid.
9. Otto Plath. *Bumblebees and Their Ways.* New York, 1934, p. 70.
10. LH p. 13.
11. LH p. 23.
12. LH pp. 27–28.
13. J pp. 298–99.
14. J pp. 299–300.
15. J p. 266.
16. Ibid.
17. J p. 267.
18. "Electra on Azalea Path."
19. J p. 129.
20. Ibid.
21. TH in AA p. 157.

Chapter 3. *Dearest of Mothers*

1. LH pp. 4–5.
2. JP p. 118.
3. LH p. 19.
4. LH p. 29.
5. Letter from Aurelia Plath to Elizabeth Compton, May 18, 1976.
6. JP p. 119.
7. J p. 26.
8. J p. 34.
9. LH p. 64.
10. LH p. 109.
11. LH p. 113.
12. LH p. 30.
13. LH pp. 30–31.
14. LH pp. 26–27.
15. LH p. 104.
16. LH p. 220.
17. LH p. 134.
18. LH p. 137.

19. LWM p. 37.
20. LH pp. 132–33.
21. J p. 116.
22. EB p. 45.
23. BJ pp. 129–30.
24. AS p. 48.
25. AA pp. 215–16.
26. AA p. 102.
27. J p. 143.
28. J pp. 265–66, 275–77, 288–97.
29. J pp. 266–67.
30. J p. 82.

Chapter 4. The Hostile Self

1. R.D. Laing. *The Divided Self.* London, 1960, pp. 76–78.
2. J p. 56.
3. LH p. 36.
4. J p. 14.
5. J pp. 40–41 and LH p. 85.
6. J pp. 18–19.
7. LH p. 86.
8. J pp. 50–51.
9. Letter to Marcia Brown, LWM p. 110.
10. J p. 56.
11. LWM p. 84.
12. LH p. 91.
13. J pp. 58–65.
14. J p. 66.
15. LH pp. 97–98.
16. LH p. 101.
17. LWM p. 91.
18. BJ pp. 100–103.
19. J p. 66.
20. LWM p. 95.
21. LH p. 103.
22. LH p. 105.
23. LH pp. 109–13.
24. LH p. 114.
25. LH p. 115.
26. LWM p. 97.
27. AS p. 42.
28. Television program in "Voices and Visions."
29. LWM pp. 99–100.
30. J pp. 80–81.
31. LH pp. 116–20.
32. BJ p. 118.
33. LH p. 123.
34. BJ pp. 119–20.
35. LH pp. 123–24.
36. J pp. 83–85.

37. J pp. 85–86.
38. J p. 156.
39. LH pp. 123–24.
40. BJ pp. 150–51.
41. LWM pp. 104–5; AS p. 46.
42. LH p. 125.
43. LH p. 131.
44. NHS p. 21.
45. LH pp. 129–32.
46. LH pp. 125–26.
47. JP pp. 271–72.
48. LH pp. 177–78.

Chapter 5. Boys

1. J p. 269.
2. NHS p. 17.
3. LWM p. 111.
4. NHS p. 33.
5. NHS p. 32.
6. J p. 15.
7. J pp. 48–49.
8. LWM pp. 48–49.
9. LWM p. 55.
10. LWM p. 59.
11. J p. 18.
12. J p. 16.
13. LWM p. 69.
14. J p. 16.
15. J p. 29.
16. J pp. 29–30.
17. J p. 44.
18. Letter from Eddie Cohen, Sept. 16, 1951.
19. BJ pp. 65–70.
20. BJ pp. 70–71.
21. J p. 459.
22. J pp. 38–44.
23. LH p. 87.
24. J p. 67.
25. LH pp. 99–100.
26. LH pp. 100–01.
27. J p. 68.
28. LWM p. 94.
29. EB p. 33.
30. J pp. 73–74.
31. J pp. 74–75.
32. J pp. 75–78.
33. J p. 80.
34. EB p. 37.
35. NHS p. 56.
36. J p. 102.
37. LH p. 161.

38. LH p. 223.
39. J p. 290.
40. Peter Davison.
41. BJ pp. 237–43.
42. NHS pp. 33–47.
43. J pp. 91–92.
44. J pp. 91–93.
45. J p. 94.
46. J p. 96.
47. J p. 97.
48. J pp. 99–102.
49. J p. 100.
50. Davison.
51. AS p. 61.
52. LWM p. 122 and EB p. 124.
53. EB p. 163 and AS pp. 61–62.
54. EB pp. 164–65.

Chapter 6. Female Support

1. EB pp. 42–43.
2. EB p. 48.
3. EB pp. 53–57.
4. LWM p. 102.
5. LWM pp. 106–7.
6. BJ pp. 195–96.
7. Letter from Olive Higgins Prouty, March 1957, AS p. 85.
8. LH p. 136.
9. NHS p. 17.
10. NHS pp. 19–20.
11. NHS pp. 30–31.
12. NHS p. 31.
13. NHS pp. 33–51.
14. NHS pp. 50–51.
15. BJ pp. 224–27.
16. J p. 194.
17. J p. 232.
18. J pp. 269–70.
19. LWM p. 215.
20. LH p. 243.
21. LH p. 251.
22. EB p. 50.
23. EB pp. 51–53.
24. EB p. 56.
25. EB p. 60.

Chapter 7. Marriage

1. Arthur Miller. *After the Fall.* New York, 1964.
2. In the *Observer,* June 10, 1990. Subsequently a letter from TH was published, denying the truth of another anecdote in Clive James's article.
3. Interview with John Horder in the *Guardian.*

4. AS p. 76.
5. AS p. 312.
6. J p. 163.
7. J pp. 112–13
8. J p. 113.
9. J p. 116.
10. AS p. 78.
11. AS pp. 76–77.
12. LWM p. 130.
13. June Anderson.
14. Letter from Olive Higgins Prouty, January 1956.
15. LH p. 243.
16. LH pp. 247–48.
17. J p. 153.
18. LH p. 263.
19. AS p. 94.
20. J p. 145.
21. J pp. 145–47.
22. AS p. 95.
23. LH pp. 268–69.
24. LH pp. 269 and 285.
25. Newman p. 182.
26. Ibid., pp. 183–85.
27. *New Statesman,* April 23, 1976.
28. EB p. 56.
29. J p. 156.
30. J p. 166.
31. J p. 163.
32. LH p. 287.
33. AS p. 314.
34. J p. 154.
35. AS p. 314.
36. J pp. 151–52.
37. J p. 152.
38. J p. 168.
39. J pp. 168–69.
40. J pp. 165–66.

Chapter 8. Panicky Wife

1. AS pp. 109–11.
2. J p. 168.
3. J pp. 162–64.
4. J p. 170.
5. J pp. 171–73.
6. J p. 173.
7. LH p. 324.
8. LH p. 342.
9. J pp. 176–79.
10. LH p. 329.
11. AS p. 116.
12. J pp. 179–80.

13. LH pp. 329–30.
14. LH p. 331.
15. J p. 182.
16. J p. 183.
17. J pp. 184–85.
18. J pp. 185–87.
19. J pp. 186–98.
20. J pp. 189–96.
21. J pp. 199–200.
22. J p. 214.
23. J pp. 201–6.
24. LH p. 336.
25. J pp. 210–13.
26. J pp. 212–13.
27. J pp. 218–20.
28. J pp. 221–22.
29. J pp. 231–32.
30. J pp. 232–34.
31. LH p. 342.
32. J p. 236.

Chapter 9. Boston

1. J p. 174 and "Mussel Hunter at Rock Harbor."
2. AS pp. 315–16.
3. J pp. 245–46.
4. AA p. 155.
5. J pp. 239–49 and LH p. 345.
6. J pp. 249–61.
7. J pp. 243–49 and LH p. 347.
8. J p. 251.
9. LH p. 346.
10. J pp. 262–64.
11. JP pp. 17–33.
12. JP pp. 74–91.
13. J p. 265.
14. J p. 269.
15. J p. 264.
16. J p. 265.
17. J pp. 265–66.
18. J p. 266.
19. J p. 268.
20. J p. 271.
21. J pp. 270–71.
22. J pp. 272–83.
23. J pp. 272–73.
24. J pp. 276–83.
25. J pp. 275–76.
26. J pp. 278–85.
27. J pp. 285–90.
28. J pp. 289–90.
29. J pp. 286–99.

30. J pp. 278–90.
31. J pp. 292–95.

Chapter 10. *The Poetry of Death*

1. Letter from Robert Lowell to T. L. Rosenthal.
2. Robert Lowell. *Selected Prose.* London and New York, 1987, pp. 123–24.
3. CP p. 198.
4. TH "Notes on the Chronological Order of Sylvia Plath's Poems," in Newman pp. 187–95.
5. J p. 183.
6. J p. 295.
7. J pp. 292–99.
8. J pp. 295–97.
9. Robert Lowell. Introduction to *Ariel.* New York, 1966.
10. Newman p. 178.
11. J pp. 303–4.
12. J pp. 279–85.

Chapter 11. *Pregnancy*

1. Letter to Lynne Lawner, Sept. 30, 1960, published in *Antaeus* No. 28, Winter 1978.
2. J p. 322.
3. J pp. 310–11 and LH p. 352.
4. JP pp. 94–105.
5. LH p. 352 and AS pp. 159–61.
6. LH p. 352.
7. Grace Schulman in AA pp. 165–77.
8. LH p. 353.
9. AS p. 163.
10. LWM p. 163.
11. J pp. 314–24.
12. LWM p. 164.
13. J pp. 313–18.
14. J pp. 317–18.
15. Newman p. 191.
16. J p. 321.
17. J p. 326.
18. J pp. 322–30.
19. J p. 322.
20. Newman pp. 192–93.
21. AA pp. 165–66.
22. Television program, "Voices and Visions."
23. AS pp. 176–78.
24. AS pp. 180–81.
25. LH p. 362.
26. LH p. 363.
27. Alvarez pp. 20–21.
28. LH pp. 363–64.
29. AS p. 189.

30. LH p. 373.
31. LH pp. 368–70.

Chapter 12. Close Quarters

1. LH p. 467.
2. LH p. 386.
3. LH p. 381.
4. LH pp. 384–85.
5. LH pp. 387–91.
6. AS p. 198.
7. LH pp. 392–96.
8. LH p. 398.
9. LH pp. 399–402.
10. LH pp. 402–3.
11. AS p. 204.
12. LH p. 405.
13. LH pp. 406–7.
14. LH p. 410 and LWM p. 182.
15. AS p. 334.
16. JP pp. 185–98.
17. LH pp. 408–9.
18. AS p. 212.
19. LH p. 408.
20. J pp. 331–40.
21. LH pp. 412–14.
22. BJ p. 257.
23. AS p. 214.
24. AS pp. 337–38.
25. AS pp. 336–42.
26. AS p. 219.

Chapter 13. In Devon

1. LH pp. 420–27 and AS pp. 218–22.
2. LH pp. 421–28 and note by TH in CP p. 292.
3. LH pp. 431–35.
4. LH pp. 439–40 and J pp. 351–53.
5. LH p. 437.
6. LH p. 439.
7. LH pp. 439–40.
8. LH pp. 441–44.
9. LH pp. 444–45 and JP p. 229.
10. LWM p. 198.
11. Conversation with Suzette Macedo.
12. LWM pp. 201–2 and AS pp. 240–41.
13. Newman p. 193 and note by TH in CP p. 292.
14. Elizabeth Sigmund (formerly Compton). "Sylvia, 1962: A Memoir," in the *New Review*, May 1976.
15. LH p. 454.
16. Conversations with Suzette Macedo and with Julia Matcham and Angela Landels.

17. Julia Matcham letter of Nov. 24, 1989, to the *Independent.* Unpublished.
18. Conversations with Julia Matcham and Angela Landels.
19. Letter from Assia Wevill to Sylvia Plath, May 22, 1962.
20. Ibid.

Chapter 14. Infidelity

1. AS p. 246.
2. LH pp. 450–53.
3. AA p. 192.
4. Elizabeth Sigmund. "Sylvia, 1962: A Memoir."
5. Ibid.
6. Conversation with Elizabeth Sigmund, Jan. 20, 1991.
7. LH pp. 458–59.
8. AS p. 253.
9. AS p. 349.
10. AS pp. 350–53.
11. AS p. 257.
12. LH p. 461.
13. AS p. 353.
14. LH p. 464.
15. LH pp. 463–64.
16. LH p. 464.
17. LH p. 466.
18. Letter to Ruth Fainlight, Oct. 22, 1962, AS p. 262.
19. AA pp. 194–95.
20. AA p. 193.
21. LH pp. 478–79.
22. AS p. 278.
23. LH p. 476.
24. AA p. 195.
25. Conversation with A. Alvarez on Nov. 8, 1990.

Chapter 15. Cul-de-sac

1. AA pp. 205–6 and conversation with A. Alvarez.
2. JP pp. 125–33 and Trevor Thomas.
3. AS p. 353.
4. AS p. 286.
5. AA p. 1.
6. Note by TH in CP p. 265.

Chapter 16. Posthumous Life

1. *London Magazine,* March 1961.
2. *New Statesman,* Jan. 25, 1963.
3. *The Listener,* Jan. 31, 1963.
4. *The Review,* No. 9, October 1963.
5. Elizabeth Sigmund. "Sylvia, 1962: A Memoir."
6. Marjorie Perloff. "The Two Ariels: The (Re)Making of the Sylvia Plath Cannon."

7. TH in Newmann pp. 187–95.
8. TH Foreword to JP.
9. LH p. 471.
10. LH p. 472.
11. TH Foreword to JP.
12. Conversation with Julia Matcham.
13. Letter from Fay Weldon to the author, May 17, 1990.
14. Conversation with Brenda Hedden.
15. Letter from Fay Weldon.
16. Quoted by Ian Thomson in the *Independent*, March 12, 1988.
17. The *Observer*, Feb. 29, 1989.
18. *Michigan Today*, vol. 22, no. 2, April 1990.
19. *Western Morning News*, Nov. 1, 1989.
20. *Michigan Today*, vol. 22, no. 2, April 1990.
21. Interview with Libby Purves in the *Times* (London), July 5, 1989.

Select Bibliography

By Sylvia Plath

The Colossus (London, 1960; New York, 1962).

The Bell Jar (London [under pseudonym Victoria Lucas] 1963, [under own name] 1966; New York, 1971).

Ariel (London, 1965; New York, 1966).

Crossing the Water (London, 1971; New York, 1971).

Winter Trees (London, 1971; New York, 1972).

Letters Home: Correspondence 1950–63, ed. with a commentary by Aurelia Schober Plath (London, 1975; New York, 1975).

The Red Book (London, 1976; New York, 1976).

Johnny Panic and the Bible of Dreams and Other Prose (London, 1977; New York, 1980).

Collected Poems, ed. Ted Hughes (London, 1981; New York, 1982)

The Journals of Sylvia Plath,, ed. Frances McCullough and Ted Hughes (New York, 1982).

About Sylvia Plath

Alexander, Paul, ed., *Ariel Ascending: Writings about Sylvia Plath* (New York, 1985).

Alvarez, A., *The Savage God* (London, 1971).

Axelrod, Steven Gould, "The Mirror and the Shadow: Plath's Poetic of Self Doubt," in *Contemporary Literature*, Fall 1985.

Butscher, Edward, *Sylvia Plath: Method and Madness* (New York, 1976).

Butscher, Edward, ed., *Sylvia Plath: The Woman and the Work* (London, 1977; New York, 1979).

Davison, Peter, *Half Remembered: A Personal History* (New York, 1973; London, 1974).

Hardy, Barbara, "The Poetry of Sylvia Plath: Enlargement or Derangement?" in Martin Dodsworth, ed., *The Survival of Poetry* (London, 1970).

Heaney, Seamus, "The Indefatigable Hooftaps," in *The Government of the Tongue* (London, 1988; New York, 1989).

Holbrook, David, *Sylvia Plath: Poetry and Existence* (London, 1976).

Kroll, Judith, *Chapters in a Mythology: The Poetry of Sylvia Plath* (New York, 1976).

Lane, Gary, ed., *Sylvia Plath: New Views on the Poetry* (Baltimore, 1979).

Lowell, Robert, "Sylvia Plath's Ariel," in *Collected Prose* (New York and London, 1987).

McGlatchy, J. D., "Staring from Her Hood of Bone: Adjusting to Sylvia Plath," in Robert B. Shaw, ed., *American Poetry Since 1960: Some Critical Perspectives* (Cheadle, Cheshire, 1973).

Newman, Charles, ed., *The Art of Sylvia Plath* (Bloomington, Indiana, and London, 1970).

Perloff, Marjorie, "The Two Ariels: The (Re)Making of the Sylvia Plath Canon," in *American Poetry Review,* Nov.–Dec. 1984.

Steiner, Nancy Hunter, *A Closer Look at Ariel: A Memory of Sylvia Plath* (New York, 1974; London, 1974).

Stevenson, Anne. *Bitter Fame* (Boston, 1989).

Wagner-Martin, Linda W., *Sylvia Plath: A Biography* (New York, 1987; London, 1988).

Index